PREACHING

OTHER BOOKS BY JAMES W. COX

The Ministers Manual (editor)
Biblical Preaching: An Expositor's Treasury
The Twentieth Century Pulpit, Volumes I and II
Surprised by God
A Guide to Biblical Preaching
Minister's Worship Manual (coeditor with Ernest A. Payne and
     Stephen F. Winward)
Learning to Speak Effectively
God's Inescapable Nearness (coauthor with Eduard Schweizer)

Preaching

James W. Cox

1817

Harper & Row, Publishers, San Francisco

Cambridge, Hagerstown, New York, Philadelphia
London, Mexico City, São Paulo, Singapore, Sydney

FIRST EDITION

Library of Congress Cataloging in Publication Data

Cox, James William.
  Preaching.

  Bibliography: p.
  Includes index.
  1. Preaching.   I. Title.
BV4211.2.C65   1985   251   84-48214
ISBN 0-06-061600-8
85 86 87 88 89 RRD 10 9 8 7 6 5 4 3 2 1

To my sons,
David Allan Cox and Kenneth Mitchell Cox,
whose genuine interest, unfailing
encouragement, and sound advice have added
to my joy in writing this book

And to my wife, Patricia Parrent Cox, who
has lovingly contributed her special
affirmation and inspiration to this project
and to every aspect of my ministry.

Contents

Preface

The traditional sermon seems destined to keep an honored place in Christian worship and in evangelism. The sermon has outlasted dire predictions of its demise and various experiments with its omission or replacement.

This book attempts to help ministerial students and practicing pastors to preach well: that is, to preach with solid biblical and theological content; to preach sermons that engage both heart and mind; and to preach interestingly, persuasively, and with integrity.

This is not a book that favors a narrow concept of method. It recognizes that preachers have personalities that differ and that congregations have differing needs and capacities. Therefore, this book attempts to set forth a variety of ways to communicate Christian truth. This is, of course, a concession to individual personality differences, but it is also an effort to suggest alternative ways of "getting the message across," so as to make the preparation of every sermon a challenge to be creative and effective.

There is hardly a place to begin when attempting to express gratitude to individuals and institutions for their part in the writing and publishing of a book like this. My students, the faculty and staff, and the administration and trustees of The Southern Baptist Theological Seminary have made distintive contributions. The late Charles L. Wallis, editor of *Pulpit Digest* and *The Ministers Manual*, and Editor John Shopp of Harper & Row both urged me to write this book, which would have no doubt appeared earlier, except for the unexpected death of Mr. Wallis, whose editorial duties I took over and added to my already full schedule.

Special thanks should go to *Pulpit Digest*, to *The Princeton Seminary Bulletin*, and to Claude A. Frazier, M. D., editor of *Should*

Preachers Play God? and to Independence Press, for permission to use extensive excerpts from my writings in their publications.

I have attempted to give credit where credit is due for numerous ideas and quotations, but in addition there are doubtless many ideas that entered my thoughts whose origin I could not trace. It will be clear that I am heavily indebted to specific persons, such as John A. Broadus, Arthur E. Phillips, and James T. Cleland, whose influence on my own thought is unmistakable.

Introduction

Preaching is here to stay. From time to time observers and critics have questioned its value. They have noted popular preference for other means of communication. They have witnessed the failure of preaching at times to deal effectively with certain important issues. Yet the return of people again and again to the word of the pulpit, as they seek answers to at least some of their questions, demonstrates the durability of preaching.

The chief factor in its favor is its content, not its practitioners. Unworthy, uninformed, and unskilled preachers have not been able to put preaching out of business, for its message has always stood in judgment on even the best preachers. In this way, preaching has maintained a kind of independence of the forces that would diminish its role in society.

Also, preaching survives because of its very humanness. From the earliest times, people in groups both large and small have listened while someone with an important or interesting message spoke. It is a natural way of getting needed facts, arguments, inspiration, or motivation. While preaching has its special qualities, it nevertheless has qualities in common with the most elementary and necessary means of communication of one human being with another.

Preachers and their preaching, however, and not the content alone, are important. The message comes through human beings with their strengths and weaknesses and thus is magnified or diminished. At any given time, this may explain in part what is right or wrong with preaching. Undoubtedly other factors are at work in the society that affect the way preaching is perceived.

This book is concerned with the preacher, the message, and the methodology—with the factors determining success over which the preacher has control. Every God-called preacher has the potential to accomplish what the One who called intended. But this achievement cannot be reduced to a stereotype.

The dean of a divinity school compared two teachers of preaching. Of one he said, "He tries to bring out every student's individual best." Of the other he said, "He turns out little carbon copies of himself." The approach in this book is that of the first teacher. It seeks to avoid an inhibiting reductionism. It encourages the freedom and potential creativity of the individual preacher to find the best way for himself or herself, yet it offers options of approaches that have proven useful to many effective preachers. The poet John Ciardi has said that one value of reading poetry is that it gives vicarious experience—that is, it stretches one's capacity for life. Similarly, the options I present will suggest to you alternative methods for size and comfort; then you can decide whether one is useful or effective for you, at the moment, or whether through experimentation and practice it can *become* useful or effective. Some preachers prematurely seize upon a method of sermon preparation and delivery that works passably well and then proceed to make every sermon by that pattern. They may survive or even do better than survive, yet they may fail to reach the maximum strength that freedom and variety promise. In some instances, unusually successful preachers among us make a strong impression with their idiosyncratic sameness. They invite imitation, which has been called the sincerest flattery. They, of course, have compensatory qualities that make up what is lacking in their sameness of approach in preaching. But their impressive characteristic way of doing things often imposes an unnecessary burden on their would-be imitators, who have gifts of their own that can be developed in different directions. This is not to say that imitation is homiletically taboo. In truth, it is by imitation that we learn most of the skills we know. Imitation becomes a problem when it is reduced to learning one prominent trait in a person or in a process and ignoring many other traits worthy of evaluation, of experimentation, and perhaps even of emulation.

It should be clear, however, that freedom and variety do not imply that "anything goes." Not at all. Freedom that is worth the name is always within bounds; variety is only a richer expression of a reality that has discrete integrity. One writer on homiletics has said that the preacher needs not so much to be formed as freed. In the context of this book, these words mean that homiletical options attempt to call out the individual preacher's unique gifts for the most effective service.

I. THE IMPORTANCE OF PREACHING

1. The Nature of Preaching

Behind the concept of preaching stands the ancient belief that *word* had power. This belief prevailed both in the extrabiblical world and in the world of the Old Testament. We see this particularly in the idea of blessing and cursing. A word spoken *with strong intent* was creative or destructive and could build up with blessing or tear down with cursing. So powerful was such a word that it was thought to have an independent life and could go on to do its work long after it was uttered.

In the Old Testament, creation is pictured as the work of the Word of God. The message of the prophet is called the Word of the Lord. The shape taken by history is the manifestation of the Word of God. Even nature is caught up in this process. Also, the written word of scripture comes to be invested with mysterious power. In the fullness of time, God speaks his decisive and supremely revelatory word in the person of his incarnate Son, Jesus Christ.[1]

The New Testament does not represent the work of the spoken word and the written word in quite the dramatic terms of the Old Testament. The New Testament, however, depicts for us the progress of the "unhindered gospel" as it spread from Jerusalem toward the uttermost parts of the earth. Who can deny the power of *that* word, "the word of faith, which we preach" (Romans 10:8)?

There are four words that will help us understand the nature of what we call preaching and the different ways in which the power of the Word of God comes to expression today: proclamation, witness, teaching, and prophesying. We shall consider each of them in some detail.

PROCLAMATION

Preaching is proclamation. It is the presentation of a message of good news, indeed, the presentation of the living Christ himself. To say that Christ is living and that we have business with him today is to say that God is victorious, that the enemies of God who persecuted and crucified Jesus did not win out, that the cross was not the end of him. It is to say, then, that God raised him from the dead and that he is forever alive.

This is good news in another sense also. The fact that Christ is alive and comes to us—or is brought to us—means that God is for us, still for us, undefeatedly for us. This assures us that we belong in God's scheme of things and that we are important to him. More than that, it means that we share his life and that we participate in the "life and immortality" that he has brought to light.

All of this is made possible for us because Jesus Christ died for our sins and rose again for our justification. God did something in the cross and resurrection that forever puts behind us the penalty of sin. A new day has dawned, and those who have sinned can through God's grace enter into the benefits of what Christ has done and, beyond that, into what he offers in the new age.

The New Testament writers associate a number of significant Greek words with this proclamation. The message is the *kerygma*, "news, declaration, decree, command, proclamation of the victor." The messenger is the *keryx*, "the herald, the one who brings the message." It is his responsibility to pass on unchanged what he has been commissioned to declare. The word denoting what the messenger does in giving the message is *keryssein*, "to proclaim."

Another word, a more important one, is *evangelizesthai*, "to proclaim the good news." This word is more important because it suggests the nature of the message: The messenger brings *good* news. The good news is the *evangelion*, and the bringer of it, the *evangelos*. Among the ancient Greeks, the evangelos might come from the field of battle by ship, by horse, or on foot. In any case, he would appear to the people who anxiously awaited news of the battle. A garland about his head would indicate that the news was good. As he approached he would raise his hand and cry, "*Chaire, nikomen!*" ("Greetings, we have won!")[2]

The preacher brings a report from the battlefield of the conflict between Christ and Satan. The news is that for the whole of humankind Jesus Christ has won the victory in his death and resurrection.

This announcement or proclamation implies invitation, an invitation to believe the message that the preacher has brought, an invitation to accept the truth and implications of it as settled fact, and an invitation to participate fully in all that God's victory means for the entire world.

WITNESS

Preaching is witness. Before Jesus' ascension, he reminded his disciples that everything written about him in the ancient scriptures had to be fulfilled, meaning specifically his crucifixion and resurrection and a worldwide preaching of repentance and forgiveness of sins in his name. Then Jesus declared, "You are witnesses of these things" (Luke 24:48). As Luke puts it in Acts, Jesus said, "You shall be my witnesses in Jerusalem and in all Judea and Samaria and to the end of the earth" (Acts 1:8). Here Jesus was referring to witnesses who were eyewitnesses to the facts of history.

Peter gave the criterion for an apostle to replace Judas Iscariot. As a witness he must indeed be a witness of the events of Jesus' life and passion. "So one of the men who have accompanied us during all the time that the Lord Jesus went in and out among us, beginning from the baptism of John until the day when he was taken up from us—one of these men must become with us a witness to his resurrection" (Acts 1:22). Luke states that "with great power the apostles gave their testimony to the resurrection of the Lord Jesus, and great grace was upon them all" (Acts 4:33).

So, early in the book of Acts, the word *witness* was reserved for those who were "there" when Jesus was crucified and raised from the dead. This aspect of witness has been of crucial importance to the preaching of those who were not eyewitnesses. Christian preaching through the centuries and our preaching today has relied on their testimony. No one living today can be a witness in the sense of "eyewitness."

However, preaching is witness in another sense. Later references in Acts designate as witnesses persons who were not eyewitnesses. These persons had believed the truth of the good news and gave testimony to it. They may not have had a special vision, as did Saul of Tarsus, who was told, "You will be a witness for him to all men of what you have seen and heard" (Acts 22:15), yet they have had their own encounter with him through the Word and the Spirit. Paul, quoting from his prayer in the Temple, referred to "Stephen thy witness" (Acts 22:20). In this meaning, whoever takes a firm stand for Jesus Christ and his gospel, confessing him openly and boldly, becomes a witness. "Now I rejoice in my sufferings for your sake, and in my flesh I complete what is lacking in Christ's afflictions for the sake of his body, that is, the church, of which I became a minister according to the divine office which was given to me for you, to make the word of God fully known, the mystery hidden for ages and generations but now made manifest to his saints" (Colossians 1:24-26).

Not only is the word of preaching intended to set forth what has happened once for all for the world's salvation, it is intended also to do something in the lives of those who transmit the message. The kerygma is like the metal of which a coin is made; witness is that metal with the image and superscription of the messenger upon it. What the gospel does to the messenger, therefore, becomes a part of what is preached. When the Apostle Paul spoke of "my gospel," was he perhaps speaking of the gospel as he had experienced it? The degree to which the messenger, then, is changed or not changed by the message, to that extent the good news is helped or hindered. Let us be clear: The essential message does not change. Paul could rejoice that Christ was preached even by unworthy messengers with questionable motives. H. H. Rowley's image is helpful here. He said that the Word of God that came through the prophet was wholly marked by the personality of the prophet, like the rays of light that pass through colored glass. It is the same light, yet it is wholly modified by what it passes through.[3] So it is with the Word through the preacher. While Paul could rejoice that Christ was preached even from envy and rivalry, he admonished Timothy, "Let no one despise your youth, but set the believers an example in speech and conduct, in love, in faith, in purity" (1 Tim. 4:12). What L. H. Brockington said of the Old Testament prophet is true also of the preacher of the gospel: "Because of his entire submission to the will of God his acts are fully taken up into the divine purpose and become part of the creative process."[4]

Phillips Brooks stated it impressively in his classic *On Preaching*:

The truth must come really through the person, not merely over his lips, not merely into his understanding and out through his pen. It must come through his character, his affections, his whole intellectual and moral being. It must come genuinely through him. I think that, granting equal intelligence and study, here is the great difference which we feel between two preachers of the Word. The Gospel has come *over* one of them and reaches us tinged and flavored with his superficial characteristics, belittled with his littleness. The Gospel has come *through* the other, and we receive it impressed and winged with all the earnestness and strength that there is in him. In the first case the man has been but a printing machine or a trumpet. In the other case he has been a true man and a real messenger of God.[5]

TEACHING

Preaching is teaching. What one declares calls for explanation, perhaps for argumentation. After the preachers have proclaimed their message, declaring also what it has meant to them personally, it will not be long before someone will ask, "How did this come about? . . . Why are you telling me? . . . How do you know this is true? . . . What else can you tell me about it?" In fact, teaching is necessary as preparation for the proper hearing of the good news, as part of the proclamation of the good news, and as follow-up of the good news. We can make no absolute distinction between gospel proclamation and Christian teaching. Still, we can profitably highlight the didactic element in preaching.

Alfonso M. Nebreda, indicating the focus of a conference at Bangkok in 1962, has stated "the three stages which normally characterize the journey of an adult to faith" as follows:

1. *Preevangelization*: a stage of preparation for the kerygma that, taking man as he is and where he is, makes a human dialogue possible and awakens in him the sense of God, an indispensable element for opening his heart to the message.
2. *Evangelization* or *kerygma*: the dynamic heralding of the substance of the Christian message, having as its goal personal conversion or initial acceptance of Christ as the Lord.
3. *Catechesis proper*: a stage that leans on the conversion achieved by the previous stages and systematically develops the message. Its goal is to initiate man into Christian life and build within him a Christian personality.[6]

Praeparatio evangelica or preevangelization enables potential believers to listen seriously to the gospel. The principle of incarnation works effectively at this stage. The preacher prepares the way for proclamation by the distinctiveness and appeal of an authentic Christian life. Charles Haddon Spurgeon said, "A man known to be godly and devout, and felt to be large-hearted and self-sacrificing, has a power in his very person, and his advice and recommendation carry weight because of his character."[7]

This will mean that we truly identify with the people among whom we live, that we share their hurts and hopes, that we work to help them (and help ourselves as well) reach goals that will improve our common life. Circumstances may throw us more with one group or "class" than another, but we will work for understanding, justice, and cooperation and will refuse to sanctify oppression on the one hand or destructive protest on the other.

Some persons may oppose any efforts the preacher makes toward changing oppressive social structures, because they are costly to themselves, but others, who are helped or at least impressed by efforts made in the spirit of Christ, will thank God for the preacher's concern and courage.

Again, the preaching of the gospel may require that we simply impart information necessary for making the gospel intelligible. People do not make valid decisions of faith in an intellectual vacuum. After interest in the Christian faith has been aroused, a long period of instruction may be needed before a commitment is made.

This has been standard procedure on mission fields where converts have come to Christianity from other religions. Also, "taking instruction" fills a need for others who may know the rudiments of the Christian faith but who bring with them many misconceptions of it. Sometimes the pulpit fulfils these needs, but when it does not, it can support other means of preparation for the gospel. In any case, simply because inquirers or potential converts have a mass of data, we cannot assume that they have grasped its meaning. Studies have isolated seven steps in the communication process. 1. *Transmission* takes a message and moves it. 2. *Contact* occurs when a person hears the message. 3. *Feedback* returns reactions to the sender for refinement or elaboration of the message. 4. *Comprehension* occurs when the message is actually understood. 5. *Acceptance* occurs when the hearer assents to what is understood. 6. *Internalization* makes what is believed a part of one's appropriate conduct. 7. *Action* translates inner commitment into appropriate conduct.[8]

A minister told of an experience that exemplifies this process. A man who came to hear him preach sat on a pew in the back of the sanctuary. After a particular sermon, the man raised questions that challenged the preacher. These questions became the starting point of the sermon on the following Sunday. Then more questions came, and the preacher responded in the next sermon. As this heart-to-heart, mind-to-mind struggle continued, the man moved closer and closer toward the front of the sanctuary, until he sat right before the preacher. This dramatic incident suggests what ought to occur in every pulpit, though perhaps less dramatically, as preachers take seriously their teaching task in the spirit of John the Baptist to "prepare the way of the Lord."

Christian apologetics has its place not only in a theological seminary curriculum but also in the work of the evangelist and of the pastor. Karl Barth did not see such a need. He said, "It is not easier and it is not more difficult for modern man [to hear the word of God clearly in the Bible], because for all men God is a stranger and God can only be heard and understood in so far as He Himself speaks to him."[9]

I once heard Emil Brunner asked how he compared himself with Barth. He answered, "Professor Barth is a preacher to the Church; I am a missionary." It is precisely this missionary function that requires *someone* to give a reasonable account of the Christian faith. Often it is the parish minister who must do this.

Helmut Thielicke wrote:

To me, the greatest miracle of the gospel has always been that it includes *all* these human possibilities and seeks out everyone in his own individual "far country." It knows how to find the prostitute in her pitiful degradation and the rich young man in his glittering poverty. It addresses both the opportunistic Pontius Pilate and the despairing Canaanite woman. It reaches a Luther wrestling with his conscience, and it wrings one last hope of peace from the unhappy Rufus who, in James Baldwin's *Another Country*, plunges to his death with a curse on his lips. They are all held safely within the gospel, embraced by it. Their addresses are all written on the great all-inclusive envelope.[10]

Preevangelization, therefore, requires different kinds of help or teaching for different people.

Sometimes it is simply a matter of seizing the propitious moment. Though this moment of "vulnerability" may become a favorable time for unethical exploitation by a religious predator, it may be God's opportunity. John Baillie saw in the threatened collapse of modern thought a judgment of God but more: "God's judgments are . . . intended to lead us, not to despair, but to repentance and amendment of our ways; and signs are not lacking that the series of severe jolts which have lately been suffered by those who have supported their spirits by the hope of a natural and necessary upward progress of our earthly society is actually leading some of them to open their minds more hospitably to what I have called the Bible view of history."[11]

The divine command—the Law—likewise prepares the way for the gospel; indeed it is a function of the gospel, or as Karl Barth put it, it is "enclosed in the gospel."[12] In any case, the Apostle Paul concluded that the law functioned to produce knowledge of sin. Thus it had and has the role of *paidagogos*: It is a custodian in whose charge we are temporarily, on our way to Jesus Christ who justifies the disobedient by his forgiving grace (see Galatians 3:23-26).[13] When one of the Ten Commandments or some teaching of the Sermon on the Mount confronts us and we hear it not as a free-floating moral precept, but as the Word of God, we recognize our alienation, our need. Thus we may see ourselves as estranged from God, from our neighbor, and from our own self. The law of God, when we are face to face with it, deepens our sense of sin and may, as in the case of Paul, increase the sin (Rom. 5:20), for "law turns one inward and makes him more and more egocentric."[14] Thus the hard soil of the human heart is broken up and made ready for the seed of the gospel: "Where sin increased, grace abounded all the more" (Rom. 5:20). Spurgeon reported that old Robbie Flockhart, one of his mentors, used to say, "It is of no use trying to sew with the silken thread of the gospel unless we pierce a way for it with the sharp needle of the law."[15]

Teaching also bulks large in the actual proclamation of the saving gospel. The accounts of early Christian sermons are loaded with didactic material. We cannot draw a sharp line between *kerygma* and *didache*. We can be sure that those who make intelligent and valid commitments upon hearing the gospel have received and weighed data from faithful teaching. Whether the vital decision was made after hearing an impassioned plea devoid of teaching or after a carefully reasoned and documented message is unimportant. Teaching went on somewhere, sometime, and became a part of the preaching.

We are likely, however, to associate teaching with what follows the commitment to discipleship. Certainly teaching at that point is a proper emphasis. Again, proclamation—*kerygma*—is its basis, yet it is explicitly and consciously teaching—*didache*. What the pastor is supposed to do is to teach, for the pastor is the chief teacher of the congregation. Elton Trueblood said that every church ought to be a little seminary. Indeed, when Ephesians lists the special ministries given to persons in the body of Christ, one category is "pastors and teachers," probably referring to one office. Some pastors neglect their obligation, passed on to them from the apostles, to teach the followers of Christ to observe all that he commanded (see Matthew 28:20).

It may seem easier and more enjoyable to prepare and preach sermons to stir the emotions than to stimulate the intellect. Yet preachers willing to work at it have learned how to do both and have thereby achieved unusual success (in the best sense of the word) in the pulpit. George Dana Boardman (1828-1903) got wide recognition of his ability as a pulpit orator—whatever that might include—in his early ministry. When he changed pastorates, however, he launched into a preaching style characterized by its teaching aim and continued this method to the end of his life.[16] Jesus, we must remember, did not disdain the title Rabbi, Teacher, when he was so addressed in John's Gospel. To be sure, he went everywhere "preaching (*kerusson*) and bringing the good news (*evangelisomenos*) of the kingdom of God" (Luke 8:1), but he also "opened his mouth and taught (*edidasken*)" (Matthew 5:2). In what is known as the Great Commission, Jesus brings together three inseparable charges to his messengers:

make disciples, baptize them, and teach them (Matthew 28:19-20).

PROPHESYING

A fourth emphasis of preaching is what might be called in Pauline language "prophesying" or as William Barclay preferred, "forthtelling." In the sense in which I use the term, it does not mean foretelling the future: It means giving a message perceived to meet a present need. This is what was going on when Jesus said in the synagogue of Nazareth at the outset of his ministry, "Today this scripture has been fulfilled in your hearing" (Luke 4:21). Jesus' words as well as his presence were the timely application of what Isaiah had written centuries before.

Paul contrasted speaking in tongues with prophesying, saying that the former is a religious exercise for one's own good but that prophesying is for the good of the church. He went on to denote what prophesying is: It is edification; it is exhortation; it is consolation (1 Cor. 14:3). There is here a "heart-to-heartness," an aspect of preaching where "deep calleth unto deep." With this emphasis, preaching becomes most personal. Dialogical spirit, if not actual conversational exchange, takes over. An "I-thou" relationship between preacher and hearer prevails. We hear not only what God, the Bible, Christian tradition, and our own hearts may say; we hear also what the people to whom we preach are saying, as we know the temptations, the guilt, the sorrows, the sufferings, and the doubts of these people. We read the lives of these people from what we see of their everyday living, their casual conversation, their requests for counsel, and even their demeanor during the act of preaching. Thus the message comes alive with reality. If it is faithful to both poles of this heart-to-heart preaching encounter, can the event be called anything less than the work of the Holy Spirit?

One preacher may sound one note, while another preacher may sound a quite different note. We might say that this preacher is evangelistic, that preacher is prophetic; this preacher is devotional, that preacher is expository. In the history of the church, each of these specialists has been useful in a particular place at a particular time. It is also true that preachers have been mismatched with circumstances. They have been devotional when they should have been prophetic, evangelistic when they should have been expository. This obviously calls for acute sensitivity to the needs of church and community, so that a creative response can be made, perhaps by utilizing the services of specialists with precisely the emphases needed.

It is a tremendous challenge, but a worthy goal for every preacher thus to respond to all types of need, whether by enlisting outside help or by learning to preach with such versatility that the entire spectrum of homiletical response will be reflected. One aim of this book is to indicate ways in which the preacher can broaden his or her concerns and preach with appropriate variety as needs demand.

2. The Preacher's Authority

Thinking people will sometimes ask, "What right does the preacher have to say these things?" The question may not have to do with the truth of the message or of parts of it but only with the legitimacy of the preacher as the fitting communicator of the message. It is a proper question. Individuals do arrogate to themselves authority to speak for God or for the church. Apparent strength of conviction, generous use of the Bible, a loud voice, perhaps even a dogmatism that brooks no contradiction can lead those who hear a speaker with such qualities to believe they hear a message from God. Admittedly, this does constitute a certain kind of authority, though a specious one, if God is not somehow involved in the process.

SOME SOURCES OF AUTHORITY

Several factors determine the preacher's authority as it is perceived by a congregation or by sympathetic people generally. Some of these factors are perceived primarily by the preacher but are to be believed by others; other factors are objective and obvious for all to see.

For the preacher, *a divine call* may be utterly decisive. Some prophets in the Old Testament and the Apostle Paul in the New Testament took pains to show that their office or mission was not of their own choosing, but of God's. Others did their work without leaving a written record of some dramatic summons. Nonetheless, confirmations of a genuine call are not lacking as one examines the record of this latter class.

Contemporary preachers can point to unusual experiences of the call of God, experiences that match in color and tone those of the men who spoke for God in biblical times. At the same time, other moderns go about their speaking for God with the calm, settled assurance that they have answered a heavenly summons, though their experience of it was perhaps a gradual dawning of purpose and mission. Let the tree be judged by its fruits!

Ordination gives public recognition by the church to the ordinand's gifts and commitment to special ministry. This puts the weight of community and continuity behind the individual. When that person speaks, it is not the preacher alone who speaks. It is the voice of the church, to the extent that the preacher is faithful to the purposes for which he or she was appointed. Ordination signifies stability of character, genuineness of personal religious experience and of commitment to service, and soundness of theological beliefs. A hospital chaplain goes into the room of a patient who needs special help and is able to give it after answering affirmatively the patient's question, "Are you the man of God here?" In the same way, a preacher gets heard in the sanctuary; the listener may feel unconsciously, "This man, this woman, speaks for God!"

Associated with ordination is the administration of what are variously called the sacraments or ordinances. I refer here in particular to baptism and the Lord's Supper or Eucharist. Word and sacrament have long been associated, both in practice and in theological statement. The locus of authority, in one expression, is where the Word of God is faithfully proclaimed and the sacraments are properly administered. The proclamation of the gospel normally leads to faith that is expressed and confirmed in baptism and reaffirmed by participation of the baptized believer in the Eucharist. Where such things authentically happen, there is the church. Thus the preacher who works in that context attracts a certain authority; the church apparatus in operation lends to the celebrant the authority of divine institution.

Education contributes to the sense of authority. Granted, there are those who are "ever learning, and never able to come to the knowledge of the truth" (2 Tim. 3:7), yet to have studied the Bible and the contemporary world thoroughly and to have reflected on their relationship places the preacher in a position to get his or her own beliefs, convictions, and behavior taken seriously. Thinking people demand more than "a gift of gab," even if it is interesting and grammatical gab. Charles Spurgeon noted that "verbiage is too often the fig-leaf which does duty as a covering for theological ignorance."[1] Sooner or later, however, the winds of crisis and change blow away the specious camouflage. It is the truly informed preacher who commands the respect of the people.

Experience lends authority. This can be of two kinds. First, there is the experience gained in a time of crisis. In what matters most, the preacher has firsthand knowledge. Before he had been a Christian very long, the Apostle Paul could get a hearing by recounting what happened to him on the Damascus Road and immediately thereafter. Reference to a dramatic conversion experience or to some other extraordinary but believable experience often commands credence and respect.

Moreover, growing, cumulative experience is most important. When the preacher gives evidence of growth in the grace and knowledge of our Lord and Savior Jesus Christ, those who have observed and felt this progress take the preacher seriously.

Whenever we speak on the basis of personal experience of the truth affirmed, what we say carries unusual weight. "The wounded healer" possesses an immense advantage. It would be wrong, however, for us to assume that we could not honestly preach about truth not personally experienced. Were we to draw a circle around our own experience and ignore what others have experienced, we would preach a meager gospel. The fullness of God's grace cannot be capsuled in any one person's experience.

Yet it is of utmost importance that the preacher possess a solid integrity of *character*. We may not be perfect, but our morals must be healthy, commanding the respect of all. The Apostle Paul advised Timothy, his son in the ministry, "Make yourself an example to believers in speech and behaviour, in love, fidelity, and purity" (1 Tim. 4:12). If the ancient rhetoricians like Aristotle, Cicero, and Quintilian believed that the orator's chief means of persuasion was his *ethos*—his character—how much more should this be true of the preacher whose great concern is the salvation of souls and the formation of character.

Preachers are often parent figures to many in the congregation. The people look to them in much the same way they have regarded their own biological parents. We know quite well the devastations wrought, first, by parents who do not back up their preachments by honest and sincere efforts to live up to the life they recommend to their children and, second, by parents who make no pretense to morality and expect and get none from their children. There is an old saying, "Like priest, like people!"

The biblical text lends authority to the preacher. If we cannot come before our people on Sunday morning with a fresh oracle prefaced with a "Thus saith the Lord," as did the ancient prophets, we can come before them with a biblical text, which is in a real sense "the word of the Lord." Pity the preacher who appears with only personal opinions! To be sure, preachers have sometimes misused the Bible: faulty exegesis, biased interpretation, and use of the text as a mere motto have in some quarters lessened respect for the Bible. However, most congregations take seriously the preacher who takes the biblical text seriously enough to wrestle with it honestly, to look squarely at the problems it raises for acceptance today, and to listen for its possibly relevant but often unwelcome message. When we use a text worthily, we are supported both by the revelation of God and by the accumulated wisdom and devotion of God's people across the ages. When people make a mess of things, whether as individuals or as a society, they often yearn for old verities that worked in the past, verities now ignored or scorned. Thus the ancient text stands with imperious promise and lends authority to preachers who ally themselves with it.

SPECIAL AUTHORITY

It is the instrumental authority of the text that at last is decisive and that has to do with the Holy Spirit. The Holy Spirit is God at work, especially in the church. The Holy Spirit makes truly alive every aspect of the preacher's authority. But there is perhaps no more elusive concept in the New Testament than that of the Holy Spirit. Individuals have used the term to indicate a hunch, an ecstasy, a feeling of grim courage, peace that passes understanding, religious conviction, illumination, and so on. No doubt each and all of these experiences can be and are associated with the work of the Holy Spirit. Yet the temptation of many has been to reduce the Spirit's work to a perception of God's activity in individuals. So we sometimes hear persons who (no doubt sincerely) say things like, "The Holy Spirit spoke to me and. . . ." And there is no reason to doubt that the Spirit has spoken and does speak to individuals, sometimes in opposition to a strong consensus of pious, praying people. But the Holy Spirit seems usually to work in community, "where two or three" or more "are gathered together." The Jerusalem Church once made a significant decision saying, "It seemed good to the Holy Spirit and to us" (Acts 15:28).

To achieve this kind of authority in preaching we cannot rely on personality traits, on academic achievements, and, as Simon Magus found out (Acts 8:18-24), on the power of money. This authority arises from a genuine participation in what God is attempting to do in a particular group of people, and it requires caring for them, praying for and with them, and paying the price in self-denial to discover and do the will of God. R. E. C. Browne, in his classic *The Ministry of the Word*, has said, "Authority is not the static manifestation of power at one particular point in time giving unquestionable directions to all generations. Authority is the name for an element in a living relationship and consequently eludes exact definition."[2]

Our authority as preachers is no authority at all unless it points beyond ourselves to the One for whom and in whose name we speak. Often it is our individual weakness and uncertainty that establish our true authority. When we are face to face with our true self, we know that we are nothing. We then cast ourselves utterly on God for better or for worse, realizing that despair of autonomous authority is the ground of our hope of becoming an instrument of the authority of God.

Interestingly, different people get in touch with the authority of God through one aspect or another of the preacher's authority. For one person, it may be enough to know that we have received "the call." For another, that we have been ordained. For another, that we have been educated for the ministry. For another, that we are persons of continued and consistent religious experience. For another, that we sincerely explain the Bible. And for still another, that we "have the Spirit." Any one of these aspects of the preacher's ministerial life may represent "the near end of God" to an individual.

FURTHER CONSIDERATIONS

In connection with the sources of the preacher's authority, more must be said.

Authority may be conferred or imposed. That is, authority accrues to certain leaders placed in strategic positions in institutions or organizations. In the church, an apparatus exists with which ministers, once they have assumed their office, have authority. Their work is more or less decisive in certain defined and undefined areas. This applies whether they have been appointed to their office by hierarchical decision or by congregational ballot.

Authority may be earned. In the case of Jesus of Nazareth, no ecclesiastic appointed him. No congregation elected him. Yet he spoke as one having authority. Of course, authority had been conferred by God the Father, but the perception of his authority was a cumulative conviction based both on his words and his deeds. Even the preacher who has received formal authority in one way or another may achieve among the people authority based on criteria less objective but just as real as formal credentials. Because of certain formal qualifications we may speak with the tongues of men and of angels and be admired for it, but because of our genuine love for our people that time and circumstances have proven again and again, we may speak and find people willing to follow us to the death. The "greatest" among Jesus' disciples would not be those who sought and exercised power in the spirit of the pagans. They would be those who became the willing servants among those whom they led.

Authority may be shared. Although the Holy Spirit has distributed special gifts to certain persons in the Christian community and has thus endowed them with leadership in particular areas, the Spirit really belongs to the entire community. Authority is a shared experience. The preacher cannot function apart from the support and cooperation of the people. The preacher's great gifts may be widely acknowledged, yet they are empty of meaning unless they are exercised in the Spirit of Jesus Christ.

And finally, *authority can be lost.* The Apostle Paul said that he buffeted his body and brought it under subjection, lest after he had preached to others he himself might be rejected. Individuals can come and go, but the Word of the Lord endures forever.

I conclude this chapter with another important word from Browne: "What ministers of the Word say may seem too little to live on, but they must not go beyond their authority in a mistaken attempt to make their authority strong and clear. That going beyond is always the outcome of an atheistic anxiety, or a sign that the man of God has succumbed to the temptation to speak as a god, to come in his own name and to be his own authority."[3]

II. THE CONTEXT OF PREACHING

3. The Cultural Context

Preaching must be as old as the truth it proclaims and as modern as the day it is done. The message emerges from eternity, yet it is as fresh in its application as this morning's newspaper. And that is precisely the problem. How can we who preach make meaningful for the present age anything that is so ancient and time-bound to the past?

THE SCIENTIFIC AGE

Our present age is characterized by its scientific and techno-logical preoccupations. We have "come of age." This means for some that we have supposedly outgrown our need for God. By our scientific and technological knowledge and skills we can now get for ourselves what we once looked for from God. We evaluate so many aspects of our existence on the basis of scientific evidence. We have been taught to believe in nothing but that for which hard evidence can be produced. Other things may be true, but we must suspend judgment until the case for them has been proven. What has been taken for granted in the Bible is now believed by many to be a stumbling block to true knowledge and we would be better off to abandon the Bible with its "prescientific" views and get on with something more congenial to our modern ways of thinking.

This has a powerful appeal to youth, and at the same time it produces inner conflicts. Their heads tell them one thing while their hearts may plead for something mysterious, elusive, and yet true, which is hidden beneath the strangely out-of-date accounts of Holy Writ. As reported by psychologist Carl Rogers, a young man in therapy said poignantly, "I'm a pagan intellectually and in my heart, but in my guts I'm a perfect puritan."[1]

At the same time, these contemporary secularist views have had a profound effect on the value systems of many. A rigidly scientific view of the universe, which allows no place for God, raises serious questions about the grounds for meaning and morality in life. If God does not exist or if God is just some unfeeling law operating in the cosmos, then many matters once considered important are not important at all. In the end, it makes little difference whether we lie, cheat, steal, kill, and the like. We may choose on grounds of prudence not to do such things, but in the last analysis the concepts of right and wrong have no appeal.

Also, social and political realities impinge upon preaching. The same social and political situations produce both fearless prophets and moral cowards. They produce people of cautious courage as well. In truth, preaching is sometimes in a position to work changes in the social and political structures. At the same time, social and political forces are frequently effective in changing the direction and tone of preaching. It is remarkable how often the pulpit reflects in many ways the prevailing political temper. Thus truth may be compromised, and the oppressed and unfortunate may go without help. We have only to look back to the time of the Civil War and the events that preceded it. On the slavery issue, the pulpit usually echoed the political sentiments that prevailed in the community. The voices of some were not compromised but were silenced by threats of physical violence.

THE LANGUAGE AND CONCEPTS OF PSYCHOLOGY

Psychology, one of the least exact of the sciences, has come to play a dominant role in our society. Some of its principles are as old as the human race. Aristotle identified certain psychological principles in his *Rhetoric*, in which he analyzed the motives for human behavior. Yet psychology as a discrete field of human knowledge has come into its own within just a comparatively few recent decades. No aspect of life today is untouched

THE CULTURAL CONTEXT / 31

by it. Because of progress in the understanding of human personality, some pages of Holy Writ that were virtually closed to us now make more sense and more clearly mirror our own contemporary situation. A cleric went so far—perhaps too far—as to say that the language of modern depth psychology is for many people today better clothing for the gospel than Greek philosophy or Hebrew messianic language.[2]

One major Protestant denomination requires all its ministers to have a thorough psychological workup before they are full-fledged pastors. Various denominations require psychological evaluation of missionary volunteers before they are sent out to foreign mission fields. Increasingly, pastors of local churches seek to become equipped to do routine counseling more effectively and to recognize danger signals and make appropriate referrals. These same pastors also make greater use and often singularly effective use of the principles of conflict management. All of this affirms that psychology is here to stay. The sooner ministers learn what they can about it and come to understand and appreciate its possible service to religion, the more effectively can they communicate the gospel in its full-orbed splendor.

However, a misuse of psychology can obscure the gospel. One parishioner complained of a minister who was something of a specialist in psychology: "He analyzed us to death!" The knowledge of psychology can promote a trendy and dangerous kind of legalism—the perfectionism of ceaselessly touted normality, contrasted with the depressing revelations of neurosis everywhere. The "law" can so abound that grace is pushed aside. We are not saved by insight, though insight encompassed by the grace of God may be helpful in the process.

The more important matter for souls needing God is not what their past has been or what crippling conflicts rage within them now. The matter of supreme importance is the available forgiveness of God and the grace to resolve or triumph over the conflicts. With such an experience, the past can be looked at and put in perspective, and current problems can be faced with courage. Even the experience of conversion can profit from wise psychological debriefing. That may go on in the pulpit as well as in the privacy of the minister's study.

Programs of clinical pastoral training have proven helpful both to students for the ministry and for established pastors. They have helped these men and women to gain insight into themselves in an atmosphere of acceptance and encouragement and at the same time to gain skills in dealing in greater depth with the problems their parishioners face in everyday life. In his *Exploration of the Inner World*, Anton Boisen, the founder of the clinical pastoral education program, described how he was motivated for his work by the way he saw ministers relate to patients in a mental hospital. The ministers would come to the hospital ostensibly to help the patients, yet for the most part they were out of touch with the realities of the situation. When they might have said a word of encouragement and healing, they preached on such subjects as foreign missions. Boisen resolved to change that—and did!

EXPECTATIONS OF MINISTERS TODAY

In addition to these hectoring forces, the modern minister has to do the work of the pulpit often amid the harassment of multiplied parish and community expectations. The apostles faced a similar problem in the early church. They had come to the point of spending so much time in necessary administration of a program for the poor that they were neglecting their personal intellectual and spiritual growth. At the same time, they were hardly effective in the administration they attempted. The expectations of the people would not permit abandoning their social ministries—complaints were rife already. Thus necessity compelled the delegation of certain services for the community.

Demands upon the minister's time today are numerous and more complex. Many laborsaving devices actually add to the minister's burden. If we become slaves to demands so easily articulated on the telephone, there is no end to our troubles.

Unfortunately many ministers welcome interruptions and multiplied parish duties: These things offer plausible and justifiable escape from the discipline of study and sermon preparation; they also offer a ready excuse for Saturday night plagiarism. However, on this, ministers are both sinning and sinned against. Their hectic activity and going in circles may be the result of their failure to organize efficiently the time available to them. On the other hand, this culpability may be exacerbated by the congregation's failure to see a genuine need for more help to meet the extra demands of parish and community and to provide that help. But this must be said: Ministers do find a way through, around, or over the many demands made upon them. Their life expectancy as a professional group does not suffer by comparison with other professional groups, however much their sermons and those who listen to them may suffer.

What the congregation expects of the minister may be unrealistic and unfair. The detractions of cultural competitors in the forms of scientism, social and political pressures, and psychological reductionism may leave little room for God. Notwithstanding, the cry of human need continues to go up. Somehow we must fight our way through the administrative clutter to go to those who need the Word that we are called, ordained, and, presumably, trained to give. Likewise, we must acknowledge any debts we have to modern science, welcoming truth from whatever quarter it may come; we must work within a social structure of which both we and our people are functioning parts; we must use in the interest of our faith whatever psychology has to teach us of the dynamics of human behavior. Out of the incompleteness of life viewed only in three dimensions, out of the anguish of human striving in murderous competition and conflict, and out of the many frustrations common to the human family come questions, signals, pleas, and demands that the minister cannot turn away from. If we are sensitive to them, they will order our priorities. We will know what we have to preach on. And we will know how preaching must relate to all of life.

DEALING WITH PEOPLE TODAY

We are well informed about the sources of divine revelation and about the records of that revelation. But what are the sources of the revelation of the human condition? How do we come to know of the emptiness, the conflicts, and the nagging needs of Everyman?

Pastoral counseling provides the living human documents. Whether the setting is formal and the atmosphere that of the confessional, or informal and the atmosphere that of a chance conversation, pastoral conversation can uncover layer after layer of need. One noted preacher's sermons were regularly suggested by what people said to him in counseling sessions. He never violated confidences, yet he was able to see problems in the raw that drove him to the Bible for answers that he could share with a larger audience. He could safely assume that what troubled one person was likely to trouble many. Thus his preaching was, in part, ordered by what he heard in his study.

The *arts* mirror the human condition and suggest, for those who have eyes to see, the need for some kind of help. Ah, but those eyes to see! Regrettably, many of us fail to see the disparity between what is and what ought to be. For some of us, whatever condition exists is that which necessity has placed upon us. The "is" almost becomes the "ought." Whatever happens to be the case at a given point in time is normal. We may, of course, debate that in theory while defending it in practice. The best state of personality is an acceptance of life and the world as we find them!

Admittedly, the arts as a medium of disclosure of how things are with us is an elitist source of insight. What percentage of the people ponder the profound implications of Picasso's *Guernica*? How many have heard a message in *The Death of a Salesman*? Or in *Waiting for Godot*?

The negative revelation is important in our times, though the revelation appear in a corner. Even the cheaply conceived and executed offerings of sex and violence tell us volubly what we

are and what we want. All such intimations of the human condition pose questions for the Christian faith to answer. As Paul
Tillich puts it, "None of us is asked to speak to everybody in all
places in all periods. Communication is a matter of
participation."[3]

This emphasizes the necessity of *engagement*, of dialogue, of
struggle. I once asked D. T. Niles how a Christian should approach someone of a different tradition. His answer: If you are
going to board a moving train, you have to be moving as fast
as it is. One has to be as willing to listen to what God has to
say through the other person as to be willing to speak for God
to that person. It is better if the two of you can look away to
Christ and listen to what he has to say to the both of you.

This engagement, dialogue, struggle, and perhaps meeting of
minds is essential. Participation there must be. Yet there has to
be a Word from the outside. Tillich reminds us, "We can speak
to people only if we participate in their concern, not by con-
descension, but by sharing in it. We can point to the Christian
answer only if, on the other hand, we are not identical with
them."[4]

As to the participation—this is what the incarnation teaches
us. "For we have not a high priest who is unable to sympathize
with our weaknesses; but one who in every respect has been
tempted as we are yet without sin" (Hebrews 4:15). D. L. Moody
said somewhere, "I never read infidel books." His reason was
that he had prayed so fervently for faith and now had found it.
Thus, it would have seemed to him a blasphemy or a tempting
of God to expose himself to ideas that might upset his hard-
won faith. Yet he was a man of such generous spirit that his
personal problem did not cut him off from his doubting and
unbelieving fellows. Obviously, however, he was severely limited in his ability to minister to certain persons. *That* he had to
leave to others. Someone has to prepare to help the agnostic
and the atheist. And that may be painful. The rigors of preparation to do surgery are apparently impossible for some people.
Yet someone, in order to save lives, has to work through the

raw flesh and blood as unpleasant as that may be. Some persons find clinical work with the mentally ill so unsettling that they cannot do it. Yet someone has to descend to the hell of the insane in order to bring the light of hope and health.

One person cannot be everywhere at the same time or do everything anyone else can do. We do what we can and learn by suffering to do more than we believed possible. One who preaches effectively cannot live an ivory tower existence. Even if a congregation permitted it, the very nature of preaching would forbid it. Yet most of us exercise our ministries with special gifts and special attainments in which true human engagement at some important level puts us in touch with all levels. After all, the body of Christ has many members, not all with the same role, but individually working with the others to function as a vital part of an organic whole (1 Corinthians 12:12-31).

As to the separateness, our participation must mean putting the people with whom we dialogue and share in touch with Christ's world, the world we represent. Always the danger lurks that the messenger will be drawn to the other side. The believer could succumb to the skeptic's doubts. The surgeon could collapse at the operating table. The psychiatrist could grow insane himself. A good person could be lured into sin. These are the kinds of risks that Christians have to take in order to make Christ's world accessible to people who are actually seeking such a world under the guise of other allurements.

4. The Worship Context

"This world can be saved from political chaos and collapse by one thing only, and that is worship." So said William Temple, then the archbishop of Canterbury. Temple acknowledged that this sounds outrageous, but clarified his assertion as he continued: "[Men] are to find their fellowship with one another as their hearts are given to God in response to that divine love which Christ showed to men in His life and in His death."[1]

Somehow it is easy to set worship in opposition to something considered more vital. What has been called worship has been under suspicion from the earliest times, and often for good reason. Something was wrong with Cain's worship, so that God rejected it. Something was wrong with Israel's worship, so that God said, "I hate, I despise your feasts, and take no delight in your solemn assemblies" (Amos 5:21). Something was wrong with the worship of Jesus' contemporaries, so that he said, "Is it not written, 'My house shall be called a house of prayer for all the nations'? But you have made it a den of robbers" (Mark 11:17).

Thus the situation is at least somewhat confused. Yet worship has been demonstrated to have a positive impact on preaching.

POSITIVE VALUES

A service of worship *provides the occasion for preaching.* Something that deserves to be talked about goes on when a congregation gathers and worships. An activity, a scripture, a duty needs explaining or discussing. That, at the very least, is understandable and, we might say, only natural. Christian worship has much in common with the synagogue worship of New Testament times. Four main elements in this worship were: reading from the Law and the Prophets, exposition of these scriptures, public praise, and prayer. Luke gives us a glimpse into the early synagogue, where we see the appointed lesson being read and a sermon delivered by Jesus of Nazareth. Justin Martyr, writing about A.D. 140, gives us a more comprehensive and detailed picture. He reports that after the memoirs of the apostles or the writings of the prophets were read, the president of the assembly verbally admonished and invited all to imitate such examples of virtue.[2] In the history of the church, all liturgies have not had a sermon. Yet in all of them the possibility of a sermon existed. Archbishop Yngve Brilioth, in his *Brief History of Preaching*, has taken as a starting point the assertion that three basic elements emerge in the history of preaching as a golden link between Jewish proclamation and the Christian sermon: the liturgical, the exegetical, and the prophetic.[3] In other words, the preaching of the church appears within a worship context.

A service of worship *provides the best atmosphere for preaching*. It offends some of us to hear whatever precedes the sermon called "the preliminaries," as if nothing really significant is happening until the sermon begins. We ought to be offended. Yet the acts of devotion that go before the sermon *do* lend a certain atmosphere or prepare the mind and heart to receive the preacher's message. Karl Barth believed that most sermon introductions could be eliminated because "the successive acts of worship are sufficient introduction to the sermon—which is their culmination."[4] Actually, the sermon both receives from what goes before and contributes to what follows. It prepares the mind and heart for the dedication of person and money; for the receiving of communion; for the prayers of intercession; and for the daily living of the liturgy outside the walls of the church, as a "living sacrifice, holy and acceptable to God, which is your spiritual worship" (Rom. 12:1b). The Old Testament tells of an impressive worship scene: "And when the burnt offering began, the song to the Lord began also, and the trumpets" (2 Chron. 29:27). So it is today: The trumpets of proclamation begin to sound with a firm, sure note when all that is within the worshiper blesses the Lord's holy name.

This works two ways. The congregation makes a better response to the explanation, affirmation, and application of the Word of God in the sermon. At the same time, the preacher does the work of the pulpit at a high level of inspiration. We can understand the feeling of the preacher on a Sunday morning when worship was poorly attended. With a long face he looked about, noting the apparent apathy of the few persons present, and said, "And I don't even have a choir to back me up!" This same preacher, on a different and more encouraging Sunday, observed, "Great congregations make great preachers." Perhaps we could modify that to say more helpfully: Congregations that worship in spirit and in truth make preaching an event! A multitude does not have to be present to make that happen. Raymond Abba relates this story. An English colonel billeted in a French village during the First World War delighted in badgering the old village priest for one reason or another. One Sunday morning, as a mere handful of worshipers were leaving mass, the colonel said to the priest at the door, "Good morning, Father. Not very many at mass this morning, Father—not very many!" The priest replied, "No, my son, you're wrong. Thousands and thousands and tens of thousands!" He had in mind the words of the Sanctus: "Therefore with angels and archangels, and with all the company of heaven, we laud and magnify thy glorious Name; evermore praising thee, and saying: Holy, holy, holy, Lord God of hosts, heaven and earth are full of thy glory: Glory be to thee, O Lord most high."[5]

Worship that has in it "the shape of large design" *suggests the most important themes for preaching*. This is preaching guided by the Christian year. The congregation is to be pitied that has its spiritual diet determined by the personal tastes and limited experience of the preacher. This is not to say that preachers and congregations who have not heard of the Christian year are necessarily spiritually impoverished. Some preachers take their congregations beyond their personal whims by preaching straight through books of the Bible or at least through large connected sections. All of the important themes will have to be considered and preached on or deliberately ignored—and ignoring them is hard to do! Yet the use of the Christian year has certain other advantages. The Christian year is, of course, based on the Christian church's most important festivals, which have a commemorative character. Josef A. Jungmann has pointed out that this character is unusual: "In civil commemorations men celebrate some particular event of the past and recall it to mind by means of words and actions. It is not thus that the Church commemorates; with her the commemorated event is brought, in a mysterious manner, from the past into the present. Not in itself—as if what happened long ago takes place again now in the moment of celebration—but in its effects and source."[6]

George M. Gibson has noted four guiding principles in the development of the Christian year: the principle of reiteration, which "recognizes that religious constancy comes through faithful repetition"; the principle of appropriateness, in which "a certain spiritual psychology of association is at work"; the principle of "separation between sacred and profane"; and religious preparation, which is "a running theme throughout the Christian Year."[7] On the basis of what was said earlier, we could add a fifth principle, or perhaps preface Gibson's four with it: the principle of confrontation. For it is important that the preacher and the congregation be confronted with the entire range of Christian truth. When Paul Scherer gave the Yale Lectures on Preaching, he said, "For almost twenty-five years now I have done most of my morning preaching on the pericopes, . . . those selections of epistle and gospel worked out for all the Sundays of the church year with an eye to the whole round content of the Christian faith; and I have never felt them to be a hindrance or a slavery. It has been one of the most amazing facts of my experience to find opening through them one avenue after another, vista upon vista. Nothing else has so persuaded me that these familiar words of Scripture hold enshrined within them the inexhaustible riches of God."[8]

Preaching itself *may be an act of worship*. Whatever spiritually meaningful response the preacher and the congregation make in worship, it happens because of God's coming to the worshipers. He offers himself, with his forgiveness and redemption, in the preaching of the Word. As Martin Luther put it, "It is through the sermon that Christ cometh to you and you will be drawn to Him: for the preaching of the divine Word is not our word but God's."[9] God comes to us also in the Eucharist, but that is another theme, though definitely related to the sermon.

In the German language, the word for worship is *Gottesdienst*, meaning "the service of God or divine service." While it may refer to our service before God, it may also refer to his service to us. A dialogue takes place in worship—*Wort* and *Antwort*, "word" and "response"—and we do nothing apart from what God has done, is doing, and promises to do.

There is another sense in which the sermon is an act of worship. The sermon itself may celebrate the mighty acts of God and praise him in such a way as to be comparable to a hymn, an anthem, a chorale. As Roy Pearson notes, "At its best a sermon is not only surrounded by worship; it is also one of the acts of worship. And he who does not worship while he preaches has denied himself both most of the reason for preaching and most of the power. The ties between the service and the sermon are not of adoption but of blood. The sermon does not merely tolerate the service: Preaching can no more exist without worship than the diver without air."[10]

Although we may agree with Luther that in a sense the sermon is not our word but God's, it is also true that it is our word, a human word, an offering—let us hope—of our best to God.

The preacher's sermonic offering to God becomes, in turn, the occasion of the congregation's praise. When the preacher says homiletically, "Bless the Lord, O my soul; and all that is within me, bless his holy name," then the people, identifying with the sentiment, worship too.

P. T. Forsyth said, "Preaching . . . is part of the cultus. . . . The sermon has always been regarded as an integral part of the service by a Protestantism which knew what it was about. It is the Word of the Gospel returning in confession to God who gave it. It is addressed to men indeed, but in truth it is offered to God. . . . Like all the rest of the worship, it is the fruit of the Gospel." No wonder Forsyth called preaching "the organized Hallelujah of an ordered community."[11]

Now what has been said here about worship in its relationship to preaching may have sounded utilitarian, and we may justify it in part on utilitarian grounds. But that aside, worship has a deontological basis, that is, it is a duty. The word *worship*, in its English derivation, is from the Old English word *weorthscipe* and denotes the reverence or veneration paid to God. There is that in God deserving our worship whether we personally get anything out of it or not. We would surely do the concept and practice of worship a disservice if we tried to justify it solely on the grounds that it improves our preaching and the way this preaching is heard. Moreover, worship is necessary also because there is that in our human nature that seems to demand that we do it. What the Apostle Paul saw as he gazed upon the idols throughout ancient Athens was typical of all peoples of all times, civilized or not. In fact, in many ways we humans are very religious. Johan Huizinga has shown how the play element in culture passes from children's games to the rituals of sacred performances. Those who have played—and who has not?— will also worship.[12]

The issue, then, comes down to this: What kind of worship is being offered? Does the worship do anything salutary for preaching? Even when worship is of a high order, are there tendencies, omissions, or exaggerations that stultify preaching?

NEGATIVE CONSIDERATIONS

Let us now go back over the points that have been made and examine some negative evidence on them.

It was stated that "a service of worship provides the occasion for preaching." While the continuity of regular worship in a place dedicated for that purpose offers extraordinary opportunity for preaching, *effective preaching can happen without it*. John

Wesley acknowledged that at one time he would have thought it almost a sin to preach anywhere but in a church building. Yet he preached in a cemetery from his father's grave, in village squares, in open fields—wherever people would gather to hear his message. Admittedly, the songs and hymns of his brother, Charles, together with whatever prayers were offered on the occasion, could be called a service of worship, even if it took place under the open sky.

Who can begin to measure the amazing positive results of extrachurch preaching through the centuries? Yves Congar, a Roman Catholic priest, has said, "I could quote a whole series of ancient texts, all saying more or less that if in one country Mass was celebrated for thirty years without preaching and in another there was preaching for thirty years without the Mass, people would be more Christian in the country where there was preaching".[13] Congar goes on to cite Humbert of Romans (thirteenth century), Saint Bernardinus of Sienna (fifteenth century), and Johann Eck (sixteenth century). Today, the good news can be proclaimed over radio and television and via the printed page—without the benefit of prayer, song, and sacrament. While we rejoice that Christ is preached through all the media available, we might wish that all extrachurch preachers were interested in getting their listeners into local churches.

Now to go a step further. It was stated that "a service of worship provides the best atmosphere for preaching." Unfortunately, worship, as it has been practiced in some eras of church history, *can hinder preaching*, at least, preaching in the regular services. In the later centuries of the Middle Ages, preaching flourished and became a high art as it was practiced by the Scholastics in the monastaries. Also, preaching by traveling friars was received with popular enthusiasm. This could not be said for the preaching in the Mass. There the people heard significant preaching usually only during fast or festival. Priests preferred to preach on the saints rather than on the gospel lessons. According to Brilioth, "It is no exaggeration to speak of a divorce between preaching and liturgy. And that meant that the healthy interaction between the ritual and the spoken word had ceased to operate, to the detriment of both."[14]

It seems that the importance of the liturgy exclusive of the sermon was emphasized to such an extent that preaching generally went into decline. So it was easy for *Hoc est corpus meum* to become "hocus-pocus," for mystery to be superceded by superstition. The insights contained in the liturgy, which were to be transmitted, were more or less veiled.[15] Thus Vatican II directed that "the ministry of preaching is to be fulfilled with exactitude and fidelity. The sermon . . . should draw its content mainly from scriptural and liturgical sources. Its character should be that of a proclamation of God's wonderful works in the history of salvation, that is, the mystery of Christ, which is ever made present and active within us, especially in the celebration of the liturgy."[16]

These lessons, which were learned the hard way by the Roman Catholic church, should be taken seriously by Protestants who are rightly concerned about the barrenness of their liturgy and eager to enrich it but oblivious to the possibilities of overemphasis in some directions. During the Vatican II sessions, a Roman Catholic scholar observed that in their worship Catholics were moving toward emphases that had long characterized Protestants and that some Protestants had taken an unusual interest in traditional Catholic preoccupations. He concluded by saying, "I hope Catholics and Protestants will meet and not pass each other on the way!"

Moreover, the values in preaching that is guided by the Christian year were highlighted. But that has another side. The standard lectionaries endeavor to cover the whole round of Christian truth—in broad strokes, of course—in one year; and to cover a large part of the Old and New Testaments in two or three years. And it makes a good, reasonable balance of themes and texts. However, the question is sometimes asked, "Doesn't this tend to *limit the work of the Holy Spirit*? Suppose there is some pressing need in the church or nation or world, and the lessons do not fit or suggest anything helpful—what do you do?" And this! In the Reformation and some time thereafter, the Calvinists rejected the Christian year as a liturgical guide. They chose individual books of the Bible and preached straight through. This did not permit the preacher to ignore passages that might judge either preacher or congregation. Also, it enabled the people to gain a more intelligent view of the Bible in general and the book preached in particular. Note, however, that Paul Scherer, as quoted earlier, said that he did *most*—he did not say *all*—of his morning preaching on the pericopes. This was why he could say that he had never felt them to be a hindrance or a slavery. A preacher can still read the lessons for the day and then proceed to speak on a different text that seems more urgent. One can, in fact, devise a lectionary with the continuing and special needs of a specific congregation in mind, making adjustments when it is necessary and desirable. We should be free, but free to use as well as not to use the lections of the Christian year.

Once again, it was said that preaching is an act of worship. The very fact that it is such might make it appear that preaching is *an end in itself*, that its purpose is achieved when it is done and heard. Worship was never intended to turn in on itself or to be merely a dialogue with deity. "What then is the event that we usually call 'divine service?' " asks Eduard Schweizer. He answers, "It is simply the 'coming together' of the church in which it is served by its God. This means that it is primarily the occasion of listening to him, enabling us to praise him and to carry his service into the world. Thus, divine service remains what the term actually says, God's service, which always flows on a one-way street, from Jesus Christ to his church and from the church on to the world."[17]

Thus, to come to church just to "receive a blessing" is not enough; to come to receive and return to God a blessing is better but still insufficient; to come to receive God's blessing, praise him for it, and share it with brothers, sisters, and outsiders—this is true worship. Too often sermons minister to egotism, narcissism, and greed, thus becoming an aid to more successful and entertaining idolatry.

One has to take seriously the critics who say that they cannot accept the concept of worship as a duty, whether because we say that God requires it or because it seems that our human nature calls for it. Some have said that they can do without public worship, even do better without it. They point to glaring inconsistency in church between pronouncement and performance, to conflict and schism, to the superiority of radio and television sermons over the regular fare in the average church.

Paul wrote to the Corinthian church: "When you come together it is not for the better but for the worse" (1 Cor. 11:17). It is not unreasonable to believe that one may be better off without some so-called worship services, and we do not have to go so far as to mean the cults of Satan worship. We recall the church at Laodicea. To that congregation the living Christ said, "You say 'How rich I am! And how well I have done! I have everything I want.' In fact though you do not know it, you are the most pitiful wretch, poor, blind, and naked" (Rev. 3:17). What could a church like that do for a person who really wanted to worship God?

As we have gone back over the points, we have seen the dark side, to the extent that there is one. If we see some of the main problems clearly, perhaps this clarity will direct us to ways of making the impact of worship on preaching more significant, problems notwithstanding.

SUGGESTIONS FOR IMPROVEMENT

In his book *The Worship of the Early Church*, Ferdinand Hahn has explored what both the Old Testament and the New Testament have to say on worship and has distilled what he considers to be the crucial principles that must prevail in any renovation or restructuring we may do. He concludes: "The proper form of worship is always proper only to its age, because only thus can the missionary function of worship and its function in equipping the faithful for service in the world be taken seriously."[18]

Here, according to Hahn, are the essential points:

• The church meets for worship on the basis of "God's eschatological saving act in Christ." This demonstrates its power today in the activity of the Spirit.

• Worship has a missionary function, for it is in worship that the church is built up.

• Worship takes place in the real world, not in cultic isolation.

• Worship must always make room for the work of the Spirit, though this does not exclude a flexible kind of law and order.

• Worship remains open to what God will do in the future.

If Jesus Christ alone is Lord, if he seeks to bring us in worship more generously to love one another, if we make a place for the expression of differing spiritual gifts, if we consider the time and the place in deciding what is appropriate, and if we do everything to the end that the church might be edified by ministering to believers and unbelievers as well, then sermons will be meaty, mature, relevant, inspiring, and life-changing. They will more surely be the word of God for the times; they will be in a real sense sacramental.

Not only should we find help for our preaching from a better understanding of the worship in biblical times but we should also find help in the experience of the church since. We ought to know our own worship tradition well—and the reasons for it. No distinctive tradition exists without some rationale behind it. The originally good reasons may no longer exist, and the time for change may have arrived. The reasons may still be valid, and only renewal and modest updating required. In other cases, something more drastic may be needed. On October 20, 1962, the Second Vatican Council approved and released this message: "In this assembly, under the guidance of the Holy Spirit, we wish to inquire how we ought to renew ourselves, so that we may be found increasingly faithful to the gospel of Christ. We shall take pains so to present to the men of this age God's truth in its integrity and purity that they may understand it and gladly assent to it."[19]

It is this kind of self-study that every Christian group should do continually and periodically. At least, individual ministers can join other concerned colleagues and explore ways and means of renewal in local churches, if not in an entire denomination. Improvement will not come by way of adding pretties gleaned from church bulletins. Mere ornaments are a hindrance. Whenever changes seem desirable, they should answer to real need; whenever changes are made, they should reflect study, discussion, and understanding.

With the freeing up of certain aspects of liturgical practice in the Roman Catholic church and with concomitant experimentation within some Protestant groups, a new and different situation often confronts the preacher today. John Killinger began his introduction to his book on worship, *Leave It to the Spirit*, with these words: "Something drastic must surely happen to the church's worship during the next few years. Too much has happened to the world around us during the last half-century, and to the way we perceive reality, to permit the church to go on uninterruptedly conducting worship the way it has for the past three or four hundred years."[20] Because of our ever new situation, there are some different things that we should do and that—given some imagination, comradeship, and courage—we *can* do.

How can the preacher discover these different things—the methods of worship and preaching that would have the most salutary effect of the one upon the other? In truth, there is no way of doing it apart from the help of the congregation. The pastor, of course, is the key figure in it all. But pastors will fail if they inflict their personal tastes on the people, apart from any effort to get them to see matters with appreciation from the pastor's point of view. Pastors must share with their people from their special research and knowledge, and they must follow the leadership of the Spirit. The people must think along with the pastor, and they too must follow the Spirit's leadership. It should be clear: The Holy Spirit is given not to the pastor alone, but to the whole church; every believer in the body of Christ can contribute to the designing and execution of the kind of worship that meets the needs of the worshiper and glorifies God.

When a church undertakes to enrich its worship practice, it should proceed in a deliberate, orderly manner. David Randolph put it well: "The process of change in worship may be more important than the product of change." Randolph suggests the following steps for achieving liturgical change. First, we begin with worship itself, recognizing where we are and what we already have. Then we go into small study groups, perhaps utilizing a workshop and the expertise of specialists. Here the biblical, theological, and cultural bases of worship are explored. After that, a study group gathers data from those who worship in their church and from potential worshipers. Next, the group reviews and creates resources for worship. When that has been done, the group designs the service with these criteria in mind: the biblical basis, historical consciousness, personal and corporate authenticity, theological perceptiveness, missional sensitivity, and liturgical wholeness. This is a tremendous responsibility and must be reviewed and the input of the congregation taken seriously as revision is made on the basis of actual worship experience.[21] What Randolph has suggested is not the only way to gain a more meaningful experience of worship with a congregation, obviously. Some situations will require more informal plans. In any case, the primary need is the desire for something better.

What do we seek to do? It is neither a nostalgic return to the practices of a classical period nor a rootless celebration of the present. Rather, we seek to maintain what Geoffrey Wainwright calls a "diachronic identity," to keep alive, in worship, our vision of God.[25] "The Church believes its vision to be true: it believes its vision to have been decisively revealed in and through Jesus Christ: the envisaged God is believed to have a universal and lasting concern for humanity. For these reasons the church seeks for its liturgy *both* substantial identity through time *and* culturally appropriate forms which vary with human history."[22]

And can we not say that the preaching of the church, as it reaches back to the ancient sources and shows their adaptability to the present, offers a paradigm for all that we attempt to do whenever we gather together for worship?

5. The Sharing of Meaning

The purpose of preaching is to get what is in the mind and heart of the preacher into the mind and heart of the hearer. This suggests that preaching is a one-way street, a one-directional kind of communication.

Preaching *is* one-way communication. We have received a message, and we have to pass it on. The gospel is called the *kerygma*, that is, a message proclaimed by a herald. The preacher as defined by this role is more propelled by the message and/or its source than drawn by the audience.

Preaching also has a function in which the audience plays a role. The work of a herald presupposes a hearer. Furthermore, we assume that the hearer will respond. Both herald and hearer eventually share the message that both receive. If it is an important message that pertains to their vital interests, they will not be neutral or indifferent. The hearer may respond with a question, a different opinion, an elaboration, or a celebration that engages the attention of the herald. The hearer may also react with disbelief, resistance, hostility, or rejection. Thus ideas, opinions, and feelings flow in the opposite direction.

The response of the hearer, then, may elicit in turn a response from the herald. Words and feelings begin to fly back and forth in dialogue. In such an exchange, vital decisions may take place, obedience may follow. Early Christian preaching, though carrying the force of "Thus saith the Lord," nevertheless was followed by inquiry and discussion. Sometimes it resulted in faith and obedience; sometimes in unbelief and disobedience to the message.

PROBLEMS IN COMMUNICATION

What makes the communication of the message problematic? The difficulty may lie in *the attitude of the preacher*. The preacher may come across as *authoritarian* and may cause the message to sound like a kind of verbal bludgeon to compel assent. There will always be people who submit to such treatment, and their surrender makes the method appear to be successful. All the while, others silently turn away unmoved. In neither group has a true meeting of minds taken place. There has been no dialogue, no sharing of meaning.

Harry Guntrip, a psychologist, has described the authoritarian preacher in this way:

A man who, in private life, is intolerant of contradiction and disagreement, who gets heated in argument against those who will not accept all his views, who must be always right, who identifies himself with fixed opinions and is not prepared to change or learn, can find an easy rationalization for all these stubborn, resistant, and at bottom anxious attitudes by identifying himself with an unchallengeable Word of God which he proclaims, and for which he demands unquestioning acceptance from his hearers. The intolerant championship of an orthodox creed and the attempt to impose it on others provides what seems a justified outlet for the urge to dominate. This tells us nothing about the question of theological orthodoxy, but much about some temperamental weaknesses that can shelter behind it.[1]

No wonder communication is hindered!

The difficulty may lie in *the method*. Preaching as normally practiced is monological. It is one person speaking to one or more persons who do not enter verbally into the speaking situation. Pulpit preaching is not designed for dialogue. Words, phrases, and even whole paragraphs slip past the hearer uncomprehended. Questions go unasked. Feelings are suppressed. Sometimes sleep takes over even before boredom has done its perfect work. These weaknesses of the monological method can be mitigated. Many preachers do make their message clear, maintain audience attention, and achieve remarkable rapport. Yet the task is not easy, for the monological method has built-in limitations.

The difficulty may also be in a related matter—*the impersonal character of the preaching*. The monological method helps to produce this phenomenon, but the increasing size of the congregation augments the problem. The sermon may be no longer a heart-to-heart event between people who know and care for each other. It may be a kind of recitation to a sea of faces. The ultimate insult of the impersonal is epitomized when listeners begin to believe that the preacher they hear on the radio or television does not truly care for them but is interested only in their financial contributions. First, the glassy eye and then the disembodied voice will make communication difficult.

Finally, the difficulty may be *the difference between the preacher and the members of the congregation.* At an elementary level, the preacher may speak one language and the hearer another. If the preacher speaks only English and the hearer speaks only Korean, communication is extremely difficult, though not impossible. Certain gestures can convey feelings of goodwill, or desire for food or drink, but without words the preacher's most important message does not get through. Halford Luccock said, "Seminary students learn Greek and Latin and forget English."[2] The language of the academic world or the technical language of theology, may be virtually a foreign tongue to the man or woman in the pew. Sometimes a preacher who is only obscure gains a reputation for being deep. Big words may be a screen for paucity of ideas.

Similarly, cultural differences hinder communication. Politicians know this and emphasize whatever common bond they can affirm or exaggerate to make it appear that they understand the people they wish to influence. Then we smile when those politicians unwittingly show that they live furlongs away from the people. The preacher who lives in a world of literature, art, music, theology, to say nothing of Bible study and prayer, would appear to be out of touch with the day-to-day existence of most people. This preacher may or may not be out of touch. Yet he or she can hardly avoid some cultural insularity.

Experience also classifies persons and separates them. The Apostle Paul admonished his ministerial protegé Timothy, "Let no one despise your youth." Not only character defects but also sheer lack of experience of some things can undermine perceived authority. On the other hand, it could as well be said to a mature minister, "Let no one despise your age," for young people may believe that no one of an older generation could possibly understand them and appreciate their needs.

One of the strongest forces at work against the meeting of minds and hearts is the pressure of the group to which we belong. Family, religious denomination, political party, social club, vocational group—all create biases and preoccupations that often make communication between competing groups difficult. We tend to hear ideas and data as, let us say, Smiths or Joneses, Protestants or Catholics, fundamentalists or liberals, Republicans or Democrats, Rotarians or Jaycees, management or labor, or any other contrasting or distinctive groups.

MUTUAL RESPECT

Nevertheless, despite all hindrances, communication does take place—understanding dawns; conviction takes hold; emotional barriers fall; grace reigns. How does this come about?

First of all, we recognize or posit the existence of objective truth. Jude called for this when he urged his fellow believers "to join the struggle in defence of the faith, the faith which God entrusted to his people once for all" (Jude 3). We begin, therefore, with the message that we have received and make that the the common ground of our meeting. At the outset, this meeting of preacher and hearer may be stiff and formal: They may agree only on the claim of the truth of the Bible, of a particular text, or of a creed, not on the meaning. But that is enough; the preacher does not have to require the hearer to agree that the Bible is the Word of God before communication begins. The hearer has only to recognize some prior claim of truth in the Bible and let that become the basis of communication. A scientist, who was a convinced Christian, spoke informally to a group of seminary professors. He said that it is impossible to lead a person to faith by simply arguing the classical "proofs" for the existence of God. He said, however, that this was a proper subject for a believer to discuss with an unbeliever, the believer hoping that while discussion proceeded, something more important would happen. The living God does not appear—poof!—in the final term of a syllogism, but in the experience of the Holy Spirit, which is never really in isolation, but in community.

We hope for ourselves and for our hearers a response of faith and obedience. Living in the presence of God's truth can lead to faith and produce the fruits of obedience. What we read and hear does not necessarily overwhelm the intellect with arguments—it only nudges us into the stream of redemptive history, so that we are swept along in the current of God's movement in the world. Faith takes hold, and before we know it inner certitude has calmed our doubts and fears. This goes on when preacher and hearer are able to look beyond themselves and see and hear a *word* that judges and can save them both. At last the word that they question and debate speaks to them with the force of "thus saith the Lord!" and they are awed and silent in the presence of that word.

Such a result occurs because it is aided and abetted by a genuine quest for understanding. Truth seldom travels on a one-way street. The most effective proclaimer of God's truth can hardly fail to be enriched with precious insights while imparting this truth to others.

Minds and hearts are able to meet when mutual respect prevails. Surprisingly, this respect comes to those who recognize that we are all sinners. The hearer may take a pharisaical attitude toward the speaker: "Can any good thing come out of his mouth?" Or the hearer may think more highly of the speaker than the speaker deserves. To get to the truth, the Apostle Paul and his colleague Barnabas had to declare to people who wanted to deify them, "Men, what is this that you are doing? We are only human beings, no less mortal than you" (Acts 14:15). We achieve mutual respect when it is clear who it is that speaks and who it is that hears, without illusions on either side.

This mutual respect is enhanced when both sides recognize the freedom of God to communicate his truth *where, to whom,* and *as* he pleases. Call your partner in dialogue what you will—

opponent, adversary, prospect—this person may have received *from God*, the Author of all truth, some aspect of truth that can enrich the dialogue and add to the messenger's apprehension of truth. To make an *a priori* assumption that God is locked into the messenger's theological system and no longer free to speak outside that system, makes dialogue impossible and may effectively silence God, who refuses to be the prisoner of any man or any system.

We have much in common with our fellow human beings. Ordinary honesty reveals this. Shylock, in Shakespeare's *Merchant of Venice*, while making a clever defense, spoke truth. He said, "I am a Jew! Hath not a Jew eyes? Hath not a Jew hands, organs, dimensions, sense, affections, passions? Fed with the same food, hurt with the same weapons, subject to the same diseases, healed by the same means, warmed and cooled by the same winter and summer as a Christian is?"[3]

Many of the facts and rituals of everyday life are the same for all people. Likewise, basic goals are similar. Professor H. H. Farmer made a poignant confession. He said that as a minister of the gospel, he had gradually lost some of the power that he was sure he once had of "seeing and appreciating men and women objectively in their peculiar and total individuality." He had come to see them all "primarily as sinful men and women needing to be changed," and that meant that he was no longer able to see in them "that which love would not want to see changed." He said,

I caught myself once in something of the same attitude, when travelling in a train. Some men got in and immediately settled down to play cards for money. Then as they played they began to talk about their homes and children and gardens. I was horrified to notice flit across my mind a faint feeling of disappointment. My unexpressed thought had been that nobody who is so sinful as to gamble enthusiastically could have so decent and clean an interest as delight in children and gardens; if they ran true to pattern, my pattern, the pattern that is to say of one who had got into the way of thinking of men first and foremost as people to be saved, they ought really to beat their wives.[4]

Mutual respect, and the honesty that belongs to it, will reveal not only what all of us share in common but also what are our differences. We are not all alike, and in many ways we are not even remotely similar. Sex, nationality, religion, politics, age, occupation—these are some of the areas where differences actually exist. No amount of wishful thinking, sloganizing, or argument could change all of those differences. However, when we acknowledge differences and relate them to something that can transcend them, then minds and hearts can meet in creative understanding.

Notwithstanding, preachers who believe that they have been sent from God on mission will not permit their conviction and their message to be dissolved in a sea of conflicting opinions. We can be respectful of others and their views; we can recognize that we are bound together in the common bundle of life; we can honestly acknowledge our many differences—yet we have to get on with the business for which God has sent us. If God has spoken, then we must say, "Thus saith the Lord!" and tell what he has said. This may sound overbearing to some who hear us, but "if the trumpet give an uncertain sound, who shall prepare himself to the battle?" Nevertheless, regardless of how straightforward we may have to be, this is indispensable: We must do what we have to do and say what we have to say in love. Love is as important as anything we say or do; indeed, that is our message. Love, says scripture, covers a multitude of sins. In the interest of communicating God's truth, we could also say, love covers a multitude of differences and outlasts every human opinion, every human achievement, and every human failure.

III. THE CONTENT OF SERMONS

6. The Text

The text is there to be understood, believed, and applied to personal and social need. The approach to interpretation, therefore, must be clarifying, convincing, and practical. This does not rule out our recognizing the incompleteness of any hermeneutical work that we may do. The language of the text may point to vast and impenetrable mysteries, and we may only stand in wonder before the text. Still, it is the interpreter's duty to make the truth, to whatever degree we can grasp it, accessible to as many of our hearers as possible.

By theological training and vocational interest the preacher is expected to command greater knowledge of "the things of God" than does the average person. Knowledge of the biblical languages, of ancient cultures and customs, as well as of systematic syntheses of biblical truth, places the preacher in a special position of authority. However, this should not make the preacher a gnostic guru, dispensing bits and pieces of esoteric knowledge beyond the reach of ordinary people. Some preachers who dabble in eschatological mysteries often speak with the brashest confidence about the shapes and times of things to come and gain for themselves unwarranted respect among the gullible.

Responsible biblical interpretation recognizes mystery where it exists and seeks a proper attitude toward it; it dispels mysteries that are subject to understanding; and it exposes the manufacturing and use of spurious mysteries. Biblical interpretation needs the ripest scholarship available. This, however, should result in freer access to the Bible for the average person and not put barriers in the way. Much will depend on the interpreter's motivation and way of working. Inevitably, any person who makes a specialty of a particular field of study will be to an extent "set apart." That person will know or should know more about that specialty than does the average person. Yet this does not have to present insurmountable problems of communication between interpreter and hearer. Responsible preachers will present truth not to shock, mystify, or anger, but to edify.

Whenever we stand before an audience, we may expect to be challenged by various types of hearers. There will be the heavily biased, who bring with them such a burden of prejudice as to make anything we say difficult to hear clearly. Either they reject our interpretation outright or they fit it into their own scheme and claim its support. There will be the confused, who are people of goodwill, yet who bring with them a mass of misinformation or no opinion at all. Then there will be seekers, who are eager to know the truth and ready to make strong commitments to it. Clearly, the process of textual interpretation is not just a matter of intellectual understanding. It is also a matter of emotional reaction, response, and experience.

SELECTING A TEXT

If, then, the process of interpretation is emotional as well as intellectual, we need to lower the emotional voltage so as to get the facts clearly understood. Truth, when it is perceived as truth, can remove prejudice and the many distortions that go with it. Is there an approach to the sermon text that will help bring this about? Is there a way of selecting a text that will be so objective as to eliminate at least the suspicion that we use only scriptures that seem to support our personal biases?

The use of a good lectionary can deliver the preacher from hobby preaching and give—eventually—a well-rounded view of biblical truth. The prechosen lessons, not the preacher's whims, will determine the message. Of course, we can import our prejudices into any text, but facing portions of the scriptures that are broadly representative of the entire Bible will be a safeguard. Another method can deliver the preacher from a too subjective approach to preaching: the habit of preaching straight through a Bible book or through large portions of one (for example, the Sermon on the Mount). Again, the preacher, even with this method, can still wrest the scripture to accommodate personal bias.

Having said all of this in favor of two rather objective approaches to preaching, something remains to be said for the preacher's highly personal choice of texts. This can be at least an occasional method. We all have our individual angle of vision of truth. (Moreover, acute needs that present themselves demanding to be addressed require subjective response.) As we read the Bible, we sometimes dream dreams and see visions. As John Robinson, the Pilgrim preacher, said, "God has yet more truth to break from his holy word."

The more personal method of text selection can group texts for treatment in a series under a broad theme. Or, the preacher can simply respond to a perceived need, choosing a text that will "throw light upon a shadowed spot."

INTERPRETING THE TEXT

What shall we make of particular texts?

To begin with, we should *avoid spurious texts*, that is, texts that are not supported by the best biblical scholarship. A comparison of Bible versions will send one quickly to the commentaries if there are apparent discrepancies. However, variant readings may be occasionally helpful, for they represent early understandings of the texts, though we should not base sermons on them.

We should *be careful not to misunderstand the text*. Again, a comparison of versions will help. For example, "prevent" in the King James Version (1 Thessalonians 4:15) did not mean what the word means today. In 1611 it meant precisely what its Latin components meant—"to come before."

We should *not be bound by authorized interpretations*. While remembering the confession of one's family of faith when examining a text, we must keep in mind that the Holy Scriptures judge our confessions and dogmas.

We should *avoid allegorical interpretation*, that is, a kind of interpretation that arbitrarily makes one thing in the text stand for something else. No less a theologian than Augustine asserted that church doctrine must be founded only on the clear teaching of scripture, though he believed that a spiritualized interpretation of some texts could be supportive of those clear teachings. In practice, however, this method does not come off too well. The line between the literal and the spiritual meaning becomes blurred. It appears, however, that such a story as the stilling of the storm (Matt. 8:23-27; Mark 4:35-41; Luke 8:22-25) was meant to have an extended application to such storms as those of persecution and so on, in addition to its literal meaning. With these texts we have to proceed with caution.

We should *use typological interpretation very carefully*. Typological interpretation differs from the allegorical. In classical typology things set forth in the New Testament are prefigured by things in the Old Testament and are sometimes regarded as preplanned. Yet the interpreter must be judicious here also. The Apostle Paul employs typology in Old Testament interpretation (1 Cor. 10:1-11; Gal. 4:21-31), and in his relating of the events of Jesus' life to the life of the Christian (Phil. 2:5-11; Rom. 6:35).[1]

The safer course for the preacher, however, would be to leave typology to the biblical writers and use only their types in preaching. This would not hold if one adopted Gerhard von Rad's understanding of types: "Wherever one of God's dealings with his people, or with an individual, is witnessed to, the possibility exists of seeing in this a shadow of the New Testament revelation of Christ. The number of Old Testament types is unlimited."[2]

Too much fanciful exegesis makes typological interpretation as traditionally understood and practiced a dubious undertaking. Hear the wise counsel of G. W. H. Lampe: "Our safest guide to the very difficult task of distinguishing what is of permanent value from what can only at best serve as a homiletic embellishment would seem to be found in the insistence that typology must rest upon authentic history, interpreted in accordance with the biblical view of the divine economy and with due regard for the literal sense of Scripture and the findings of critical scholarship."[3]

TOWARD RESPONSIBLE INTERPRETATION

Now we shall look at ways and means by which we may be able to avoid at least some of the mistakes we can make as we attempt to interpret the scriptures for our hearers. To begin with, it is absolutely indispensable to know the biblical data and, besides knowing the facts as they are set forth in the text, to know what the text meant when it was written.

KNOW THE BIBLE

The Bible is the preacher's primary textbook; therefore, we must make every effort to know that book. Even a seminary education cannot guarantee that; such knowledge requires a lifetime of study. No part of the Bible can be interpreted rightly if we do not have a knowledge of other parts. The question or issue raised in our text for a particular sermon may be dealt with better or more fully in another part of the Bible, though our text may need to be emphasized so as to bring the larger truth into sharper focus. This cannot be done without a well-rounded knowledge of the totality of scriptural teaching. One of the purposes of systematic theology is to give a comprehensive knowledge of what the Bible teaches. However, such abstract statements are no substitute for a knowledge of the scriptures themselves, upon which systematic theology is based.

Many heresies or occasions for controversy through the ages could have been avoided if every interpretation of scripture had been subjected to the test of total scripture. To give supreme visibility to isolated and obscure texts, while ignoring the broad meaning of the Bible, is to invite trouble. Dwight L. Moody, the evangelist, had limited formal education, yet he said with true wisdom that he followed a simple principle of interpretation: he let one scripture tell him what another meant. The love of God was for him the central theme of the Bible, and that theme was always present, standing watch above his use of any Bible text. One has only to read his sermons, however, to see that his concept of love was informed by the way the love of God has been expressed by God himself, not by pale, weak contemporary notions of what love is like.

However, to regard every text on the same level of usefulness as every other text is to misuse the Bible. Depending on one's definition of inspiration, one may say that the scriptures of the Old and New Testaments are inspired in all their parts, including statements attributed to Satan or to the fool who says in his heart, "There is no God." But that is not to say that what is revealed in the words "an eye for an eye, and a tooth for a tooth" shows as much of the heart and mind of God as the words "love your enemies." Therefore, some have properly advised us that we must take account of what they term "progressive revelation." Some prefer to speak of mankind's increasing perception of what God has been revealing all along. No matter! We have to hear Jesus as he says, "You have heard that it was said . . . But I say to you . . ." (Matt. 5:21-22).

Some books of the Bible give a better and fuller account of the central teachings of the Bible than others. Likewise, the New Testament in comparison with the Old offers us the fuller revelation. The author of Hebrews puts it well: "In many and various ways God spoke of old to our fathers by the prophets; but in these last days he has spoken to us by a Son, whom he appointed the heir of all things" (Heb. 1:1-2).

Know what the Bible meant. Krister Stendahl has rightly asserted that the task of the pulpit can be carried out only if we know what the text *meant.* When this is the case, when the church and its teaching and preaching ministry are exposed to the Bible in its original intention and intensity, then they will be exposed in every way to its "ever new challenge."[4] It will not do to read our own way of thinking back into the text. Not until we have let the text speak in its own language are we prepared to translate it into our contemporary tongue.

How can we, then, know what the text meant? Of first importance, we have to deal with the text as it has been received in its canonical form. The scriptures we have now of the Old Testament and the New are what we have to work with. They have been made available to us in their canonical form because they were adjudged to have been certified by their usefulness to the community of faith as they stand. Historical and critical research can sometimes go behind these texts as we have them and discern an earlier form, and that may be useful in our interpretation. Whatever historical study of the scriptures has to offer of value we should welcome. However, the text as it stands before us will inevitably have the greater claim upon us.

In our interpretation, we work with the meaning of individual words. The interpretation often turns on the meaning of a single word. For determining the importance of particular words, the use of a book like A. T. Robertson's monumental *Grammar of the Greek New Testament in the Light of Historical Research* can prove helpful. From a different approach, the preacher will find Gerhard Kittel's *Theological Dictionary of the New Testament* a valuable aid. Similar books are available for the study of the Old Testament.

Interpretation, however, does not proceed so much on atomistic meanings found in individual words and metaphors as on related meanings in a syntactical context. The problem is usually not what this or that word or phrase means, but what the sentence or story as a whole means. Often the meaning of the individual word derives as much, perhaps more, from the immediate context as from the original root from which it sprang or from other contexts in which the word has been used.

When we interpret a passage, we must remember the special time and circumstances. Since Christ has come, we would not interpret certain laws that were obligatory for the ancient Jews as binding upon us today. Even certain directions given to the apostolic church for reasons valid in the first century were so geared to existing conditions, which no longer prevail, that they do not apply now. Still, even behind those transitory directives may lie a principle or message that is relevant in our own time.

We must be careful to take every biblical text seriously. That does not mean that we have to interpret each text literally. Some texts are clearly intended to be understood figuratively, certain parts of the book of Revelation being the indisputable examples. Other texts appearing to be historical narratives may, in fact, have been intended from the beginning to be regarded as something akin to parables. This, however, is often difficult to determine and becomes the source of controversy when it is feared that if we regard some scriptures as symbolic rather than literal, we are undermining the authority of the Bible. On the other hand, not to regard some scriptures as symbolic of something greater than what lies on their surface may be a stumbling block to certain inquiring minds. The responsible interpreter will avoid a cavalier dismissal of any biblical text or an attempt to make it what it is not. Sometimes, however, a responsible decision of faith has to be made in what has been termed "the freedom of the Holy Spirit."

It is important for interpretation to see the ethical and theological refinements that cumulative knowledge of the ways of God have made. This applies, first of all, to the biblical times. However, we may also receive enriching insights into God's truth from interpreters of the scriptures who have lived since the canon closed. While the scriptures were normative for them, they were not exhaustive. Augustine, Francis of Assisi, Luther, Wesley, Spurgeon, and Barth have enriched the legacy of God's Word. An insight from one of them may be especially illuminating as we confront a modern problem in the presence of the biblical text.

"EXECUTE THE TEXT"

With all due regard to the text and its original intent and to its history as it has touched life through the centuries, our task as interpreters is not primarily the exposition of the text but its execution. It is not nearly so important that the text should get explained as that it should get carried out. I recall a conversation with Professor Gerhard Ebeling at the Hermeneutical Institute in Zurich. We talked about his play on two German words— *auslegung* ("exposition") and *ausführung* ("execution")—as a most important distinction for preaching. In one of his essays he uses the analogy of the judge and the accused. What matters to the man standing before the judge is how the judge applies the law in his case, not the judge's explanation of it, though, in fact, the judge may deem it wise and necessary to explain the law before pronouncing sentence.[5] The most important thing that could happen when I speak about a text or read or hear a discussion of one is this: God may be speaking to me or to those who hear me through the text.

Other important things may happen also. Different sermons have different objectives, and different hearers may get different messages from the same sermon. Some sermons do have as their main business the explanation of a text or an argument for the truth of what the text says, though the ultimate, long-range aim may be to put the hearers in personal touch with God. Thus the sermon may not be so direct an assertion as we find in Karl Barth's sermon on Jesus' words as recorded in John 14:19, "Because I live, you will live also." After citing the text, he begins, "My dear brothers and sisters, *I live*. Jesus Christ has said that, and he is now saying to us again: 'I live.'"[6]

Whenever the hearer perceives the text to be a message of God for him or her, interest mounts, for the hearer has a personal stake in it. The message may come as comfort or challenge and can hardly be received with a ho-hum attitude. This happens even with a biblical story obviously out of the remote past. The preacher may narrate the story with such a depth of insight and with such lively imagination that the people hear it as their own story. It may be about Adam and Eve or Abraham and Sarah or Moses or David, but it is about me also. I have "overheard" the message, as Fred Craddock suggests in his *Overhearing the Gospel*. It has hit me perhaps more forcefully because it came to me indirectly, when all my usually effective defenses were down.

The interpreter must put many kinds of questions to the text: Everyday practical implications of the text for the individual have to be considered. Social and political issues have to be confronted. The Bible is concerned with all aspects of life, and the preacher has to weigh the significance of even apparently "unspiritual" matters for those who are trying to "walk by the Spirit." It is noteworthy that ethical imperatives and very practical advice grow out of the kerygmatic passages in the Pauline epistles.

What the text has to say cannot always be found in the text itself. A simple, clear example of that is the question in the book of Job, "If a man die, shall he live again?" (Job 14:14). Obviously the answer lies elsewhere. Perhaps a partial answer lies in the book in which the question is raised. The fuller answer, however, is in the New Testament in a word of Jesus or of the Apostle Paul.

A more difficult matter is the extrapolation of a truth from one context to another or the application of the truth to two different classes of people. For example, the relevant truth for the disciples with Jesus on the Sea of Galilee was that the God revealed in Jesus is Lord of nature and thus they were in his safekeeping even when the fiercest storm arose. This very truth may also have comforted travelers at sea in times of extreme peril. However, it perhaps had its most pointed meaning for different generations of disciples when storms of persecution arose, threatening to capsize a little congregation or some daring prophet of God. The word of Christ brought a great calm. As to the application of the truth to two different classes of people, consider the story of the Israelites' crossing of the Red Sea. James Sanders has noted that we may preach on such a text in two different ways. We may preach it to comfort the oppressed, or we may preach it to warn the oppressors. To use his words, we may preach *constitutively* or *prophetically*. We need, of course, to know our audience in order to preach with this sort of relevance.[7]

Sometimes we may go from a general or universal truth, like

"God is love," to its application to a specific case or to various instances. Or we may take a specific biblical instance and go to a general or universal truth that in turn explodes in application in various directions.

Eric Routley has warned us against taking Jesus' direct and exhaustive command, "Let the dead bury their dead; but go thou and preach the kingdom of God," to entitle a man at once to desert his dying wife or brother and enter a theological school.

> You must first translate the situation of the hearer of those words into your situation, and must further interpret the passage in the light of Christ's total teaching as the Gospels record it before you make your decision on the passage; this you must do because you are aware of the necessity for taking all possible precautions against willful misinterpretation of scripture such as may be dictated by your own unregenerate impulses. In *your* case, looking after the incurable invalid may be a disagreeable hardship, to which the preaching of the Gospel presents an attractive alternative.[8]

The Second Coming of Christ, the blessed hope of Christians, has become, unfortunately, the occasion of the most fanciful misinterpretation and misapplication of scripture imaginable. The motivation for this is hardly more noble than that of the man Routley has described. This doctrine especially and others do not need hermeneutical fantasies for support. We should let the *clear* teachings of scripture suffice. One scripture may lawfully interpret another and extend or qualify its message, but it may never lawfully violate the integrity of that scripture.

Some of the language of the Bible is strange to our ears today and describes figures and events outside the real or imagined experience of most people. Terms such as myth, historical image, metaphor, symbol, parable, and poetry have been applied to these phenomena. Such terms have sometimes offended certain believers, for parts of the Bible appear to be dismissed as mere fiction. And these terms have led others not only to discard the language but also to miss the truth that the language represents.

However, rather than naively accepting a label or image at face value just because it appears in the Bible, we should try to understand its significance and present its truth if possible in the dynamic of the language and thought forms of our own time. For instance, many biblical cases of "demon possession" are what today we would call insanity.

The important fact in the gospel stories is that Jesus brought healing and happiness to many who were thus tormented. The preacher's difficult but necessary task is to help the people think biblically while maintaining their solid footing in the modern world. This effort may produce struggle in both preacher and people. It is not easy to mesh the two worlds. We have to impart understanding without subverting faith and encourage faith without promoting credulity. After all our effort, however, we may discover that God in his mysterious way has completed what we began but were powerless to finish.

A part of the interpreter's task may be to present the truth of the text in the form of the text itself. Meaning can be at least partially contained in the literary or liturgical configurations of the text. John Ciardi compiled a volume of poetry with the title *How Does a Poem Mean?*, arguing that to attempt to squeeze out the essence of a poem can detract from its meaning. Some—but not all—biblical texts lend themselves to homiletical or liturgical forms that reflect the image of the text. If the sermon follows the inner movement of the text, the sermon may take on the shape of scripture, without necessarily using the exact words of the text or simply paraphrasing it. The homily, when it is done well, can be such a sermon; likewise, the story or biblical incident. The homily will follow the scriptural passage verse by verse; the story will move through the dynamics of the narrative, from the situation through the complication to the resolution (or illumination). If we take our cue from the form of the text and do not try to force every sermon into the same homiletical mold, then we may not only heighten interest by molding form to the variety of biblical material but may also convey more of the meaning of scripture.

QUESTIONS TO AID TEXT INTERPRETATION

Biblical interpretation at scholarly levels requires attention to technical matters that arise in the various types of biblical criticism. These proper concerns, however, have not been the primary focus of this chapter. They do intrude to one degree or another in the early stages of sermon preparation.

The list that follows was put together from certain questions raised by some of my mentors,[9] as well as from questions that I wished to ask the text myself. These questions may lead to investigation of technical matters of biblical criticism, or they may not. Certainly this list does not pretend to be exhaustive or to ask every specifically pertinent question germane to homiletical interpretation. It offers a place to begin. Not all of the questions need be posed for every text. If the text is preachable for the time and audience, more material can be turned up than could possibly be used in any one sermon.

1. *What is the text about?* Give the text a general theme from systematic theology, (for example, eschatology, worship, or doctrine of God).
2. *What does the text mean to you?* This question may seem to be premature. Should we not do careful exegesis and look at the history of the interpretation of the text first? Not necessarily. Your first impression is likely to be the understanding of the average reader of the text. So it is a good place to begin. If further investigation proves that the facts will not bear out your first impressions, you are none the worse for it. We learn by contrast as well as by comparison. Besides, you will be aware of the average person's interpretation and can work from there.
3. *What crucial exegetical issues in the text might bear on a correct interpretation?*
4. *What is the significance of the text in relation to Jesus Christ and the history of redemption?* This applies to both Old Testament and New Testament texts. Remember the words

of Gerhard von Rad: "Wherever one of God's dealings with his people, or with an individual, is witnessed to, the possibility exists of seeing in this a shadow of the New Testament revelation of Christ."[10] Moreover, the ethical teachings of Jesus and the apostles have to be seen as *a part of* and not *apart from* the movement of God's grace toward us and toward all people in the Christ event. Christian preaching is always within the context of God's purpose revealed in Jesus Christ.

5. *What has the text meant to other interpreters?* This question points to such interpreters as Augustine, Chrysostom, Luther, Calvin, and Barth. Though the contexts of their interpretations were different in some respects from our own, their insights can enrich our personal understanding of the text. The older interpreters were not so well equipped for a scientific study of the text as we may be in our day, but they were well equipped to expose the spiritual depth of the text. Protestants have rightly never felt *bound* by the interpretations of "the Fathers," but they have too often wrongly ignored them.

6. *What is the point of immediacy? Where does the text strike closest home in your life?* The point of immediacy could be at one place one time and at another place another time.

7. *What is there in the text that would make it difficult to communicate?* What makes it difficult for you to accept it? You can anticipate some of the problems of your hearers as you honestly face your own. It would be a mistake, however, to assume that everyone, or even that any other member of your audience, asks *your* question. However, some of your hearers may have different problems. Here a bit of spiritual "clairvoyance" is called for.

8. *Can the truth in the text stand alone, or does it need to be seen in relation to a counterbalancing truth?* Preachers do not have to offer a complete compendium of Christian truth each time they speak. Nor must every one-sided thesis be brought into synthesis with its antithesis. Often, however,

the latter is helpful, perhaps even essential. Nevertheless, "a too well-balanced sermon does not really convey its message."

9. *What are some of the causes of the condition or situation discussed or suggested in the text?* The most interesting sermons ordinarily are those whose relevance is unmistakable—they deal with a *present* problem or difficulty. Just as it is often helpful to know the cause of a disease in order to treat it successfully, so it may be helpful to recognize the etiology of a need in the course of prescribing a remedy. In addition, when you recognize the causes of an ordinary human situation not necessarily sinful or unpleasant in itself, this may point toward the need for a higher goal.

10. *What are the theological implications or practical duties that grow out of the truth of the text?*

11. *What objections may be raised to your conclusions about the implications and applications of the truth of the text?* Anticipate emotional reactions and intellectual problems. Preaching that does its work cannot be taken for granted. Often we can keep emotional reaction from becoming harmful or destructive. Moreover, we can often keep an intellectual problem from bogging down the sermon if we simply recognize the existence of the problem and pass on to matters that we and our hearers are more competent to deal with. Perhaps the pulpit is not the proper place for in-depth or technical discussion of some issues. But it should be noted that the ancient rhetoricians made a place in a discourse for "answers to objections." The preacher, more than anyone else, will be expected to be warmly considerate and scrupulously fair.

12. *What would be the results of knowing or failing to know, believing or failing to believe, or doing or failing to do what the text suggests?* To consider the consequences of our decisions and actions is to be realistic. Often our flagging wills need the extra boost of fear of punishment—not necessarily arbitrary punishment—or expectation of reward.

This may not be the highest or most desirable motivation, but it is a recognizable part of human experience. The Bible is not unwilling to give us the *total* picture.

13. *What must you do to make the message of the text real and true in your own life?* This is the point at which *kerygma* ("message") becomes *martyrion* ("witness"). The gospel becomes incarnate and is revealed through our own experience of it in the dimensions and shape of our own need.

14. *What is there in general literature, in biblical resources, in personal counseling, and in personal observation and experience that will exemplify or illustrate the truth of the text?* The finest argument pales beside the strength of an actual instance of a truth. Moreover, human interest stories are endlessly fascinating.

7. The Emergent Truth

The central idea of the sermon is a statement of the truth that emerges from a study of the text and that determines the content of the sermon. Every sermon has a central idea or at least a constellation of related ideas. This is called by various names: proposition, theme, subject, message, and so on. The central idea is a theological or theologically shaped statement. It generates and controls the conceptual development of the sermon.

It seems better to use the term *central idea* because this can include ideas that are not argumentation, as would be suggested by the term *proposition*, as well as subjects, which do not carry a complete thought, and thus do not merit the term *proposition*.

VALUE OF THE CENTRAL IDEA

The central idea will come from a careful effort to put into a brief statement or a subject that which the text seems to want said in a particular sermon. We can say several things in favor of the use of such a statement or subject.

First of all, a central idea stimulates the preacher's creativity. It gets the ideas flowing, which will expand into the finished sermon. Many preachers preach quite acceptably without formulating a central idea. If they are biblical or expository preachers, the text itself, or a part of it, will serve as the central idea. However, we find many preachable passages in the Bible that do not lend themselves to consecutive treatment or that do not locate their center of gravity in one verse or in a part of a verse. In these cases, the preacher has to try to extract a statement that will best represent the thought in the text. Once this is done, the ideas begin to percolate up from this idea in such a way that the truth of the text can make its best showing.

The idea that appears may, by its very nature, suggest a particular type of treatment. Or the audience to whom the message will be preached may suggest the necessary treatment. Some truths simply call for elaboration. They need to be spun out into a more highly developed form. This sometimes requires meticulous definition of terms or extended explanation. Analogies and examples aid in this process.

The first thing you may wish to do after you have determined the apparent intention of the text is to contradict this "truth." You may wish to do this because of your personal resistance or because you perceive that a negative reaction will be the first response of your hearers. Of course, you will go on to attempt to compose those differences, for, after all, it is your business to set forth what the scripture teaches, not just what you or someone else may approve at the moment. On the other hand, you may wish to prove the truth of the text. Perceiving some skepticism or potential skepticism in your hearers, you may feel that the credibility or practicality of the text can be enhanced by arguing for them. You will then seek for logical arguments to support this central idea or for analogies or examples that carry power to convince.

Asking questions is a stimulus to creativity. As we have seen, the putting of a series of questions to the text can produce more ideas than you can use in a single sermon (see Chapter Six). However, once the central idea is determined, this, in turn, can be queried so as to produce more ideas, ideas that are more sharply defined. Then comes the need to ask the question of relevance: So what? What are the practical applications of this theologically shaped statement? If it does not tie in with life today, we should ask if this is an idea worth discussing. It may be trivial or inconsequential. If this is true, we should abandon the idea and go on to something else that makes a difference. However, we should not abandon an idea simply because its relevance is not immediate or obvious. Some ideas are highly relevant in the long run. The trick is to discover which are and which are not. Nevertheless, the effort to discover the practicality of the central idea can be highly productive. Austin Phelps noted: "If your inventive power is sluggish, restriction of theme will stimulate it: if it is active, restriction of theme will give it scope. Invention exercised on a restricted proposition is microscopic. It discovers much, which, in ranging over a broader surface, it would lose. It is penetrative. It goes in to the heart of a theme. . . . The preacher speaks from a full experience of its richness in his own mind."[1] The central idea *gives weight* to the sermon. As Henry Grady Davis has shown, the central idea answers two questions: What is the preacher talking about? What is the preacher saying about it? The first question gives the subject; the second, the predicate. Both taken together yield a sentence that is the gist of the sermon, the sermon in a nutshell—the central idea.[2] This gives weight to the sermon because the sermon must be about that, nothing more, nothing less. Sermons that are not bound by a central idea are often a kind of weightless fluff made up of ideas from anywhere and everywhere, and going nowhere. Such ideas may be true, even biblical, but they do not belong in these particular sermons. If they had been germane to a different central idea, they might have given solidity and weight to that sermon. But when they are misplaced, they trivialize the sermon.

The central idea *gives portability and direction* to the sermon. The central idea carries the homiletical genes that determine the essential characteristics of the sermon. When the sermon is full-grown, it will be only what the central idea promised. *Where* the sermon lives and moves and has its being is a somewhat different matter. Yet the very nature of the central idea limits the uses that can be made of it—the sermon will move in certain general directions, regardless of audience and occasion. It will never be self-contradictory. Whether the theme *God is love* be explained, argued for, or applied to personal or social matters, it will always mean that God is a God of love, nothing less.

The central idea *gives unity* to the sermon. If we take the central idea seriously, the sermon must be about that. This will not guarantee that the sermon will be interesting, but it will increase the likelihood of more than ordinary attention and of unusual effectiveness.

SOURCES OF THE CENTRAL IDEA

Two great events have shaped the theological concepts of both Jews and Christians: the Exodus and the Christ event. To be sure, certain noteworthy events and experiences preceded even the Exodus, but it was the Exodus that gave shape and significance to them. Biblical theology traces and describes the etiology and history of the main themes that wind through the Bible. Systematic theology discusses these same themes—and perhaps others—in relation to certain philosophical and historical concerns. Some biblical theologies are, however, strongly influenced by systematic concerns, and some systematic theologies by biblical concerns. Thus certain great theological concepts become touchstones of textual interpretation.

The concerns of biblical theology and of systematic theology have from time to time come to a focus in a creed or confession of faith. A theological crisis of greater or lesser degree called forth these statements. Thus they are historically conditioned. Notwithstanding, they are important because they embody serious and significant thinking that deserves consideration whenever these same issues are confronted again. Martin Luther believed that popes and councils had erred and therefore that every creed and papal declaration had to be tested by the Word of God. The same is true today. Nowadays no one has to insist that this task is necessary. It is being done and will be done, regardless of who objects. The problem today may be to get our contemporaries to refer matters of faith to these creeds and confessions for reflection and perhaps for guidance in settling some important doctrinal question.

An examination of the scriptures inductively will lead to certain conclusions about the main teachings of the Bible. These conclusions used deductively will yield systematic treatments of these teachings. Therefore, whenever any individual verse or passage forms the background of the central idea, the classical creeds of Christendom, the confession of one's own family of faith, as well as the perceived teachings of biblical and systematic theology, must form a part of that background. This does not have to stifle creativity and relative originality, yet it must stand in judgment always. "No prophecy of scripture is a matter of one's own interpretation" (2 Pet. 1:20).

A further source of theological truth is in the believing community, sometimes even among unbelieving members of the larger community. A widely neglected resource for sermons is the person who will hear the sermon or who is a potential hearer. The wise preacher will let the people who hear the sermon help to set the theological agenda. Their help may be no more that that of asking the right questions, to which the biblical texts and the propositional formulation of its truth attempts an answer. Eduard Schweizer said that the less pious of his hearers asked the best questions, for they were the people to whom the gospel was first of all addressed.[3] Thus the central idea has a chance of being more surely what God wants said, since it is determined not only theologically but also anthropologically. Both God and man have input!

The challenge to the theologically concerned preacher is to discover and facilitate the ways in which, as John Robinson said, "fresh light shall yet break from God's Word."

THEMES AND FORMS OF THE CENTRAL IDEA

With regard to themes, the preacher must tell the story or stories, explain the events and ideas, set forth the arguments, offer inspiration and support, and call for responsible decisions—all within the guidelines of a carefully worked-out theology. This theology will be responsive both to the biblical record and to philosophical and practical issues of the day. These are some of the theological guidelines that mark the boundaries of the sermon:

• God is a God of love, holiness, and power, who has revealed himself as Father, Son, and Holy Spirit. He created the universe, standing above it in his transcendence and penetrating it in his immanence.

• Man, the special creation of God, was made, male and female, in the image of God. Man, because of weakness and willfulness, was found in a state of sin—alienation from God, from his fellow creatures, and from himself. Because man was unable to put himself in a right relationship with God and because God loved his creature in spite of sin, he took the initiative and did what was necessary to redeem man. This salvation came to its fullest expression and its universal application in Jesus Christ, the Son of God, who, by his death at the hands of men and resurrection by the power of God, was God's good news of hope and salvation for sinners.

• Salvation, in its personal and corporate experience, and in its temporal and eternal dimensions, is available to all who respond in faith to God's free offer.

• The life of faith is characterized by a state of peace with God and growth in character, by personal and corporate worship, and by service to fellow human beings. This life of faith is possible through the providence of God and through the constant influx of his grace that comes to believers at the time of decision and baptism or confirmation and in the continual experience of the Eucharist, as well as in numerous acts of providence, known and unknown.

• The consummation of our salvation is eternal life in the presence and under the blessing of God. All is of God's grace, from beginning to end.

Such guidelines are obviously incomplete, and the ideas that flow within them will move at different speeds at different times and will take on changing colors and tones. Theologian Joseph Sittler put it well:

The task of theology, as I understand it, is to make statements which clearly, intelligibly, and in just relationship set forth the content of the

Christian faith as that faith is known and celebrated in the church. This definition requires that we understand theology both as a content and a task. It is a content because there is a sameness in the issues, divine and human, which it talks about, and a continuity in the substance of what it affirms about them. But it is the purpose of such statements to be intelligible; i.e., to say what is said in such a way as to communicate clearly to another mind precisely what the claim is. And because this activity goes on in a world where canons of clarity, requirements of intelligibility, and the nature of immediate human needs are in constant flux, the task of theology is a never-ending one.[4]

The content of the sermon can be expressed in several basic forms. Each of these forms can express a separate aim that the preacher has for the particular sermon.

EXPOSITION

The preacher may need to give information. The conveying of data is an important function of communication. This may include, of course, what you know, what you believe, what you feel, what you decide or do. Exposition, then, is a setting forth of information. It is also explanation of something. When we preach on a biblical text or deal with an idea, we may first of all simply lay out the facts. After that, we explain what we have said. We may include definitions, examples, comparisons, and the like, so that our hearers know not only the facts but also what the facts mean. Take the brief text "God is love." Your exposition may include a definition of your terms: What do we mean by the word *God*? What do we mean by *love*? What does the entire sentence mean? Or we may rephrase the biblical text, so that we say, "God loves us." The approach here is similar, yet the very phrasing of the sentence may dictate somewhat the form that the exposition takes. For example:

Central idea: God loves us.
General end: To explain.
Specific intent: To help my congregation to *understand* that God loves us.

ARGUMENT

The preacher may need to argue for the truth of the text or of the theme derived from the text. A simple setting forth of the facts or an explanation of what the facts mean may not be sufficient. Often prejudices have to be removed. Also, open-minded people frequently need evidence for what they are asked to accept. They must have a case made for the proposition offered for faith. Such argument, then, is the next step after exposition. Argument is not always necessary or essential to bring exposition to completion, for, when an issue has not been raised, exposition can stand on its own feet. But argument always presupposes facts, data, information. Argument builds on exposition. Occasionally, of course, a clear explanation is the best argument. Often more is needed. Let us now take the same text or theme: "God is love" or "God loves us." In argument, your main concern is to treat the idea as an issue. For some people, the idea is debatable. They need evidence before they will believe. Therefore, the same idea, when it is used to secure belief, requires a quite different form as it is fleshed out. We may base our "proofs" on several kinds of evidence. We may appeal to scripture, to tradition, to authorities ancient and modern, to intuition, to experience, to reason, to faith, and the like. Admittedly we can misuse what we construe as evidence; we can be unfair; we can even be deceptive. On the other hand, we can be careful, fair, and honest, and our argument may help someone find God. In the process, our effort will have caused the sermon to take a particular form.

Argument can take the form of exploration. The theme takes the form of a question: "Does God love us?" Many persons are not sure that God really loves us; therefore, we can treat this as a legitimate issue. We can take seriously the skepticism of our bewildered hearers and begin with them a quest that will lead down several paths of investigation. We will do our best to deal fairly with all our hearers' questions and then arrive at what we believe to be the right view of the matter. This is an inductive approach that will have an unusual appeal to those who like to think through their problems rather than shelve them with a glib answer that pretends authority. This approach does not or should not imply that the preacher does not have the answer until the end of the sermon. Obviously the preacher will be imitating induction or showing the inductive process by which a conclusion was reached while preparing the sermon. For example:

> *Central idea:* God loves us.
> *General end:* To convince.
> *Specific intent:* To help my congregation to *believe* that God loves us.

INSPIRATION

The preacher may wish only to use the text or theme to breathe new life into the congregation. The preacher assumes that the people know what the text or theme is and that they know what it means. The preacher further assumes that the people know and understand. What then? It remains for the preacher to point to text or theme as a source of hope, courage, confidence, comfort, or aspiration. Consider this example:

> *Central idea:* God loves us.
> *General end:* To revitalize.
> *Specific intent:* To help the people to *find comfort and strength* in the fact that God loves them.

PERSUASION

The preacher may wish to bring people to a decision that leads to action. The preacher (or someone else) has presented the facts and explained what is essential and has credibly argued the case. Now the hearers need the opportunity and motivation to bring to a decision what they have learned and have come to believe. It is a time of new beginning. Here the preacher must unpack the text or theme—"God is love" or "God loves us"—in its urgency, calling for decisive trust, definite acceptance, and grateful obedience and service. For example:

> *Central idea:* God loves us. (Or, to be more specific: Because God loves us he offers us his saving friendship.)
> *General end:* To actuate.
> *Specific intent:* To lead uncommitted people in my congregation to *accept and live by* God's love for them.

STYLE OF THE CENTRAL IDEA

The central idea should be *relevant*. It is best stated in timeless language, language that is always timely. It is historically correct to say, "When Simon Peter denied his Lord, he dishonored Jesus and brought remorse upon himself," but it is homiletically better to say, "When we deny our Lord, we dishonor Jesus and bring remorse upon ourselves." Even when we preach on the sovereignty of God or on his transcendence, we should set forth the central idea in such a way that the subject is somehow related to human experience today.

The central idea should be *complete*, that is, it should contain the essence of the entire sermon, both subject and predicate. Obviously it cannot comprise all extensions, details, and applications, yet none of these would be out of place within its bounds. One exception is what H. Grady Davis called "A Subject Discussed."[5] In this case, the central idea does not take the form of a complete sentence. The central idea is a subject. The main points of the sermon constitute a "distributed predicate." These points are therefore necessary to make the central idea complete. Other statements of the central idea have both subject and predicate by implication.

The central idea should be *simple*. We ought to avoid heavy theological or philosophical language. A bit of care will enable us to put our thought in language that our hearers can readily understand.

The central idea should be *lean*. We achieve this quality by omitting unnecessary adjectives and adverbs as well as unnecessary qualifying phrases and clauses. The discussion in the sermon itself is the place to deal with the subtleties and nuances of our thought, so that the central idea only furnishes "a center of interest."

The central idea should be *literal*. Figurative language sometimes obscures thought or commits the preacher to pursue a dominant image throughout the sermon, which restricts the natural movement that the sermon would otherwise take.

The central idea should be *striking*. This might seem to be an impossible achievement if we must avoid figurative language. Yet, it can be done by writing and rewriting the central idea— trying the idea first one way and then another—until it is both impressive and able to be fixed in the hearer's memory. To achieve either of these goals, the central idea has to be brief. The longer the sentence, the fuzzier the meaning and the more difficult the remembering.

SOME WORTHY EXAMPLES OF THE CENTRAL IDEA

These statements of the central idea of particular sermons come from preachers who have served in widely ranging times and circumstances. The statements are clear, are relatively brief and uncomplicated, and are promising of interesting or significant discussion to follow.

Robert South: "Good intentions are no excuse for bad actions."

F. V. Reinhard: "Faithfulness in present duty qualifies for higher functions."

Austin Phelps: "Men who are deeply interested in religion as a theory often revolt from it as an experience."

Thomas Chalmers: "The power of the gospel to dissolve the enmity of the heart against God."

Horace Bushnell: "Obligation to God is a privilege."

Nathaniel Emmons: "A man's religion may be his ruin."[6]

D. M. Baillie: "We can find the whole Christian gospel summed up in this mysterious doctrine, of three persons, Father, Son and Holy Spirit, in one God."

Harry Emerson Fosdick: "The sacred and the secular are inseparable."

G. Earl Guinn: "The Christian religion stands or falls with the resurrection of Jesus."

J. Wallace Hamilton: "Conversion is that process, through which the redeeming power of God brings all the powers of your being into perfect focus and co-ordination."

Wayne E. Oates: "The vision of God in Christ is most vividly real in the sufferings of human personalities about us."

Norman Vincent Peale: "You can have power over all your difficulties."[7]

John A. T. Robinson: "In what sense if any should a thoughtful Christian want to maintain that Jesus was unique?"

Robert Schuller: "Turn your weakness into strength."

Paul Tillich: "You are accepted."

John Claypool: "We humans cannot have everything all at once."[8]

8. The Aim

Do we preach to carry out the purpose of God and thus get glory for him, or do we preach to do something good for those who hear us? Is preaching an end or is it a means? Is it irrelevant to human need or is it relevant?[1]

The gospel we preach did not arise from the goals and motives of men. "General psychological principles do not carry you to its heart and essence at all."[2] It has to do with another world impinging upon our own, with a transcendent purpose. The gospel we preach is the proclamation of God's saving activity for us human beings. It tells of a God to be loved, obeyed, and worshipped, and it calls forth such responses as a rightful claim. Viewed from a human perspective, the preaching may seem to be irrelevant to many of our concerns; it does not bend to our whims and preferences.

Yet, all that the gospel is has very much to do with everything that concerns us—whether as judgment upon it, affirmation of it, or transformation of it. The preaching enterprise is incarnational in purpose and form. The gospel does not have to be made relevant to us and our hearers; the relevance of the gospel has only to be discovered. However, there are ways to facilitate the experience of that relevance. The preacher can follow some very practical procedures that will bring the saving work of God very close to the congregation's actual need by awakening a sense of particular need.

Determining the objective of a sermon rests back on exegesis of the hearers. We have to know something of the need to which we preach. The best sermon is not one in which the preacher "draws his bow at a venture." If we aim at nothing, we are likely to hit nothing. If we have a general Christian understanding of universal human need, we may have a fuzzy target, but occasionally we can hit it.

Something more specific, however, is also required. The pastor routinely encounters a variety of human need in counseling and visitation. As the congregation perceives us to be approachable, unshockable, sympathetic, and helpful, the members will more and more unburden to us their hearts and consciences. We will become true confidants. Thus, in that relationship we will see an endless pageant of unfolding need. We will have something definite to aim at: a soul to be saved, a text to be explained, a doctrine to be taught, a conscience to be guided, a heart to be comforted, or a worshiper to be met with God.

Let us examine these six aims and what they imply for our preaching.

EVANGELISTIC PREACHING

Evangelistic preaching is the preaching that builds the church.

In certain quarters this type of preaching has a hard time. Some of the worst sermons imaginable have been associated with evangelism. The preacher that Charles R. Brown described epitomizes the problem. He whines, "My beloved hearers, if I may call you so, you are under some measure of moral obligation to repent, so to speak; and in case you do not, I would venture to suggest that there is a remote possibility that you may be damned as it were, to a certain extent."[3]

At a conference on worship a lecturer paid his respects to evangelism. When asked how the outsiders would learn of Christ, he replied, "Let them come to our liturgy!" His reply was unwittingly ironic. The establishing of Christianity in his part of the world was the result of imaginative efforts to take the gospel to the people where they were and to confront them with God's grace as they were.

The growth of some churches is too parasitical. If they ever get a new member who did not grow up in a church-going family, that person will likely be a convert recruited by some "less respectable" church that goes into the highways and hedges to bring people into the kingdom of God.

If our sermons are never evangelistic, could it be that we are guilty of preaching another gospel?

The "gospeler" differed from the Old Testament prophet. The ancient prophet had bad news to announce, however good might be the ultimate purpose of God for his Word. The New Testament herald announced in the midst of darkness, judgment, and destruction the best news one could hear.

All true and effective evangelism rests on solid theological foundations. How can one be led to genuine repentance and amendment of life apart from conviction of the greatness, goodness, and love of God? Human need, the forgiveness of sins, and salvation?

Evangelistic sermons will treat many aspects of the Christian faith. The basic truths can be elaborated into countless particulars. Ethical and social implications will form a wide spectrum. Yet all particulars and applications must be founded on the bedrock affirmations of a sound theology. And the relationships should be clear for the hearer. No cut-flower sophistry or moralizing will do. The Apostle Paul takes eleven chapters of theological discussion in Romans to lay the groundwork for the ethical superstructure that begins in chapter twelve. Perhaps the theological-ethical polarities in Romans are more obvious than most sermons would need. Yet everything said in a sermon should be easily traceable to the big truths.

The Christian faith is grounded in history. The Apostle Paul, writing to the Corinthian church, spoke of "the gospel which you received on which you have taken your stand, and which is now bringing you salvation (1 Cor. 15:1). What gave rise to their faith? Facts! "I handed on to you the facts which had been imparted to me" (1 Cor. 15:3).

Certain events took place on the plane of human history, especially the Exodus and the Christ event, as well as events before and after, that made plain that God had chosen a people and that he was for his people. In the words of Walther Eichrodt, "With this God men know exactly where they stand; an atmosphere of trust and security is created, in which they find both the strength for a willing surrender to the will of God and joyful courage to grapple with the problems of life."[4]

It is significant that in the decisive sermons in the book of Acts, the call to repentance and faith is preceded by detailed reference to the history of God with his people and by careful effort to link up what had happened with what was going on right then. No one was expected to profess faith in an intellectual vacuum.

Sometimes the apologetical task may be a preacher's most challenging evangelistic opportunity. Peter Gomes sees as a beckoning ideal "thinking hearts and loving minds."

People do not slide by degrees into the kingdom of God. One may be "not far from the kingdom of God," as Jesus put it. Yet one is either in or out. Those who are not far may soon be in, but until they are in they are still out.

John the Baptist, Jesus, and the apostles called for clean choices. Decision was publicly and dramatically shown by confession of faith, by baptism, and by amendment of life. The New Testament states the alternatives in terms of such contrasts as life or death, saved or lost, light or darkness, salvation or perdition. Moses put matters graphically when he spoke to Israel: "I call heaven and earth to record this day against you, that I have set before you life and death, blessing and cursing: therefore choose life" (Deut. 30:19).

There is no way to be in the biblical tradition without plainly presenting the alternatives in the vital decisions of faith and practice. It is true that we can be drawn toward what is good for us before considering the alternative. An infant seeks food long before it is able to reflect on the possible results of rejecting food. We may seek God's love and grace in something of the same way. Nevertheless, a consideration of alternatives and consequences often impels people toward what is good for them, and they may be impelled in no other way. William Temple said, "At first or last there must be a sharp break, a conversion or new birth or else there must be a series of conversions, but there is need for real discontinuity."[5] A clear picture of the alternatives is often decisive in achieving this sharp break.

William James, discussing the adopting of a new way of life, asserted that "we must take care to launch ourselves with as strong and decided an initiative as possible . . . Put yourself assiduously in conditions which shall reinforce the new way . . . take a public pledge, if the case allows; in short, envelope your resolution with every aid you know."[6]

So far as religious conversion goes, this translates itself in one of two ways: as believer's baptism or as confirmation of an earlier baptism.

Public profession of faith, even without baptism, is important. But baptism is the normative and most significant commitment to Jesus Christ. The Lord's Supper then becomes the occasion for the continual renewal of that commitment.

Immediate counseling with the inquirer should be urged and provided so that warm interest and promising resolution do not evaporate through lack of opportunity for follow-through. Not many people come to faith without the intervention of some other person or persons in a private conversation. Churches in which people are regularly making professions of faith are churches whose members actively share their faith in personal witness. And this rarely happens when the preacher does not set the example.

Personal evangelism is not easy. Those who could do it easily most likely do it poorly. One should hesitate to intrude on another's privacy, to barge in officiously, even with the good news. However, there are ways that prayer, friendship, and providence will reveal that do not have to violate the sanctity of another personality. The concerned and sensitive minister can show lay people how to do this, and they, if they are eager learners, will perhaps go on to do the job even better than the minister can do it. The problems, fears, and hesitations that emerge in personal encounter will make the preacher all the better able to deal effectively with these matters from the pulpit.

True faith, saving faith, makes a difference in how the believer lives. James put it negatively: "Faith without works is dead" (James 2:20). Motivation changes so that one is good and does good not because one has to but because one wants to.

The necessary changes do not all take place overnight. Questionable habits may be overcome gradually. Intractable problems may take a lifetime. Yet there will be a difference, and the preacher must insist on it as Paul did: "I implore you by God's mercy to offer your very selves to him: a living sacrifice, dedicated and fit for his acceptance, the worship offered by mind and heart" (Romans 12:1).

EXPOSITORY PREACHING

Much so-called expository preaching is so bad that it gives the real thing a bad name. A preacher can talk about a Bible text at length, going into its historical background and original meaning accurately, and yet preach a sermon that is a failure as exposition. On the other hand, a preacher can preach a sermon without a specific text, which is truly biblical in spirit and message, and yet present the living God far more faithfully than the preacher who imagines that biblical exposition is happening because there is much talk about the text. Both preachers may have something important to learn: the first, that true biblical exposition always keeps the present hearers in view as the scriptures are interpreted; the second, that any vital message for today is enriched and strengthened when it emerges from or is clearly linked to a specific passage of scripture.

Good, scripturally grounded preaching does not have to be "expository," as I use the word, to be soundly biblical. Biblical preaching is the *sine qua non* of the Christian preacher. Expository preaching is a form—and an important one—of biblical preaching.

John A. Broadus characterized the expository sermon as one in which explanation of the scriptures is primary. The amount of such explanation would vary in ratio to the amount of application necessary. At its best, according to Broadus, not only does the text furnish the leading ideas of the sermon but also the details.[7]

Why explain, narrate, or examine some details of the text if they contribute nothing to the sermon's dominant goal? Everything normally done in a sermon should be done because it helps the sermon accomplish what the preacher believes it ought to accomplish. Pious padding of the sermon with irrelevant material—even if it comes from the Bible—is useless, even counterproductive. Often what the sermon needs is a direct statement of the meaning of the text for present hearers without using the words of the text itself. If the text is read before the sermon or if the hearers have an open Bible before them, the exact words may not be needed. Dietrich Ritschl has suggested that we "go right ahead in our own modern way of expression. Thus we avoid the intellectual complications which arise when the gap of the famous 'two thousand years' between the Bible and the 'modern man' dominates the sermon."[8] Leander Keck asserts that "a biblical sermon is not a book report. It is a proclamation of what has been heard in and through the text."[9]

Relevance is not always immediately consumable. A sermon may be helpful "in the long run." The most interesting sermon will likely be a sermon related to the hearer's present needs, but a very valuable sermon may be related to future needs. How many persons have discovered the meaning and power of the Lord's Prayer or the twenty-third Psalm long after they learned the words! Careful narration of a biblical incident or accurate and repeated use of a significant verse or phrase of scripture has returned years later to bless a man or woman in a spiritual crisis.

The best sermons are not preached off the top of a text. The preacher's first thoughts on the text are not necessarily the best ones. An idea for a sermon that came like a flash of light may need to be subjected to the chastening of reading of the original language of the text—or at least the comparing of several translations in one's own language—and researching the best critical commentaries. This does not mean that the preacher has to discuss in the pulpit the process by which the message of the text arrived. The clear and true message itself is usually enough. Jesse B. Weatherspoon used to tell his students to take the cream of their study into the pulpit but not the cream separator. Fred Craddock would disagree. If we use an inductive approach in the sermon, an important factor of interest and education may be sharing of the process by which we arrive at the meaning of the text for today's hearer. Craddock believes that such an approach is more agreeable to the contemporary mind than the traditional, deductive approach.[10] Is it not probable that both Weatherspoon and Craddock are right in different situations and when dealing with specific texts?

The truest expository sermon will usually expound the central idea of the text. Donald G. Miller puts it this way: "Every sermon should have a theme, and that theme should be the theme of the portion of scripture on which it is based."[11] This concept applies whether the text is an entire book of the Bible, a chapter, a paragraph, or a single verse. Yet Miller's view must be qualified. Any time one preaches on the central idea in the paragraph or chapter of the Bible, one more often than not preaches on a theme subordinate to the theme of the entire Bible book. Chapters likewise may contain themes subordinate to the main theme of the chapter and offer fitting and legitimate themes for sermons. In theory, the preacher may preach a dozen different sermons on the same text, each of them true and complimentary. For example, John 1:1-18 is an admirable text for a sermon that has unity, but the parenthetical verses 6-8 provide a proper unity also.

Many times the best arrangement of the sermon's ideas can be found in the text "if its own rhythm be followed and its proportions observed." The thought processes of the biblical writer would most often guarantee a sequence of thought that unfolds in a reasonable way. However, some texts, as Walter Bülck pointed out, do not lend themselves immediately to rhetorical treatment, and the order of presentation of the verses or ideas has to be rearranged for the most effective sermon.[12]

DOCTRINAL PREACHING

The letter to the Ephesians tells us that Christ gave some to be "pastors and teachers." This does not mean two different offices but two functions of the same office. The pastor is the chief teacher of the flock.

One type of teaching is the teaching of doctrine through what are called doctrinal sermons. Some congregations greet such sermons with a shudder. Some preachers approach doctrinal preaching with dread. I can understand why. My early attempts as a student pastor were not something to write home to my parents about. I began a series of doctrinal sermons but abandoned it in the middle. More was required than I was capable of. I knew what I wanted to say, but I did not know how to say it interestingly.

But there is more to it than ability to communicate. The preacher must have earned the right to communicate what he or she wants to say by having something worthy of saying.

One could preach a helpful doctrinal sermon by using a text allegorically or analogically. Ronald Knox preached a sermon on a text from the Song of Solomon, using the text allegorically to say something about the Eucharist. Knox first described the literal meaning and then went on to spiritualize the text. What he did was to bring to the text a meaning he got elsewhere. He used the text to express the meaning more vividly and perhaps more interestingly.[13] Augustine used allegorical interpretation with greater abandon than Knox, yet Augustine believed that Christian doctrine must be founded only on the clear, direct teaching—not the allegorical interpretations—of scripture.

James Stewart preached a sermon called "Anchors of the Soul" and used an incident from the travels of the Apostle Paul as the analogical framework.[14] The meaning of the text was quite clear—during a storm at sea "they cast four anchors out of the stern, and wished for the day." That was the literal, historical truth. But Stewart used the text, whose literal, historical meaning was no doubt clear to every member of the congregation, as an occasion to talk about anchors of another kind—hope, duty, prayer, and the cross of Christ.

Perhaps what Knox and Stewart have done is lawful. They did not deny the literal meaning or ignore it. The vital question is this: Would it have been better to preach from a text that clearly teaches what they wanted to say?

Karl Barth has rightly noted that miracle stories have a proclamation value beyond their literal meaning: "The fathers were very conscious of this, and for that reason they were at this point far better exegetes than those who, in a panic-stricken fear of what is condemned root and branch as 'allegorising,' refuse to look in this direction at all."[15] A vivid example—not Barth's—of the wider meaning of a miracle is the story of the stilling of the storm. Doubtless this story was included in the gospels mainly to comfort and strengthen believers who would be buffeted by storms of persecution and suffering and wonder if the Lord they served cared whether they perished or not. This is an extension of the meaning of the text, not a denial of its historical truth nor simply a homiletical convenience.

It has been often alleged that one can prove anything by the Bible. Could this be said if all antagonists refused to identify anything as the teaching of scripture that did not have broad support in the Bible as a whole? This is not to say that a teaching has to be mentioned more than once to have validity. Yet we would do well to question our interpretation of isolated verses when it runs counter to what seem to be the mainline teachings of the Bible.

Creeds and confessions do not guarantee the truth of a teaching. Martin Luther said, "I do not accept the authority of popes and councils, for they have contradicted each other." What he asserted is true. Still, there is much to learn from the classic creeds and confessions of Christendom. They have emerged from situations of doubt, confusion, and controversy. Important issues were at stake. Conscientious, dedicated people gave their best scholarship, thinking, and devotion in drawing up formulations of faith that would preserve the historical heritage of the Christian faith and convey its timely meaning. While we should take these theological statements seriously, we must recognize that they were historically conditioned. Thus we may find ourselves in lively dialogue with them at certain points. This is especially true when we come to understand better certain parts of the Bible.

Christians—and those who are considering professing their faith—often could profit by a sweeping view of a biblical doctrine such as the doctrine of sin, judgment, redemption, regeneration, sanctification, prayer, faith, or repentance. It seems clear that the more comprehensive the sermon is as to theme, the more selective the sermon will have to be as to the details. Some questions will have to go unanswered. Some lines of reasoning will have to be foreshortened. This is necessary if the sermon is to be understood at all. Nothing could be more baffling and boring to a congregation than a tedious doctrinal sermon when the preacher was determined to leave out nothing.

After we have preached on a major doctrine of the Christian faith, we may wish later to look at it again with our congregation—this time in greater detail. The way to do that is obvious: We can preach a series of sermons on the general theme. Many years ago Harry Emerson Fosdick wrote a book on prayer that has become a classic. The chapters of *The Meaning of Prayer* might well have been separate sermons. Note how Fosdick attempted to cover the details of his theme in these chapters: (1) The Naturalness of Prayer, (2) Prayer as Communion with God, (3) God's Care for the Individual, (4) Prayer and the Goodness of God, (5) Hindrances and Difficulties, (6) Prayer and the Reign of Law, (7) Unanswered Prayer, (8) Prayer as Dominant Desire, (9) Prayer as a Battlefield, and (10) Unselfishness in Prayer.[16] It would be impossible for us to say all that we want or need to say on prayer—or on any other major doctrine—in one sermon.

Many ministers have found that interest in a sermon series is keenest when the number of sermons is limited to four or five.

Every worthwhile doctrinal sermon touches our lives directly or indirectly, immediately or in the long run. But it is the sermon whose relevance is obvious that gets the best hearing. A common way in which preachers practically apply the truth of a sermon is to tack on an application or a moral at the end, but there is a better way. The sooner the hearers realize that they have a stake in what the preacher says, the sooner they will begin to listen. The place for the application to begin is in the introduction, and application ideally should be carried through *to* and *including* the conclusion. John Dewey said the first of five steps in reflective thinking is the recognition of a felt difficulty.[17] In the sermon this does not have to be done with a heavy, obvious hand. Suggestion or allusion may be enough. If the preacher relates a story, the hearer may make personal application by identification with someone in the story.

From the earliest times the rhetoricians advocated reserving a place in the speech, after the main arguments had been given but before the conclusion, to answer objections that might be raised against the arguments. Why do so? It is the honest thing to do. There is no biblical doctrine, however hallowed by tradition, that cannot be questioned at some point. Sometimes the only answer to an objection is to admit that there is no answer. The matter must be left to that realm of mystery that awaits further revelation. To acknowledge objections and to attempt to deal fairly with them is also the prudent thing to do. We can enhance our credibility if we do not dodge the problems that lie just beneath the surface of the sermon. Yet this does not require us to treat our congregation as confirmed skeptics who question everything we assert. We simply need to be clairvoyant enough to perceive a question or objection when it is likely to arise and then to be courageous enough to deal with it. It must be said, however, that a single pattern does not have to be followed as to the location of answers to objections. There is no good reason why the preacher should not take up an objection at any point in the sermon where an honest response might be helpful. It might be well to answer objections before making a constructive statement of the doctrine itself.

Sometimes we will reach our goal when we have clearly defined a term or explained an idea. If we do that thoroughly, we may need to do little more. If we want to correct an erroneous concept of sanctification, our entire sermon may consist (1) of a definition of the term from the biblical usage and understanding and (2) of an explanation of its contemporary meaning. However, we may use the term *sanctification* incidentally as we pursue another objective. Yet it is essential that the hearer understand what we mean when we use the word. In that case, we may need to use only a synonym or at most a brief explanation in passing.

The surest way to get an idea across is to use an example of an idea in action—a genuine instance or a case. If we are trying to impress the idea that prayer changes things, we may relate a true story of someone whose life was transformed by prayer. The next best way is to use an analogy of the idea in action, that is, some parallel experience or hypothesis that will lend credibility to the idea. Frank C. Laubach called prayer "the mightiest force in the world" and pointed to the reputed achievements of telepathy as a way of understanding how prayer works.[18] Gordon W. Ireson, an Anglican preacher, writes, "I have myself made it a systematic practice for many years to supply my own illustrations when reading a theological book. 'Suppose I were trying to teach this truth to others; how would I illustrate it? What is the point or principle involved? What is analogous to it in everyday experience?' It has been an exacting but immensely profitable discipline. If I can't produce an illustration, it's because I haven't properly understood the point at issue."[19]

ETHICAL PREACHING

When our preaching is on ethical issues, we can be sure of one thing—our preaching is relevant. It is about us and what is going on in our lives. That does not mean all such sermons are helpful. They may be harmful. They may definitely touch on life today and yet give warped views of what God expects of human beings, of how these people ought to behave toward one another, and of the way we think about ourselves. They may distort the gospel as good news and make it sound more like bad news. Added to that, they may fail to respond to the creative work of the Holy Spirit by omitting to carry out the intentionality of the text in a new situation.

Why, then, ethical sermons? People need a clear picture of the teachings of the Bible on issues of right and wrong, of the experience of the church with these teachings, and of what ethically sensitive people believe to be the will of God for our lives today. The minister may be the key person in helping to make such vital distinctions.

From beginning to end, the Bible is concerned with human behavior. God has shown his love for humankind by caring about the way we act. He would fail us as Creator and Father if it did not matter how we behaved.

We find in the Bible moral absolutes. The ancient Shema, which admonishes us to love God with all that is within us, combined with the command to love our neighbor as our own self, gives us an example of fixed points on the moral compass. Other duties, equally binding, derive from these polarities.

Also we find in the Bible certain laws, rules, or practices that were binding in given situations. They did not apply and do not apply directly in every situation. Yet they did apply in certain parallel situations. Wherever these laws, rules, and practices related to love of God and love of neighbor, there was the possibility and necessity of applying them in similar cases.

Any preaching that calls itself Christian has to take biblical teaching on morality seriously, distinguishing what is fixed and what is variable. It has to surrender mere private opinion to the judgment of Holy Scripture.

As to whether a particular ethical position is supported by Christian tradition is a tricky question. Jesus asked the Pharisees,

"Why do you break God's commandment in the interest of your tradition?" (Matt. 15:3). However, all the answers we need cannot be found in the Bible alone. We can find some helpful answers in what the church experienced after biblical times. No one, either in the Old or New Testament, spoke against slavery as such. But later—much later—some persons, inspired by the love of God and man, raised their voices. They brought to a specific and timely focus what the Bible had been moving toward all along. Legal precedents give us an analogy for the way we might well handle some questions of right and wrong that we must settle.

If we cannot find support in the Bible for a particular ethical view, we need to discover what support—if any—we can find in the experience of the church in the past.

Sometimes it is too easy to get spurious support for our views in the Bible or tradition. If we are looking for a rule or an excuse, we can turn up something. Probably no type of sin or crime has ever been committed that someone, somewhere, at some time has not attempted to justify by the Bible. One person reads the Bible seeking authentic guidance; another, looking for loopholes. The preacher can be unwittingly autobiographical. What we preach against or for may reflect more of what we want to believe or do than it reflects of truth. We may have seen and experienced so much suffering from alcohol abuse that we are absolutely intolerant even of persons who drink in moderation. Or we may be so addicted to alcohol ourselves or so dependent on the approval of persons who drink that we refuse to take seriously the moral and social problems of alcohol. We are capable of such extremes on a number of other issues, and Christian truth may suffer many wounds from our personal biases.

Too often judgment has been pictured as the punishments of an arbitrary or petulant deity. God loves to zap those who disobey what look like senseless rules. What a horrible, unfair portrayal of a loving God!

Judgment follows wrongdoing as effect follows cause. "Whatsoever a man soweth, that shall he also reap" (Gal. 6:7). Much of what we call sin is sheer stupidity—though we may rightly call it sin as well. If the sermon shows the consequences of an attitude or an act or a habit, then perhaps God's disapproval may be seen as a sign of his love.

However, we cannot exhaust God's wisdom in a utilitarian approach to ethics. His ways and thoughts surpass our own. Sometimes we must obey simply because God commands, not because we fathom his reasons.

We have no reason to preach mere judgment. Always there must be something remedial in view. Only the offer of forgiveness makes true amendment of life possible.

But forgiveness without repentance makes no sense; nor is it good religion. Easy forgiveness trivializes God and the Christian faith. Forgiveness is costly to the person who offers it. God's forgiveness has a cross at the heart of it. And it is not complete until it works a change in the person who receives it.

Peter Brunner, the Heidelberg theologian, suggests that the entire service of worship, and not the Declaration of Absolution alone, must sound the note of forgiveness.[20] Ill-informed sermons on "the unpardonable sin"—whatever that is—do more harm than good, often ignoring our Lord's words, "All sins shall be forgiven unto the sons of men" (Mark 3:28).

We cannot answer every question with a snappy yes or no. Some questions can be answered only with a painful yes and no; still others, with a yes or no slowly arrived at. The Council at Jerusalem arrived at a solution for a perplexing problem after careful deliberation (Acts 15). Social and political questions with ethical implications need and deserve our best-informed thinking.

Religious duty should not carry with it automatic and repelling glumness. For example, Jesus said, "When you fast, do not look gloomy like the hypocrites. . . . But when you fast, anoint your head and wash your face" (Matt. 5:16-17). Jesus did not misrepresent his way to potential followers. He was utterly frank. He even spoke of crossbearing as a style of life for them. Yet he lived with a sustaining joy that he bequeathed to his disciples, a joy that added "luster to the doctrine of God our Savior" (Titus 2:10).

Harry Emerson Fosdick said,

There are some kinds of people whom you would walk blocks to avoid meeting. There are the conventionally good who, through a long lifetime having observed little rules of respectability, immoderately admire themselves. . . . There are the negatively good whose goodness consists in having kept the lid clamped tightly down on their insurgent badness so that they are repressed and dried up and sour. . . . There are the censoriously good whose morality is all for export, who in endless interferences with other people's business try to do us good. There are the narrowly good, who make an infinite to-do about infinitesimal matters of behavior which do not matter much and who never get their eyes on the great ethical issues of their day.[21]

It is quite an achievement when a preacher can so represent Jesus Christ and his way as to lead someone to say, "That's what I want!" The epistle to the Hebrews tells us of "Jesus who, for the sake of the joy that lay ahead of him, endured the cross, making light of its disgrace, and has taken his seat at the right hand of the throne of God" (12:2). His heroic and self-denying love points an alluring way that ought to illuminate the most challenging and demanding sermon.

Many sermons are of the "Oh, how we ought to love one another" variety. They say that if we love one another, we will have peace. Or if we are true believers, we will obey Christ in all things.

There are complicated ways of expressing Christian love. Under the circumstances of our social order—locally, nationally, and internationally—it is difficult. One person or a few may have to channel that love in spite of people who do not share it. It is like piloting a ship with a precious cargo through rocks and shoals. The expression of Christian love may take the form of law or contract.

Obedience has to take place under human conditions. Habits, environment, and physical limitations make obedience come harder for some persons than for others. Some improvement, modest achievement, even slow spiritual growth is better than none at all. As Eduard Schweizer put it, "One of [Jesus'] sayings, which perhaps we could not even repeat correctly, will not let us alone. And Jesus becomes Lord over us. Perhaps he has to fight for his place as long as we live. So much else clamors to become mightier than he. Yet he will never forsake us. Thus our heart knows in all confusion and temptation, Jesus is Lord! He affirmed me and forgave me long before I knew it. Therefore, I may joyfully come to grips with whatever is not yet pleasing to him."[22] The all-or-nothing approach is blind to reality and distorts the gospel as well.

The most solidly imperative words known to us are the Ten Commandments. But we often overlook the powerful indicative that prefaces them: "I am the Lord your God, who brought you out of the land of Egypt, out of the house of bondage" (Exodus 20:2).

The great indicatives of what God has done, what he is doing, and what he promises to do make the imperatives possible. And the best imperatives are those that emerge quietly in our own hearts without having to be spelled out for us in so many words. After acknowledging the lawful and obligatory use of the imperative mode, Henry Grady Davis goes on to say, "The *we ought* sermon is extremely common. The imperative is the mode of the dogmatic moralist and of the exhorter. Its stock in trade is admonition. Its danger is legalism, for it is law only. Its weakness lies in the comparative futility of telling someone what he ought to do—which he usually knows already. . . . So long as a man preaches in the imperative mode, this is all he has to talk about. The moment he begins to proclaim the gospel he speaks in the indicative."[23]

PASTORAL PREACHING

All preaching is in a sense pastoral—except evangelistic preaching, that is, sermons to unbelievers. But we may use the term more narrowly. Pastoral preaching is preaching that is designed to comfort, encourage, or inspire church members. It serves the caring role of the minister. Such preaching may also serve an evangelistic purpose, for when it is done well, the unbelieving listener may be drawn to the faith. He or she may be attracted by the help the gospel offers those who believe.

The biblical challenge to the preacher of today is this: "Proclaim the message, press it home on all occasions, convenient or inconvenient, use argument, reproof, and appeal, with all the patience that the work of teaching requires" (2 Timothy 4:2).

Our sermons should cover a broad spectrum of human need. Preaching often tends to be too exclusively autobiographical. We preach on what interests us, what speaks to our own need, or— yes—what avoids our sins.

These tendencies can be overcome. We can regularly base our sermons on texts in one of the standard lectionaries. Or we can preach straight through books of the Bible. Then we will have to confront all kinds of human need. The sin and hurt that our people experience, as well as what we experience, will be exposed.

It is possible to fill the time allotted for the sermon with helpful advice that has no relation to a biblical text. Every day public service radio and television programs, as well as newspaper columns and magazine articles, offer such advice. The sermon ought to be different. It should, in addition to all that human opinion can do, make available resources of faith, hope, and love as they appear uniquely in the Bible.

Wayne Oates has made this important point: "The effective preacher grounds his preaching and squares and plumbs it biblically. Thus he avoids the fate of overgeneralizing about all people on the basis of hasty experience with one or two people. The inexhaustible wisdom of the scriptures is the stuff of the revelation of God for all time."[24]

The preacher who is a person of only one book will be heavily handicapped. Conversely, the preacher who knows something of psychology, medicine, and sociology will extend his or her usefulness. Knowledge of psychology will aid in the understanding of some forms of guilt. Knowledge of medicine will give insight into problems and proper treatment of depression. Knowledge of sociology will enable one to deal with certain types of prejudice. Anyone so informed would not say to a troubled parishioner contemplating psychiatric help, as one minister did, "Go home and read the 23rd Psalm and save your money!" Nor would anyone so informed slur in the pulpit any helping agent that can make life better and more liveable. More positively, if we go to the trouble to know what we are talking about, to get informed in areas that relate to our pastoral task, then we will enhance our credibility and consequently our effectiveness.

Many of the painful problems that come to a minister's attention relate to ethical lapses. Preventive preaching is as important as remedial preaching. Thus the preacher speaks clearly of the will of God and what duty requires to make our lives fulfill the divine intention. In addition, like the book of Proverbs, the preacher articulates prudential wisdom, that is, adherence to carefully calculated morality. So, on the one hand, we challenge people to obey God for the sheer rightness of it. On the other hand, we describe the good sense of doing what is right and the stupidity of doing what is wrong. Preaching that disregards the plumb line of God's justice is no favor to tempted and broken sinners no matter how much they need comfort and encouragement.

But how shall we minister to a sense of guilt? A man in his seventies said, "My conscience hurts me all the time." The man's name is Legion, and his age actually may be anywhere between—let us say—ten and one hundred.

Guilt is tricky. One may be categorically guilty and feel no guilt at all. Or one may feel guilty and not be guilty at all—at least of the crime one feels has been committed. Unhealthy, unrealistic feelings of guilt need to be explained and—if possible—removed, not exploited. Consciousness of true guilt needs to be raised to a level where it can be seen for what it is and the cause removed. Sometimes preoccupation with guilt about little or imagined sins is a cover-up for a gross transgression or state of sin.

One of the strengths of Alcoholics Anonymous has been in the ability of fellow sufferers to help each other to a degree hardly possible to those who have not suffered. The preacher does not have to match sin with sin to help the sinner. Yet our willingness to confess our own vulnerability to temptation, our own need for forgiveness, and our own need for support from the believing community can help the hearer deal with his or her own problems more honestly and persistently. This will not require the preacher to descend to embarrassing particulars. Most of the time we may need only to say "we" instead of "you" when we speak of doubt, fear, temptation, and the like. Occasionally a personal experience tastefully and tactfully shared will prove to be unusually helpful.

One who is assured of the support of just one person can survive. How much better it is when we know that we have comradeship with an entire community. For practical reasons, the strengthening group may be a small group within a much larger group. The important thing is that this truth be realized: "All of you are Christ's body, and each is a part of it" (1 Cor. 12:17). One of the most helpful aspects of John Wesley's ministry was the class meeting. This put the person whose life had been changed by the gospel in touch with others who shared "like precious faith" and the inevitable struggle to bring this faith to expression in everyday living. The person who hears and heeds the gospel cannot grow to Christian maturity without a deepening involvement in the Christian community. It is also true that the Christian community does not achieve maturity until it cares for the least member within it.

A preacher had delivered a brilliant analysis of a contemporary situation. A listener approached him after the sermon and asked, "Now what are we supposed to do about it?" The preacher answered, "That's up to you!" Robert McCracken said that after he preached from the Sermon on the Mount, a parishioner remarked, "That was a heavy duty you laid on us. Now how are we to get up there?"[25] In this case, the preacher was sympathetic, realizing that he needed to say more. We must not deceive ourselves or our hearers by assuming that all problems have pat solutions or that all difficulties can be quickly or easily overcome. Yet our Christian faith does offer solutions to some problems. In any case, it offers grace to carry a burden that cannot be removed, to struggle valiantly with a temptation still unconquered, and to live with depression and anxiety. No one has to be left shut up in despair—never, so long as God lives.

Some problems and difficulties cannot be adequately dealt with from the pulpit. They need to be talked out and analyzed; they need to have alternatives set alongside them; they require the warm support of some caring person who knows. Fosdick believed that the test of the value of a sermon lies in the number of persons who ask to talk with the preacher privately afterward.[26]

People will not come privately to preachers who do not command trust and confidence. Those who hear us preach must be assured by the way we use illustrations—as well as otherwise—that we will not laugh at them, betray their confidences, or reject them. We do not have to approve their unsavory conduct, however, to invite their confidence. They may come to us out of a sense of need to rectify their conduct.

When a person believes that we understand his or her problem— perhaps have even faced it ourselves—then a bond of identification is forged. This can take away a feeling of isolation and give courage to fight life's battles.

Rollo May has noted that in psychotherapy the patient tends to have an unconditional trust and dependence on the therapist and that he tends to worship him as though he were more than human. The sick-souled person has found someone who will help bear his guilt and pain and the burden of his past mistakes. Something similar takes place between the preacher and certain parishioners. That is only natural. But attachment to the preacher "must be shifted to reality." If we do not attempt to do this for our people and merely seek to exploit dependence for our own ego need and greed, then we are in desperate need of help ourselves, whether we are aware of it or not. We will fail our people unless we can lead them to trust an "absolute outside" ourselves.[27]

DEVOTIONAL PREACHING

Horton Davies said of John Henry Jowett that he was "an exceptionally able exponent of the devotional type of preaching in an excessively utilitarian age, who realized better than most of his fellows that no sacrificial service for God or men is ever accomplished apart from adoration in Christian worship which is the frankincense of obedience."[28]

Weatherspoon said in a classroom lecture that the devotional objective in preaching is "the effort to improve the life in the Godward direction." Some sermons lead people to worship God immediately. Still others suggest means by which people may worship him in different ways and days. These sermons constitute devotional preaching. Still other sermons may belong in this category. A preacher's entire pulpit ministry may be characterized as devotional preaching. This type of preaching can serve other important goals—directly or indirectly. Such was the preaching of Jowett.

Doubtless some of your preaching will be intentionally devotional and some accidentally devotional. Many churches use the Christian year as the framework of their program of worship, including preaching.

The Christian year is an ordered pattern of worship tied to the major celebrations of the church, beginning with Advent and ending with the season called Trinity or Pentecost. Christian bodies, almost without exception, observe a part of the Christian year. Where is there a church that does not celebrate Christmas? Perhaps you can find a few that do not celebrate Easter, not because they do not believe in our Lord's resurrection but for other reasons valid for them.

George M. Gibson has listed these influences that bring the Christian year to our attention: revived interest in worship, the rapid growth of the ecumenical consciousness, the emphasis upon planning, and the deepening devotional search in crisis times, which is leading many to a recovery of the classic means.[29] Religious groups that once paid little attention to the Christian year now take it seriously. In this way they are discovering fuller dimensions of devotion.

Every preacher is obligated to tell what the Bible says and explain what that means. When Jesus preached in the synagogue at Nazareth, it was in a liturgical setting. He read a scripture, explained what it meant, and applied it to the present moment. Justin Martyr, as noted earlier, wrote a description of early Christian worship about A.D. 140. He reported that after the memoirs of the apostles or the writings of the prophets were read, the president of the assembly—presumably the bishop or pastor— gave a sermon in which he admonished and invited all to imitate the examples of virtue contained in what had been read.[30] In theory, nothing has changed in all the history of the church since those days. Yet it is possible to meet and celebrate—what or whom?—with little or no reading of scripture and obviously without discussion that has any theological substance. Meaningful inducement to worship will always vibrate in harmony with scripture rightly understood and faithfully explained and applied.

One thinks immediately of the Psalms. The Psalms have been called the hymnal of the Jewish church. For a time some reformed groups of Christians sang nothing in public worship except the Psalms. Much of the New Testament is composed of hymns and hymn fragments. Theology, ethics, and history can be enshrined in a devotional approach to preaching. We should remember this especially when the biblical text obviously belongs in the category of the devotional.

Before the coming of Jesus Christ, Israel's temptation to idolatry was for a time persistent and strong. God seemed remote or abstract. That became an intolerable situation, so the people filled the vacuum with idols. Any real or imagined attribute of God would be isolated and represented in some tangible, visible image. People made gods for every aspect of human existence. Such was the case among many nations.

When Christ came, the true God drew near in a personal way. The Apostle Paul wrote that "the full content of the divine nature dwells in Christ, in his humanity" (Col. 2:9). Thus when Jesus Christ is preached as Lord and Savior, when he is presented as the unique revealer of God, and when he permeates the sermon, then God becomes very personal; it should be no surprise that in the very words of the sermon, the congregation hears God speaking in a direct and loving way. Rollo May wrote in one of his early books, "People place unconditional confidence in [Christ], take pleasure in calling his form into their minds, and find joy in phantasies about him in hymn-singing and the liturgy of worship. The idea of the logos, the mind of God, coming into human form gives millions of people a splendid pleasure, and the mere thought that the Son of God could come to earth to share their life and understand their sins fills them with awe and an eternal hope."[31]

When Jesus had commissioned his apostles, he gave them this assurance: "I am with you always, to the end of time" (Matt. 28:20). This meant the presence of God in a very personal way. When the Apostle Paul said, "The life I now live is not my life, but the life which Christ lives in me" (Gal. 2:20), this meant the presence of God in his life in a very personal way. Some mystics have spoken of fellowship with God in terms of ecstasy in which the individual self melts, as it were, into the being of God, into an abyss of bliss. Thomas à Kempis described the blessed fellowship like this: "To be without Jesus is a grievous hell, and to be with Jesus a sweet paradise."

Fellowship with God may be what Paul termed "the fellowship of his sufferings" (Phil. 3:10). The way a person experiences fellowship with God is largely a matter of temperament, expectation, and preparation. Many of God's greatest saints found God most real not in raptures or unbridled emotion but in daily obedience and faithful service. Fellowship with God is available not only to the spiritually elite but also to the ordinary Christian who sincerely wants to do his will.

Regrettably, all people do not come to church bursting with desire to worship God. They come for many reasons. A line from Oliver Goldsmith has it that some "who came to scoff, remain'd to pray." It makes little difference why they come if indeed they learn to worship. Our attitude, our patient teaching, and our discovery of ways to channel response to God's initiative will in time bear fruit in the genuine devotion of at least some of those who hear.

The best praying is done at home. While corporate prayer is perhaps the oldest type of prayer, private prayer has become the prayer into which individuals put their greatest strength. The minister can teach the congregation, as Jesus taught his disciples, how to pray. We can anticipate their problems and suggest solutions. We can recognize their discouragements and cheer them on.

Preaching can lead to inverted worship or, what is more likely, sustain the worship that is natural—worship of ourselves. Joseph Sittler has named as one of the current tyrannies "the tyranny of the self."[32] The glorification and celebration of the self, fostered in part by some forms of existentialist philosophy, has cut the nerve of morality. Looking out for Number One has become a religion for many. Some forms or extensions of this false religion have been baptized and sanctified in certain sermons designed to be relevant. False prophecy is what it always was, and the issues are not altogether different from those faced in the Old Testament.

While our egocentric worship may not take the form of gross, fleshly vulgarities, it may consist of little more than sweet, empty pieties. It may be satisfied with a church-bound ceremonialism, a faith without works, a private assurance of salvation that anesthetizes the worshiper against concern for the lost and oppressed outside. Eduard Schweizer asks, "What then is the event that we usually call 'divine service'?" He answers: "It is simply the 'coming together' of the church in which it is served by its God. This means that it is primarily the occasion of listening to him, enabling us to praise him and to carry his service into the world."[33]

It would be wrong to say absolutely that a preacher who did not pray privately could never lead others to pray. It is a well-known fact that students often surpass their teachers in learning and children often outstrip their parents in achievement. The same may be true of pastor and people. Yet Richard Baxter's advice applies: "Take heed to yourselves lest your example contradict your doctrine, and lest you lay such stumbling blocks before the blind as may be the occasion of their ruin: lest you unsay with your lives what you say with your tongues; and be the greatest hinderers of the success of your own labors."[34]

Charles Haddon Spurgeon has a graphic word on the matter: "Habitual communion with God must be maintained, or our public prayers will be vapid or formal. If there be no melting of the glacier high up in the ravines of the mountain, there will be no descending rivulets to cheer the plain. Private prayer is the drill ground for our more public exercises, neither can we long neglect it without being out of order when before the people."[35]

The sermon always has the people in mind. It is designed to reach human beings with the truth of the gospel. Yet it can be an act of the preacher's devotion, like that of Jenny Lind who said, "When I sing, I sing to God!"

IV. THE MAKING OF SERMONS

9. Preparation of Sermons

How does a sermon get prepared for the pulpit? This is a question that needs a long running start for an answer. Clearly, the best preaching does not come out of a Saturday night blitz, or even from the patient plodding of the five days before Sunday.

All of us have heard sermons that sounded as if they were thrown together on Saturday night, or even produced on the spot. Sometimes carefully prepared sermons, on which the preacher obviously spent many hours over many days, failed to make a good impression. Something was lacking. In each case, the problem was that the preacher drew too heavily on what was immediately at hand. The sermon was more the residue of a shallow, muddy well, than it was the fresh or artesian spring that flowed from the depths and the distances.

GENERAL PREPARATION

The integrity of the pulpit demands a lifetime study program. We think immediately of books, and they are important, indispensable. But life itself and serious reflection on it are a most valuable part of our education.

WIDE READING

As to books, it is important that the preacher read widely and become informed on many aspects of life. To be sure, there is no single book list that would be appropriate for every preacher. The schools should indicate to us, while we are passing through, the significant books, and then we can let our own inclination lead us in this direction or that. Some preachers, while trying to become acquainted with a wide variety of literature, through their own tastes and needs specialize in one or more areas of inquiry, perhaps even become experts in those areas. It is not too much to expect the preacher to read the latest books that have to do with the newest discussions in the theological world and books on preaching, counseling, and church administration. But we should always make sure that some of our reading is for inner enrichment, for feeding the life of the soul. We can be too much and too unremittingly absorbed in our professional specialty. Charles Darwin regretted that he had not taken time out regularly for a little gratuitous exercise of his soul with the reading of poetry. After spending much time in his scientific investigations, it was almost impossible for him to work at a task for more than thirty minutes at a time. His narrow interests had dulled his higher sensibilities.

CAREFUL STORING

How valuable are those things read and felt and seen in one's intellectual and spiritual development! The earliest and most tentative thoughts may be unworthy. Though perhaps embarrassing in light of maturity, these thoughts should be written down. Some of the sermons Phillips Brooks preached at the apex of his career can be traced back to ideas he set down in his journal as early as his seminary days. The essays of Ralph Waldo Emerson were the flowering of insights gained and duly recorded in his journal, along with stimulating quotations from what he had read.

The only way for the preacher to have the apt quotation or illustration is to have stored away such an abundance of materials that the choice is always from among many possibilities rather than from among a few.

From Paul Scherer I learned a simple way of having material ready when needed for sermons. I got a big loose-leaf notebook and pasted in clippings or wrote in quotations or observations, as well as my own thoughts. Then, when I was preparing a sermon, I could always find something useful to add to my own most recent thoughts. Preachers who continue to do this will fill notebook after notebook with material that will enrich their sermons. An important part of the process of working with the material is the noting of what is important and letting it filter into the subconscious mind as well as making certain items available for use. We can bring forth out of our treasury things new and old. Though we may never look at our earlier notebooks any longer, they will have nevertheless done their work in the nurturing of our mind and soul, while we turn to our newer notebooks for the fruits of our latest thinking, reading, and observation.

Some preachers may find a method suggested by Robert J. McCracken to be precisely what they need.[1] He recommended that preachers use a spiral notebook with three sections: one for text, one for topics, and one for illustrations. The first two sections would allow two pages for each text or topic, as the notebook lies open. The third section would put the illustrations in paragraphs with brief indexing in the margins. Illustrations can be numbered consecutively and noted by number under appropriate texts and topics in sections one and two. This method is useful for long range planning, whether one uses a lectionary or not. And it is both simple and portable.

OPENNESS

The preacher must maintain an openness to life and to new experiences. "Future shock" is, of course, the lot of all of us to a greater or lesser degree. We like our ruts. We are comfortable with the way things have been and have been done. Any major deviation from the regular and normal sends shock waves through us. Nonetheless, life marches on, and we go with it, meeting whatever obstacles or challenges may appear in our way. Otherwise, we barricade ourselves in the strongholds of outlived customs, ideas, and relationships.

While life marches on, we may try to play it safe. This may be possible for some people, but not for the preacher. Jesus commanded, "Go into all the world!" He himself did not snuggle up to the conventionally religious, for he was not sent to call the righteous, but sinners, to repentance. The "people of the land," whose manner of life was in many ways an offense to the religious establishment, were the people to whom Jesus went with the good news of God's love and forgiveness. He was open to people and to ways of living that raised the eyebrows of some—to say the least. Even so, it was said of him in retrospect, "He was without sin." Therein lies the difficulty—how to be open to what goes on around one, objectively evaluate it, react creatively to it, and yet avoid wrong. In the process, one may develop strength of character and relevance of mission.

There was the pastor who upon reaching normal retirement age quit a long pastorate and began a new career as a religion teacher on the campus of a state school. He was one of the most popular of the campus personalities. The college students beat a path to his office door for friendly counsel. His secret: He kept young by his interest in what preoccupied the young people— their pleasures, their pressures, and their problems. They never thought of him as sitting in a kind of academic or ecclesiastical fastness protected from the realities of life, so he was able to help them. To be sure, this was no new-found approach that he affected after retirement from the pastorate. It was simply an extension of what had characterized him all along and had made his sermons fresh and relevant through the years.

CONTINUING EDUCATION

Continuing education is a special and essential means of maintaining this creative, productive openness. The preachers who do not fail to challenge their congregations have been for the most part those who have availed themselves of refresher courses, attended seminars, participated in conferences, and the like. The head of the medical staff at a psychiatric hospital said that he believed that medical doctors ought to be required regularly to produce learned articles or to give other significant tokens of continuing education as a requirement for keeping their status in the medical profession. If such is important for a physician, it is no less so for a preacher.

THE STUDY OF SERMONS

The study of sermons of effective preachers offers challenge, inspiration, and example. Augustine (A.D. 354-430), the first to write a formal treatise on the application of the rules of rhetoric to preaching, advocated the study of the preaching of those who preached well. He believed that this learning by example was superior to the learning of rules. Harry Emerson Fosdick indicated that he had profited from studying sermons of the masters sentence by sentence. Why should not the method of Robert Louis Stevenson for learning to write serve the preacher also? Stevenson said that in his apprentice years he "played the sedulous ape," that is, he copied the styles of several writers he admired and in this way discovered his own distinctive style. John A. Broadus rightly warned of the dangers of imitation. We have all seen and heard the ludicrous performances of people who have affected the styles of other persons, but who succeeded only in aping their eccentricities without tapping the true sources of their strength. If imitation becomes chronic and causes the preacher to become a phony reflection of someone else, then imitation is bad. On the other hand, if imitation is a matter of exploring one's potential and discovering the best that one can do, then imitation is good. Many of the world's greatest artists began their careers by copying the masters.

PLAGIARISM, BORROWING, AND ORIGINALITY

This brings us to the problem of plagiarism. Someone has said that all work and no plagiarism makes Jack a dull preacher. This was said in jest, of course. Such use of the word does not define its true meaning or indicate its problems. Plagiarism is the unfair use, legally or otherwise, of the literary property of another. By extension, it includes the unfair use of a literary production that may have been long in the common domain.

The preacher's main concern is this: Is it morally right to preach another's sermon or a large part of it? St. Augustine said, in effect: "Yes, provided the preacher reproduces accurately what the author has originated and provided that the preacher lives up to what the sermon teaches."[2] Willard A. Pleuthner, a Madison Avenue public relations executive, said that preachers with lesser gifts should adapt and preach in their own words sermons written by others with greater gifts.[3] Also, it must be admitted that the huge quantities of homiletical aids produced for centuries lead one to believe that sermons are printed to be preached again.

There is another side to this. David Poling asserted that one important means of regaining respect for the church and its preaching is to be found in our preparing our own material.[4] How can we give an effective witness if our sermons merely echo the experience of someone else? How can we grow intellectually and spiritually unless we struggle with ourselves and with the biblical material handed down to us for an interpretation and application to our own day and age? How, unless we produce our own material, can we discover what original and significant contribution we might make in the pulpit?

Surely preachers can produce one sermon per week in which the rule of originality is held inviolate. As to other sermons, a good rule for the preacher to follow is always to give credit when making substantial use of another author's material. If we do this scrupulously, we will hardly overstep the bounds of what is right and fair.

Recently two authors have recommended the occasional preaching of sermons by other preachers. This will serve to acquaint the congregation with some of the great preachers of the church and with their sermons. At the same time, it will provide some variety from the usual pulpit fare. It is recommended that these sermons—often too long for modern pulpits—be appropriately condensed. It is indispensable that the preacher openly acknowledge, whether orally or in the printed order of service, what is being done. This procedure can also benefit the preacher, by possibly improving the preacher's own style.

SPECIFIC PREPARATION

What might be even more profitable would be to go behind an outstanding preacher's sermons to learn how they were prepared. Phillips Brooks, widely regarded as one of the finest preachers of the late nineteenth century, prepared his sermons regularly in three stages. Once he had a basic idea for his sermon, he made a very brief preliminary sketch of the leading idea, perhaps no more than a dozen lines. After reflecting on that for a few days, he spent one morning making a full sketch of the sermon. This might extend to some 1,300 words, and it contained all of the ideas that would appear in the completed manuscript. This sketch, however, was written down in separate words and phrases and divided into paragraphs. Brooks wrote beside each paragraph the number of pages into which this would be expanded in the full manuscript. The third stage was to write out the manuscript completely, sticking to the predetermined number of pages exactly. Sometimes Brooks did not write a full manuscript but took a sketch into the pulpit and spoke from that. Brooks's delivery averaged 200 words per minute, beginning at 185 words with gusts up to 215 words. This meant that his thirty-minute sermon totaled 6,000 words.[5] George A. Buttrick followed a plan similar to that of Brooks and stuck to it rigidly. He felt that doing his work in measured stages aided motivation, creativity, and productivity. In a lecture he said half in jest, "I am constitutionally lazy, and I have to play all sorts of tricks on myself."

Harry Emerson Fosdick described his usual working methods in some detail.[6] He said that he began with an object—what he wished to accomplish with a particular sermon. Then he chose a significant truth to help him achieve his objective. This relevant truth came usually from a single passage from the Bible, though it might be a truth diffused through several passages. Next, Fosdick would brainstorm the subject, jotting down ideas without any particular order. Having gone as far as he could with this process of free association, he would put a series of ques-

out any particular order. Having gone as far as he could with this process of free association, he would put a series of questions to his theme to push the process still further (see also Chapter Six, "The Text"). This step required research, "without and within." At this point, the structure of the sermon began to emerge. Sometimes he saw the outline almost full-blown; at other times, he saw only where he had to begin. Then came the writing of the manuscript. Fosdick said that he had hand written every sermon he had preached.

In *The Congregation and Mission,* George Webber described a successful method of sermon preparation that utilized the members of the congregation as well as the several ministers.[7] The East Harlem Protestant parish was multiracial and included many people of limited education. A lectionary provided the scripture text for midweek lay Bible study groups and for the Sunday sermons. The following steps were involved in preparing sermons:

1. On Monday the preacher for the following Sunday studied the Bible text with his colleagues at a staff Bible study session, utilizing all critical tools needed for understanding the text.

2. At a Wednesday staff luncheon, the preacher outlined the sermon and received criticism and ideas and suggestions.

3. The preacher's colleagues, who would be attending the lay Bible study groups meeting in homes on Wednesday evening, directed discussion toward Sunday's sermon: What should be included and what topics dealt with? Such questions as the following were helpful in producing fruitful discussion: What don't you understand about the passage or what in it is confusing? What is the most important point in the passage? Do you agree with the point of the passage? How does this passage speak to our problems today?

4. On Thursday morning staff colleagues brought reports from the groups, and with the help of these reports the preacher wrote the final draft of the sermon.

church and of its proclamation would seem to require that the sermon be a joint effort between preacher and congregation. This does not mean that the preacher should preach only what the people dictate. The evils of that are only too obvious. It does mean that the preacher will take their questions, their problems, and their insights seriously. The preacher will then go into the study at the latter part of the week and work out a sermon, "alone with the Word," prepared to preach against the will of the congregation and "*against his own will and desire,* if the Word wants him to do this." Ritschl notes that preaching of this kind offers the advantage of the timeliness of a topical sermon.[8] Bishop Yngve Brilioth writes that in the Swiss Reformation preachers and theological students gathered for exegetical Bible study in what was called *die Prophezei.* One of the preachers later "delivered a devotional lecture in the church using the conversation gathered as the basis of his address."[9]

Archbishop Fulton J. Sheen described in his autobiography his own interesting method of sermon preparation. He prepared all his sermons "in the presence of the Blessed Sacrament." For Sheen, this meant working in the presence of God. After he had a basic plan for the sermon, he talked out all his thoughts to the Lord or meditated on it, "almost whispering the ideas." He felt that this procedure helped to discover both weaknesses and possibilities in the sermon. "After the material is gathered and the points formulated, I follow with either a meditation or a quiet vocalization without ever referring to notes. The material of the sermon is not wholly that which comes from the paper to the brain, but which proceeds from a creative mind to the lips. I have asked many a comedian what he thought was his best joke, and the answer was 'the one I have most often told.'"[10]

Clyde Fant has proposed the production of an "oral manuscript." His method is supported by the solid fact that communication is basically and historically in an oral style and is freely delivered. Therefore, the preacher, according to Fant, should gear his preparation to the most basic style of communication. Careful study of the biblical text in the usual manner is necessary, after which the preacher will write down on separate sheets of paper each of the leading ideas to be developed as the major blocks of thought. Then the preacher talks out the sermon. Significant ideas and illustrations are jotted down as they occur while the preacher speaks. They do not have to be put in good order at this stage; that can come later. The preacher does not think in terms of "points," but of "thought-blocks." The ideas and illustrations that have been struck off in the private brainstorming are then rearranged. Those that are worthless or at least not fitting for this sermon are omitted. Indented under each major division will be at least six to ten "directional sentences that discuss the biblical situation and the contemporary situation," or that indicate pictorial or supportive material. From three to five such sentences each suffice for the introduction and the conclusion. When this is done, the preacher rehearses out loud as often as needed for final preaching of the sermon.[11]

Each preacher will have to find his or her own best method of sermon preparation. This can be determined after experimentation. Most likely the preacher will use various methods as different needs dictate.

10. The Structure of Sermons

Should we observe any rules for the arranging of the ideas of the sermon? Ought we not to ignore stereotyped homiletical patterns and form new ones of our own? It does seem reasonable that we might work out some *new* approach, some *new* and more effective form for sermons. The sermons of Frederick W. Robertson, of Phillips Brooks, or of Harry Emerson Fosdick have uniform excellence, and yet they have distinctive, if not original, features. A slavish use of someone else's stock sermon forms would have robbed these remarkable preachers of their unique contributions. Quintilian advocated the observance of rhetorical rules, but he believed that they must be adapted to the situation: "Rules are rarely found of such a nature that they may not be shaken in some part, or wholly overthrown."[1]

Dietrich Ritschl goes further. He says, "There are no rules, prescriptions, and principles for preparing and delivering a sermon." Moreover, "the questions of the structure and technical delivery of the sermon . . . grow out of the understanding of the message of the text." He believes this because he is convinced that "the ways in which God wants to work cannot be systematized."[2]

Two homiletics professors were discussing Ritschl's excellent, provocative book, particularly his views about rhetorical rules. One of them wryly commented, "His book would have been more readable if he had paid more attention to rhetoric." And it is at this point that the matter comes into focus: If rules can help us better to communicate the message, give us rules; if rules keep us from worthily and effectively communicating the message, then take the rules away.

ARRANGING THE BASIC IDEAS

Let us suppose that you now have your basic ideas before you. They are more than likely a jumble, a hodgepodge of good ideas and poor, and there are many more of them than you could use in any one sermon. What will you do with them? First of all, you will decide what you hope to accomplish with this sermon. What do you want to happen in the hearers' minds as a result of this sermon? Next, you might consider the primary appeal. What way of thinking or feeling or deciding in the hearers can you address that will make the sermon interesting to them and that will unleash their motive power so that they can do what is required by the truth of the sermon? Though you started with a tentative central idea, you may need now to revise it in the light of your accumulation of additional ideas and in the light of the growing clarity with which you see your objective. Brooks said, "In all your desire to create good sermons you should think no sermon good that does not do its work. Let the end for which you preach play freely in and modify the form of your preaching."[3]

The basic rules for arrangement are few.

Let your structure grow out of the text or the central idea. If your objective and your appeal are clearly in mind, the central idea will take shape along particular lines. As the structure grows, it will move in this direction and not that because it is both encouraged and restrained by needs of your hearers. Why have a text or a central idea if they are not permitted to do something for the sermon?

Let your sermon have unity. Perhaps the greatest structural fault of sermons is that the parts do not fit together. Fenelon, in his *Dialogues on Eloquence,* objected to divisions of a certain kind in sermons: "Ordinarily they put there the kind of order that is more apparent than real. Moreover, they dry up the discourse and make it rigid. They cut it into two or three parts, and these hinder the speaker's delivery and the effect delivery ought to produce. No longer is there genuine unity—there are two or three distinct discourses unified only by arbitrary inter-connection."[4]

In every type of interesting composition there is unity. What is it that makes Flaubert's *Madame Bovary* a near perfect novel? Is it not that every scene, every description, every conversation contributes to the one theme that steadily unfolds and that stands out in stark clarity at the end? Many successful writers and speakers through the centuries have taken their cue from the truth enunciated by Aristotle when he said that in dramatic tragedy there is a whole which has beginning, middle, and end. He explained: "A beginning is that which is not itself necessarily after anything else, and which has naturally something else after it; an end is that which is naturally after something itself, either as its necessary or usual consequent, and with nothing else after it; and a middle, that which is by nature after one thing and has also another after it."[5] It is clear in this explanation that beginning, middle, and end belong together, that one could not exist logically without the others. A sermon that has disjointed divisions and extraneous parts may by accident do some good, but it cannot have maximum effectiveness.

One minister asked another, a highly successful pastor, what sort of filing system he used to keep his illustrations. He replied, "I have no system. I just toss the illustration on my desk, and if it's any good I can work it into next Sunday's sermon some-how." No doubt this was said tongue-in-cheek, for this minister's illustrations seem always to be highly appropriate. However, if we seriously believe that we cannot sacrifice any ideas we may have had on our sermon theme, that we must somehow put them all in, we will destroy the unity of the sermon and reduce its thrust. After meditating a theme, we ought to use perhaps only one-third or less of the ideas for a particular sermon. But we do not have to waste the rest; we can file them away for future use in other discourses where they will have a definite place.

Let your sermon achieve suitable climax. A sermon may begin in a striking manner and promise an interesting discussion and a relevant application only to die a slow but certain death. This does not mean that if such a sermon had the ideas reversed, it would be a good sermon—as if the bad egg put in first instead of last would make the omelet good. All the ideas must be worthy and significant, but we can arrange and rearrange them until they are able to produce their best effect. This will be very difficult if you draw up an outline before you have done much thinking about what you will try to say. The practice of sitting down and tossing off sermon outlines in a matter of minutes and then compelling one's thoughts to fit into the predetermined scheme has nothing to commend it.

Actually, to arrange one's ideas always in a logical order may not be best. A psychological order that takes into account the feelings, the desires, and the needs of the hearers will more surely achieve the objective for a particular sermon. A suitable climax for a sermon may be at the point where logic is left behind, where the hearer is more and more involved in the truth that logic has already presented or that is generally regarded as valid. Brooks characteristically presented his major idea first and then went on to discuss this idea in its various practical relationships and applications.[6] Fosdick did the same thing. But Fosdick worked hard at the intellectual problems of his theme in the early part of his sermon and achieved there an intellectual climax; the emotional climax came toward the end. Thus he depended on the total impact of the sermon to achieve his objective.[7] This agrees with the advice of the ancient Cicero who believed that the strongest point ought to come first, provided "the rule be kept to reserve one's outstanding resources" to the last part of the discourse.[8] Otherwise, the sermon that is "full of verve at the beginning . . . dies out by degrees in banalities toward the end."[9]

It should not be too difficult to get your ideas in the right sequence. Think of what you are trying to see happen in the minds, the hearts, or the deeds of your hearers. Then take hold of your materials and arrange them so that they can most surely accomplish this objective. Don't be afraid to shift around the sequence of your ideas. Our first thoughts are not necessarily our best ones; therefore, there is nothing sacrosanct about the first draft of your outline, even if it seemed to come in a sudden flash of inspiration. Edgar Allan Poe observed that "most writers—poets in especial—prefer having it understood that they compose by a species of fine frenzy—an ecstatic intuition—and would positively shudder at letting the public take a peep behind the scenes, at the elaborate and vacillating crudities of thought—at the true purposes seized only at the last moment." Poe indicated that he commenced with the consideration of an *effect*. He took his well-known poem, "The Raven," and showed step by step how he put it together. He wrote, "It is my design to render it manifest that no one point in its composition is referrible either to accident or intuition—that the work proceeded, step by step, to its completion with the precision and rigid consequence of a mathematical problem."[10]

Fosdick normally had his Sunday morning sermon on the way by Tuesday noon and spent Wednesday, Thursday, and Friday morning writing it. By Friday noon he was finished with it. On Saturday morning he sat down and thought through the sermon with his congregation in mind, to see if what he had prepared would meet the needs of individuals and of groups, "so as to be absolutely sure that I have not allowed any pride of discussion or lure of rhetoric to deflect me from my major purpose of doing something worthwhile with people." In view of his objective, Fosdick often cut out certain paragraphs and rearranged the order of thought "in the interest of psychological persuasiveness."[11]

The preacher must not overlook the possible need to answer objections. The ancient rhetoricians made large room for this in their recommended schemes for arrangement. After we have argued for a theological or ethical point of view, we should deal honestly and fairly with questions, resistances, and disagreements that we anticipate. This is not the place for belligerence or polemics but for sympathetic and caring "listening to the opposition" and answering with gentleness.

SUGGESTIONS FOR STRUCTURING A SERMON

Having settled the guiding principles for arrangement of the sermon, consider the following suggestions that have to do with these principles:

1. Do not always state your points or leading ideas before you discuss them. In some cases, it will help your audience to follow your line of thought if you set forth your leading ideas beforehand. This is especially the case with sermons designed to inform or convince. But you will destroy the fetching quality of suspense that makes a mystery story or a sermon interesting if you give away your main ideas prematurely. Still, if it will help you achieve your objective, then state them!

2. Do not discuss too many points. Our attention span is limited, and our practical ability to take hold of too many separate ideas is impossible. Professor Clement Rogers argued for "the rule of three." Literature, anthropology, mathematics, grammar, logic, and journalism all support the idea that a sermon with three parts, with not more than three divisions of the middle part, is ideal. For example, certain uncivilized people do not count higher than three: after three, they say "a great number."[12] However, do not stick to this as an inflexible rule. There may be very good reasons for having a half-dozen points. One of Fosdick's most helpful sermons is on "Six Ways to Tell Right from Wrong," and it has, of course, six main points.

3. Avoid wordy statement of your points. Let the points themselves be lean. Leave the intricacies of your thought to the discussion that follows. If your audience can keep your thought always in clear sight, so that it does not get lost in a forest of verbiage at any stage of the journey, they will

know where they are at any moment and can travel with safety and enthusiasm. Therefore, strip away from the points needless adjectives and adverbs, premature nuances and ramifications.

4. Do not overlap the points. Repetition or restatement is an excellent rhetorical device if used consciously, deliberately, and with discretion. But it can result in a turgid diffusion of thought if we imagine that we are discussing a new idea when we are actually discussing the same idea under a slightly different form. Hebrew parallelism, particularly in the Psalms, can lead us astray. Wishing to treat faithfully every phrase or clause of a psalm may lead us to attempt to discuss the same idea twice, thinking that we are developing a further step in the psalmist's thought. Be discerning, for all parallelisms are not so obvious as this one in Psalm 46:10: "I am exalted among the nations, I am exalted in the earth."

5. Do not make a main point of a subpoint. It throws the sermon out of balance. A sermon that treats a subpoint as a main point would be like someone with only a finger growing where an entire arm should be. Suppose you are preaching on the Trinity. The points could be: God the Father, God the Son, God the Holy Spirit. It would be a balanced sermon. But what would the sermon be like if instead of making the third point "God the Holy Spirit," you made it "The Communion of the Holy Spirit"? It would be deformed. Yet, if you were preaching on the ways we know or experience God, your outline might correctly be: The Love of God; The Grace of Our Lord Jesus Christ; The Communion of the Holy Spirit. Note the difference—in this outline, each main point has the same weight; it is of the same order.

6. Do not fail to group ideas that can be discussed under one head. Ideas that might be presented under a broad head might be discussed more forcefully by bringing them together under proper subheads. This means that we must

generalize the particulars of our sermon. We find a common center for particular ideas, then discuss these ideas in relation to the common center. This does not mean that we should limit ourselves to general ideas and suppress particulars but that we must strengthen particular ideas by giving them a center and forming them into masses. Indeed, the particulars are of vital importance: They are the aspects of experience in which the ideas touch our lives or the aspects of truth that make truth meaningful; they are the means of clear teaching, powerful convincing, and effective persuading.[13]

7. Avoid putting ideas under the wrong heading. The preacher who gathers thoughts and puts them down as they come, without regard to order, will sometimes make this mistake. This way of accumulating ideas is commendable. Ian Maclaren used it.[14] Walter Russell Bowie recommended it.[15] But some preachers cannot work this way: They can never get their thoughts marching forward in proper formation. On the other hand, preachers who lay out the design of their sermon before they begin to elaborate can make the same mistake. We may anticipate an idea that we plan to develop later or rehash one that we have already discussed. Repetition is an excellent rhetorical device, but the repetition must always fit comfortably into the immediate context. To avoid the error of putting ideas under the wrong heading, look at your work critically and be willing to make a dozen revisions if necessary.

8. Avoid artificial or strained alliteration in the wording of points. When beginning the initial or key words of an outline with the same letter comes easily and naturally, it makes for a more striking and a memorable outline. Some of the sermons of James S. Stewart have alliterative outlines. Notice how impressive are the points in his sermon entitled "A Drama in Four Acts," suggested by 2 Timothy 4:11: Act I, "Recantation"; Act II, "Remorse"; Act III, "Restoration"; Act IV, "Reparation."[16] In a book of sermon outlines covering the entire Bible, Arthur E. Dalton made wide

and often very effective use of alliteration.[17] However, the minister must exercise the care of a poet in his choice of words. Otherwise, while the words chime, the ideas will clash.

THE ALL-IMPORTANT OUTLINE

The most important single device for achieving boldness of attack in preaching is a well-constructed outline.

Most good sermons have behind them at least a carefully prepared outline. This enables the preacher to organize the ideas. We can get our ideas into their proper groups and sequences and arrange them to the best psychological advantage. This does not require us to take into the pulpit the outline that we find most helpful in preparation for the pulpit. Our study outline may be a fully elaborated outline in complete sentences, but our pulpit outline may be a series of cues that would make sense to no one but the preacher.

Following are three forms of outline that you may find helpful in organizing your ideas.

The first is the *word* outline. This lists a series of words that are keys to the ideas or the information to be discussed. The listing of words is especially useful in classification, but it has other uses also. Consider this example: "The Task of the Church," Matthew 28:18-20; Luke 24:49.

    I. Going
      A. God
      B. Jesus
      C. Church

   II. Preaching
      A. Purpose
      B. Message
        1. Good news
        2. Bad news
      C. Presentation
        1. Everywhere
        2. Everyone

III. Waiting
   A. Weakness
   B. Waiting
   C. Ways
      1. Prayer
      2. Surrender
      3. Faith
      4. Action

The weaknesses of this outline form are glaring. Only the one who has prepared it really knows what it says, and will not know long. Yet, if the preacher has no interest in keeping a record of the ideas, this may be no problem.

The second is the *phrase* outline. This is simply an expansion of the word outline. Observe what happens to a portion of the outline we have just examined:

I. The Church going
   A. The militancy of God
   B. The daring of Jesus
   C. The creativeness of the Church

The phrase outline obviously conveys more meaning than the word outline. It may represent all that the preacher wishes to preserve of the ideas for a particular sermon. This will furnish a sufficient lead to stimulate thought upon returning to the outline in the future.

Note the parallelism in form. This often serves a purpose beyond that of form: It helps in the logical disposition of main points and subpoints.

The third form is the *complete sentence* outline. Using this form, we can know whether we have anything to say about our theme. We know *what* we are going to say. And when we have said it, we know what we have said. This form is very important in developing a sermon in which reason and proof play a prominent role. Reason and proof do not proceed well by phrases or isolated words. They need carefully formulated statements containing both subject and predicate.

Now, let us examine our outline that has been expanded finally into complete sentences:

Introduction:

    A. Some of us may selfishly think that the Church belongs to us.

    B. However, the Church belongs to Christ and is for his purposes.

Christ defines the task of the Church as follows:

    I. It is the task of the Church to *go*. "Go ye . . ."

        A. God has always been on the move in this world.

        B. Jesus was bold and daring in carrying out his program.

        C. Therefore, the Church of today, which represents God's purpose in Christ, must use every honorable means to enter and make opportunities for its task.

    II. It is the task of the Church to go *with a message*. "Go ye into all the world and preach the gospel to every creature. . . ."

        A. It is not enough simply to *go*.

        B. We must go with a message.

            1. The message is good news for sinners.

            2. But it is bad news for sin.

        C. We must present the message everywhere and to everyone. Only human need determines the boundaries of our witnessing.

    III. It is the task of the Church to go with a message *in the power of God Himself*. "Tarry ye . . . , until ye be endued with power from on high."

        A. It is not enough simply to go—even with a true message.

        B. Christ commands us to let God work through us.

        C. We can do certain things that will make us accessible to God.

            1. We can pray.

            2. We can surrender our will.

            3. We can receive on faith the help of God.

            4. We can then go confidently to work.

Conclusion:

    A. Our task is clear.

    B. Will you now join me in taking the appropriate steps?

If we use the approach to the sermon advocated by Clyde Fant, we do not attempt to develop the leading ideas of the sermon by arranging subpoints in parallel or strictly logical form. Working with thought blocks rather than points, we have perhaps under each main heading from six to ten "directional sentences" actually to be spoken, leading into exposition, argument, illustration, and so on. This is somewhat different from the examples of outlines just given, in which the illustrations are not listed as if they are on a par with the points. Fant's scheme has much to commend it and can be studied in detail in his *Preaching Today*.[18]

A further question remains. How does one indicate various kinds of supporting material in the outline? You may employ the symbols used to indicate subpoints in the outline. But if you wish to distinguish clearly your own ideas from ideas and quotations from other sources, use a different symbol.[19] One author has suggested the use of brackets at the beginning and at the end of material not original with the speaker. In any case, document at the end of the reference the source of borrowed ideas, statistics, and quotations.

ACTUAL COMPOSITION OF SERMON

Once this much work has been done, the hardest part of the sermon preparation is over. You can write your sermon or compose it mentally with a clear view of the road ahead—and you can enjoy freedom while you do it.

Henri D'Espine has written: The surest way to kill eloquence (the true, the good, that of which it has been said that it cares nothing about eloquence), is to teach it. We need not so much to be formed as to be freed, so that at least we become simple and true."[20]

Yet even simplicity and truth have their principles. It is the artist who has learned well the laws of perspective who can best convey the truth of a simple scene. It is the violinist who knows the scales so well that he does not have to deliberate before placing his fingers on the strings of his instrument who has the freedom to convey with power and verve the inner meaning of his selection. And it is preachers who have seen the good sense of a few dos and don'ts who move with greatest confidence toward their unique objective.

11. Structural Options

What is the one best thing that we can do to move with decisiveness and confidence from the central idea of the sermon to the finished sermon? For many, this requires first a careful laying out of the basic structure of the sermon. When they have done that, the sermon develops rapidly.

Some preachers, however, cannot work that way. Whatever outline their sermons have, they construct as they go along. One thought leads to another until they have finished the sermon. If that works better for them, then they should continue and strengthen the process. Yet the preacher should experiment with the other method, giving it an adequate trial, until sure about how best to proceed. In any case, the preacher will have to get the sermon in some kind of logical or psychological sequence before or after the fact. The desired response from the hearers requires it. In the long run, we preach better sermons if we regularly cut them to a pattern. We have no problem with the pattern noted by Aristotle—beginning, middle, and end. It all seems very obvious. Likewise, the development of the middle part of the sermon—especially that!—can seem natural as the ideas fall into a particular sequence. It is possible, of course, for the preacher by accident to stumble onto approaches that truly communicate. But we can shorten the journey through the homiletical wilderness by attention to the paths some other travelers have taken already. All of the sixty-four sermons in *The Twentieth Century Pulpit*, Volumes 1 and 2,[1] fall into specific structural categories. If we know these structural types and some of their subcategories, we can usually find the most fitting and effective means of setting forth what we want to say in our sermons.

Let us consider now several structural options.

EXPLAINING

Both Jews and Christians regard their faith as grounded in history, enriched in history, and always coming to expression in historical situations. Thus if the faith continues to enjoy good health, we have to know our heritage. Keeping the story alive is a monumental task for which the preacher has the primary responsibility.

The church looks to the pastor as the chief teacher. He or she cannot assume that general knowledge of the Christian heritage, ethic, and worship, or information gained in the church school will suffice. Inspirational or pleading messages that ignore factual data, therefore, cheat the congregation. For one thing, general knowledge of the Christian heritage is skimpy and spotty. Moreover, church school religious education, while good as far as it goes, is in many places notoriously inadequate. Obviously, the preacher, even if teaching from the pulpit full-time, cannot supply all that is lacking, but this contribution is absolutely necessary. Preachers have an unusual opportunity to do the most essential teaching because of the special respect commanded by their calling, training, and ongoing study.

What distinguishes expository sermons from other types is mainly that expository sermons heavily emphasize the explaining of scripture. To be sure, the detail into which the preacher goes and the length of the text will vary from sermon to sermon. The sermon may be tightly packed and heavy or, on the other hand, copiously illustrated and highly interesting. Theologians might prefer the former; an average congregation would certainly prefer the latter. In any case, biblical texts and biblical events do require explanation, and sermons can provide such explanation.

EXPLANATION OF A TEXT

One of the oldest methods of explaining scripture goes through a text verse by verse or part by part. Traditionally this has been called the *homily*, though the term has sometimes been used more loosely to denote whatever the preacher says after the gospel lesson. The homily simply takes the text as it comes, beginning at the beginning and continuing to the last verse. But just as an artist must suppress some details in painting a landscape, so the preacher of a homily must omit certain details of the text in treating a long passage. On the other hand, if the preacher focuses in on a short text as the basis of the entire message, the details will take a prominent place.

The homily has suffered a bad reputation as a sermonic vehicle, mainly because it has often been carelessly handled. Perhaps the preacher chose a long text and preached off its surface, never penetrating to its depths or finding and following its true inner movement. The result: a disjointed series of mini-sermonettes, unrelated comments suggested by isolated words and phrases from the text. But there is no reason why the homily cannot do—at least with some texts—everything that a more rhetorically structured sermon can do.

To make an effective homily, first select a text with unity and orderly progress of thought. Next, find the joints in the text and prepare each part in relation to the basic thrust of the whole. Then provide your own interesting introduction and a conclusion that pulls everything together for a final, impressive view of the meaning of the sermon as a whole. The sermons of Martin Luther, Karl Barth, and Eduard Schweizer often demonstrate the best features of the homily.

Schweizer preached on Philippians 4:4-7, which reads: "Rejoice in the Lord always, again I will say, Rejoice. Let all men know your forbearance. The Lord is at hand. Have no anxiety about anything, but in everything by prayer and supplication with thanksgiving let your requests be made known to God."[2] The introduction focuses in on the words "The Lord is at hand," which come precisely in the middle of the sermon text. Those words are the thematic center of gravity of the four sentences that make up the body of the sermon. After lifting out that focal sentence, Schweizer proceeds to take up the four sentences one after the other, relating them to the idea that the Lord is near.

Then, in a conclusion he gathers up "the truths discussed into a unity which forms the climax and goal of the sermon, its so-called 'final theme.'" Schweizer's sermon could be called "expository," for it applies the principles of rhetoric—whether consciously or unconsciously—to the construction of the sermon.[2]

Karl Barth proceeds in a similar way with a shorter text, Psalm 34:5: "Look up to him, your face will shine, and you shall never be ashamed." He simply breaks the text apart and treats each part separately, yet with a unifying thread holding all parts together. It is an Ascension Day sermon, and the first part of the text is addressed in the very first sentence. Here are the movements of the sermon:

I. Look up to him!
II. Look up to *him*!
III. Look up to him *and your face will shine*.
IV. Look up to him, your face will shine, *and you shall never be ashamed*.

In this case, there is no introduction but the one in the text, and there is no conclusion at all, except the final point, "and you shall never be ashamed," which is climactic and which sounds the appropriate note on which to end. The very last sentence, referring to a quotation from Psalm 103, simply says, "With these words let us go to the Lord's Supper. Amen." Barth's sermon could be called a "text-sermon," for it takes what is popularly understood as a text—a short passage of a verse or two—and discusses it part by part, though, like the expository sermon, it retains the main features of the homily.[3]

EXPLANATION OF A DOCTRINE

Karl Barth said: "Dogmatics is the science in which the Church, in accordance with the state of its knowledge at different times, takes account of its proclamation critically, that is, by the standard of Holy Scripture and the guidance of its confessions."[4]

Emil Brunner has pointed out three reasons why we need Christian doctrine—the fruit of dogmatics.[5] First, we have to combat false doctrine. The human tendency to take an aspect of the truth and exaggerate it or to embark upon a false course and then to seek scriptural support for it requires the corrective of an objectively derived standard of doctrinal judgment.

Second, we have to meet the needs of inquiring minds. When individuals have been awakened to the claims of the gospel, when they have encountered ideas and terms peculiar to the Christian message, they inevitably ask questions. They desire intelligent answers. Christian doctrine, carefully formulated and explained, provides these answers. While such answers may not be complete and thus not fully satisfactory to inquirers, they may be, given our human limitations, the best possible answers.

Third, vibrant Christians want more than a piecemeal view of truth. They want to see more than a particular aspect of truth as located in a lone verse of scripture. They would like to take in the broad sweep of a doctrine like that of "sin" or "grace," to know what the Bible as a whole has to say about it.

D. M. Baillie undertakes to explain the biblical doctrine of God in terms of the Trinity in a sermon simply titled, "The Doctrine of the Trinity."[6] He says, "I believe we can find the whole Christian gospel summed up in this mysterious doctrine, of three persons, Father, Son, and Holy Spirit, in one God." Then he proceeds to explain what the doctrine means:

I. There is one God, not the host of gods of the pagan world.
II. The fact of Jesus Christ brought God into human life in a new and tremendous way, so that men could speak of God as Father and Son.
III. The fact of Pentecost made the power and presence of God real even after the departure of Jesus. "So now on the Day of Pentecost they said: 'This is what Joel predicted. This is what Jesus promised. And God our Heavenly Father, who came to us in His Son Jesus, is with us now, and forevermore, in this new and wonderful way, through His Holy Spirit.'"

Baillie's sermon meets all three of Brunner's criteria for dogmatics—insofar as a sermon can do that. It struggles with false doctrine; it answers questions; it gives a comprehensive view of a biblical teaching. Baillie accomplishes this by means of explanation.

Paul Tillich's explanation of a doctrine is oblique.[7] Without laboring with the term *justification by faith* as such, he nevertheless explains it, using different terminology. He takes the words *sin* and *grace*, which appear in his text, and gives their modern equivalents or approximations. Such modulation into a more contemporary key is intended to make ancient doctrine more accessible to present-day hearers, for meaning often becomes hidden in language that gets encrusted not by neglect but by use and familiarity. The text is Romans 5:20: "Moreover the law entered, that the offence might abound. But where sin abounded, grace did much more abound."

Introduction:
- A. The words of the text as a summary of Paul's apostolic experience, his entire religious message, and the Christian understanding of life.
- B. The strangeness of the words *sin* and *grace*.
  1. Our misuse of *sin*. Sin as "separation."
  2. Our misuse of *grace*. Grace as "reunion."
- C. The struggle between separation and reunion.

I. The experience of separation.
- A. Separation from one another.
- B. Separation from oneself.
- C. Separation from the ground of our being.

II. The experience of grace.
- A. What it does not mean.
- B. What it does mean when it comes. The sense of being accepted.
- C. How it comes. Its effect upon us.

AFFIRMING

When we affirm the truths of our faith, we simply proclaim them, assuming but not arguing for their validity. Sometimes old, neglected teachings need to be dusted off and restated;

teachings currently held need to be repeated and highlighted. With "the faith once delivered to the saints" comes a whole body of doctrine that must be announced. We do not explain good news or dialogue about it; we tell it like a herald.

The outline of James S. Stewart's sermon, "Why Go to Church" (Heb. 12:22-25), offers a clear example of the heraldic approach.[8] Stewart hears the writer of Hebrews "saying five things about our fellowship of Christian worship in the Church":

    I. It is a spiritual fellowship.
    II. It is a universal fellowship.
    III. It is an immortal fellowship.
    IV. It is a divine fellowship.
    V. Is a redeeming fellowship.

Except for limitations imposed by the content of the text, Stewart could possibly have gone on to list some other aspects of the fellowship of Christian worship. This pattern is what is sometimes called the "jewel" outline, for it shows facets of a truth— some facets, that is, but not a required number.

G. Earl Guinn affirms "The Resurrection of Jesus" in three statements:[9]

    I. The resurrection of Jesus is indisputable history.
    II. The resurrection of Jesus provides inspiring philosophy.
    III. The resurrection of Jesus gives invincible hope.

The scriptural background for Guinn's sermon does not itself provide the points for discussion but clearly provides the theme that he develops in his own way.

In a sermon on the future life, "All Things New?" (Rev. 21:1, 5), Elam Davies exemplifies affirmation: "We are not asking," he says, "*whether* we believe in another world, or existence in it. For the Christian, this has been answered once and for all."[10] He continues with an unusually long introduction, recognizing some of the problems of faith. Then he sets forth the positive convictions of "the writers of the New Testament and the saints through the ages" as to the "hereafter."

I. The life to come is a life of vision.
II. The life to come is a life of service.
III. The life to come is a life lived in love.

REASONING

First Peter admonishes Christians: "Be always ready with your defence whenever you are called to account for the hope that is in you, but make that defence with modesty and respect" (3:15). The apologetical task of the pulpit is imperative. Augustine argued for it and perhaps for more. He wrote in Book IV of his treatise, *On Christian Doctrine*, that if the enemies of the truth use the weapons of rhetoric in the service of error, then the lovers of truth should not be defenseless but should themselves employ the same weapons.[11] Let this be done, however, as 1 Peter says, "with modesty and respect."

Not all preachers can fulfill this need well, and perhaps they should leave the more challenging aspects of the apologetical task to specialists. Some preachers have made themselves ridiculous in their handling of issues of science and religion because of their obvious lack of understanding of the issues they attempted to discuss.

It is not the purpose of homiletical reasoning to build a ladder of rationality to climb to God. Reasoning about the faith does two things: (1) it clears away some misconceptions and prejudices so that the truth can be seen in sharper definition; (2) it bolsters the already existing faith of the believer.

Charles G. Finney, the evangelist, was as trained as a lawyer, and he approached unbelievers in much the same way that lawyers would argue a case. He would follow one argument with another in rapid sequence, using as many as a dozen and a half in a single sermon. He left the sinner with no place to flee.

Short of such attempts to overwhelm the wills of our hearers, we can present our case effectively—"with modesty and respect." One way is to use a line of reasoning, perhaps employing extended syllogisms or enthymemes. R. C. H. Lenski deals with this by discussing "the categories of possibility, actuality, and necessity." He proposed this sermon on Luke 12:49-57, titled, "The Discord Which Christ Brought on Earth."[12]

 I. At first it perplexes us.
 II. On second thought this is entirely as it should be.
 III. Moreover, our only hope is in this discord.

Martin Luther King, Jr., followed the thesis-antithesis-synthesis model in his sermon, "The Answer to a Perplexing Question."[13] The text is Matthew 17:19: "Why could not we cast him out?" The sermon has to do with human efforts to eliminate evil. "How can evil be cast out?"

 I. Man has tried to remove evil through his own power, but unsuccessfully.
 II. Man has waited submissively upon the Lord, but this falsifies both God and man.
 III. Neither God nor man will individually bring the world's salvation. Rather, both God and man, in unity of purpose, work the miracle.

The most decisively convincing reasoning will not be found in the most cleverly arranged and executed arguments. Rather, it will be found in credible examples that resonate with the hearer's own experience and observations. For instance, we know, if we reflect on it, that try as we may we cannot remove evil in our own power, that if we sit down and wait for God to act nothing is likely to happen, and that some good things have actually happened when we prayed, trusted God, and got busy in obedience to him.

APPLYING

A common sermonic method of Phillips Brooks was to set forth the truth of a text and then show its implications. I heard an address by a noted scientist on the first chapter of Genesis. After establishing what he believed to be the truth of the text, he listed and discussed the ten lessons he drew from the text.

It was heavy-handed and straightforward, but powerful. Normally, we would go no further than five areas of application, but what the speaker was dealing with was so significant for theological orientation and for current political discussion that the long list of points was appropriate.

In Romans 12:1-2, the Apostle Paul brought his previous discussion to a head in a summary statement with a general devotional-ethical injunction: "Adapt yourselves no longer to the pattern of this present world, but let your minds be remade and your whole nature thus transformed." Then follows a series of specific ethical directions, the day-to-day implications of the tremendous theological truth—God's mercy—described in chapters 1-11. We find something similar in "The Love Chapter," 1 Corinthians 13. After discussing the various gifts of the Spirit to the church, Paul says, "The higher gifts are those you should aim at." Then he goes on to say, "And now I will show you the best way of all" (12:31). The best way of all is the way of love—*agape*, caring—which the Apostle proceeds to apply in very practical ways.

The freedom from "the Law" that Christ has brought us has not freed us from the need for ethical precedents and directions. Love is indeed the fulfilling of the law (Rom. 13:10), yet love can be mocked by sentimental, *ad hoc* private interpretations of it in moments of temptation. When we face a moral crisis, God does not saddle us with the burden of constructing a whole new personal ethical system out of the raw materials of our faith experience.

Let us consider again Eduard Schweizer's sermon, "God's Inescapable Nearness," which I gave as an example of biblical exposition.[14] It is also an example of specific application of the theme "The Lord is at hand." Here are the implications of that assertion—the theme applied:

    I. Rejoice
   II. Observe others and their needs and questions.
  III. Do not worry; pray.
  IV. Therefore, the peace of God will keep our hearts and minds.

Paul Scherer tells us what we can do when we have no directions as to what to do. His sermon is on "Creative Insecurity," and his text is Acts 9:15, 16.[15] "He is a chosen vessel unto me. . . . I will shew him how great things he must suffer for my name's sake." In Paul's experience and in our own, we are snatched from something solid and secure and thrust into something insecure. Scherer's points (in essence) are as follows:

I. We are lost in our "security."
II. We are saved in our "insecurity," that is, in our willingness to go with God, even when he says, "I will *show* you—not now, but as events transpire—how much you must suffer for my name's sake."
   A. Like Paul, we have no blueprint of the future.
   B. Yet we are chosen now for what God has in mind: We go not our own way, but where God goes.
      1. It is the way of Calvary.
      2. At least, it is the way of disciplines of life.
      3. In any case, it is a demand for obedience, come what may.

In Scherer's sermon, the only specific guidance we get is the solid reassurance that in the great events of our lives, there are no neat solutions, no pat answers. There is only the certainty that it is no strange thing that is happening to us and that, baffled though we be, God is in it all with us. Scherer had a strong conviction against using the imperative mode and expected the indicatives of the gospel to carry the weight of application. With him, it was application by implication.

Harry Emerson Fosdick, on the other hand, did not hesitate to urge specific courses of action when necessary. Appeal was a hallmark of his preaching. One of his sermons emphasized "The Importance of Doubting Our Doubts," using as a text the words of a distraught father to Jesus: "Lord, I believe; help thou mine unbelief" (Mark9:24).[16] His sermon is in two main parts.

I. Preliminary observations:
   A. The capacity to doubt is one of man's noblest powers.
   B. The sturdiest faith has always come out of the struggle with doubt.

II. The vital issue: Faith overcomes doubt by doubting our
doubts
   A. . . . about God
   B. . . . about Christ
   C. . . . about man and his possibilities.

This brief sketch does not give a full definition of Fosdick's
thought about doubt. It might seem that after praising doubt,
he turns around and sets it in a negative light. Not so. For
example, in II. A., he says, "There are many ideas of God which
ought to be doubted. The Bible itself progresses from one discarded idea of God to a nobler concept of him because men
dared to doubt." *Then* he goes on to urge us to question our
more basic doubts of God.

QUESTING

It is obviously easier to get a person to accept an answer if he
raises a question than if we thrust an answer on him uncere-
moniously. This may indicate a streak of perversity in human
nature, but it is a real factor to be reckoned with in preaching.
It dictates the preacher's treatment of some themes with any
audience and of many themes with some audiences. What is in
view here is an inductive approach in the sermon.[17]

It could be argued that true induction is impossible, for the
preacher knows where the sermon will come out. This would
be correct, of course, most of the time. But a sermon might be
open-ended. Then the conclusion would be what the hearer
contributed to the sermonic process, both by reactions during
the sermon and by reflections afterward. Conclusions would
vary from hearer to hearer. However, such sermons would be
rare.

An inductive approach is possible. We can simply describe
the process by which we arrived at a truth or a lesson, taking
the hearer into our confidence, hoping to involve him or her in
such a way as to be able to arrive at our destination together.
We must be fair; we must honestly present and weigh negative

evidence bearing on the issue. When dealing with a problem, like the problem of evil, we should be prepared to present it "in its most difficult form." If we are unwilling or unable to do that, perhaps a different approach—a more traditional, deductive approach—would be better.

Harry A. Overstreet recommended what has been called "the 'chase' technique."[18] The preacher considers several possible options, one after the other, showing the weaknesses or limitations of each, until both preacher and hearers arrive at the correct option. Of course, there may be problems even with the best option, but this one is affirmed and the sermon reaches its climax. It is hoped that the hearer has followed and heartily consents.

George A. Buttrick preached such a sermon on Matthew 7:12: "Whatever you wish that men would do to you, do so to them."[19] His first three points are rebuttals of certain implications of the notion "My religion is the golden rule." His fourth and last point is what Buttrick affirms as the proper interpretation of the golden rule. He has held us in suspense by not entirely rejecting certain ways of interpreting it, suggesting that these ways may be right under some as yet undisclosed conditions. The word *until*, followed by a pause, an uncompleted sentence, rivets our attention. We strain forward for the full answer to the question (the sermon's title), "Is It the Golden Rule?"

I. It cannot mean "whatever we wish."
II. Nobody has kept the golden rule.
III. The rule *of itself* gives us no power to keep the rule. Besides, all rules tend to alienate us.
IV. It is the golden rule only because the rule is held in the life and love of him who spoke it, who has said also, "Love one another as I have loved you."

STORYTELLING

With the sermonic narrative we move into an area that extends beyond the simple telling of a biblical story. *Story* embraces a concept of the sermon that includes the broad biblical story from creation to consummation, from Genesis to Revelation, with all of the smaller stories within that framework. Included may be stories—human stories—that are presented in such a context as to be revelatory for the purposes of God. This would embrace Jesus' parables as well as modern parables, true contemporary incidents, and autobiographical accounts. The key here is the *context*, the relationship of the stories to some purpose or action of God. It is not likely that Jesus' parables were launched like free-floating balloons to drift willy-nilly and to be subject to just any person's preferred interpretation. Rather, they were told in a context that pointed to their proper interpretation for the hearer who, as Jesus said, had "ears to hear."

The most obvious example of storytelling would be the relating of a biography or the retelling of a narrative incident. Many such stories follow a well-known dramatic pattern:[20]

    I. Situation or exposition, in which a wish, an expectation, or a purpose emerges.

   II. Complication, in which a hindrance or hindrances frustrate the achievement desired.

  III. Resolution or illumination, in which the wish, expectation, or purpose is after all achieved or abandoned—perhaps for something better.

Using such a scheme, the preacher can tell the story of Adam and Eve, or of Isaiah's conversion, or of the prodigal son, or of Peter's denial and restoration. Milton Crum, Jr., does precisely this in his sermon "The Christmas Story and Our Stories."[21] First, he says that if he were writing the Christmas faith story his own way, he would present Jesus in the most ideal situation. Next, he points out that the biblical faith story is totally unlike what he would have written. He shows the many difficulties, hardships, and so on that actually attended Jesus' birth and infancy. Finally, he admits that the Christmas faith story the Bible tells makes better sense of life than the nice one he would like to write, and it brings new results. So there it is—the biblical story with its dramatic tensions intersecting with our stories, with God at the intersection.

We should note also that a vibrant story lies just beneath the surface of many an epistle text. Think of the drama in Ephesians 2:8-10:

    I. We try to get on good terms with God by our good works. (The situation.)

    II. But works "don't work." (The complication.)

    III. God saves us in spite of our weakness, failure, and sin, saves us by his grace through our faith in Jesus Christ, which produces good works. (The resolution.)

This is a story of the Apostle Paul. It is our story, too, and the story of many of our hearers. Those who hear such a sermon can identify with at least its first movement. Who would be at church without having expected to get some "brownie points" with God for the effort, to say nothing of some other, perhaps more costly, efforts to please him? Then some of these hearers could identify with the second movement, recognizing that their efforts have brought no certitude, no clarity of relationship with God. They may even know that their best is not good enough and understand profoundly the plight of Martin Luther, whose fastings, prayers, and pilgrimages could not win a gracious God. The last movement could well be precisely the word of salvation for such hearers, the light at the end of a long, dark tunnel.

Frederick B. Speakman presents a story in a first person narrative, "What Pilate Said One Midnight."[22] This is an imagined conversation between Pilate and a Roman citizen, Gaius; it is in reality a monologue, though the way it goes suggests a dialogue between Pilate and Gaius. Details of the story are true to the facts of history and tradition, as far as these facts are known. To begin with, Pilate sets the stage for the crucial event that will involve him with Jesus, by telling Gaius what it is like to be procurator of Judea, with all the attending problems. Clearly, Pilate wishes, above all, to please Caesar, and thus he tries to cope in the almost impossible situation in Jerusalem. Second, the unwelcome appearing of Jesus of Nazareth on the scene threatens both the fragile peace that exists between Pilate and the people and the approval of Caesar. Pilate admits to actions of his own that have caused no end of trouble for himself and for his wife. Finally, something about Jesus gives him a thread of hope: "Deeper than the curse is the haunting, driving certainty that He's still somewhere near. That I've unfinished business with Him." Here we have a turbulent situation, a sudden deepening of the critical situation on a personal level (to say nothing of the political crisis), and the hint of a possible resolution of Pilate's own continuing problem.

In "Revelation and Response" the preacher, Theodore Parker Ferris, goes autobiographical by telling how revelation happened to him.[23] He explains how it may happen to another individual: "I am going to speak . . . from my own experience not because I think that my experience is unique, or that it may match yours; but rather, because the experience of one person sometimes helps another to interpret his own, whether by way of contrast or similarity." First off, Ferris quickly sets the stage for the experiences through which the revelation of God was actualized in his life. He speaks of "the small, friendly world" of his childhood, where his father and mother loved each other and loved him. Next, he depicts the struggles in his life that threatened to frustrate his burgeoning faith. "But at the center," he says, "there was still love and meaning, and I projected that upon the larger screen of the universe." Finally, he sets forth his rationale for what he has felt to be true.

COMBINING

The main thought of the sermon may follow a more or less straight course in a sequence of movements. Or it may follow a zigzag course. In either case, it must go somewhere. However, each movement may have within it characteristics that are different from the other movements. There may be a natural flow of sequences, but each sequence will have its own discrete features.

Take Alan Monroe's "Motivated Sequence,"[24] for example. This is a formula for speaking that is based on observation of the five steps that a salesman or a speaker actually takes when trying to win acceptance for a product, for an idea, or, we might even say, for his or her faith. Each of the steps, as such, has biblical support in Isaiah 55:

 I. Attention step: "Ho . . . "
 II. Need step: " . . . everyone that thirsteth."
 III. Satisfaction step: " . . . come ye to the waters . . . ; come ye, buy, and eat . . . "
 IV. Visualization step: "Wherefore do ye spend money for that which is not bread? And your labour for that which satisfieth not? . . . " "Incline your ear, and come unto me: hear, and your soul shall live. . . . "
 V. Action step: "Seek ye the Lord while he may be found . . ."

Such a scheme, though we could use it selfishly for crass, unethical manipulation, can be used from the highest motives for the highest ends with the highest standards of fairness and honesty.

That done, we can go on to observe how a sermon built on Monroe's scheme may employ different types of outlining within each separate step. I do not offer what follows as an ideal sermon—it merely exemplifies what we are discussing.

Text: "For the wages of sin is death; but the gift of God is eternal life through Jesus Christ our Lord" (Rom. 6:23).

 I. Attention step
   A. *Sin* is a word that many have dropped from their vocabulary.
   B. But it is easier to get rid of the word than the reality the word stands for: "For all have sinned, and come short of the glory of God" (Rom. 3:23).
 II. Need step
   A. Sin brings death to a sense of security in life.
   B. Sin brings death to a sense of meaning in life.
   C. Sin brings death to many promising relationships in life.
   D. Sin brings death to our spiritual self.

III. Satisfaction step
  A. Nevertheless, eternal life is a possibility for every one of us who have sinned.
  B. This is possible because of what God is: gracious—and gracious because he loves us.
  C. God works his salvation through Jesus Christ.
IV. Visualization step
  A. Death will continue to permeate your existence unless . . .
  B. Life can be radically different if . . .
V. Action step
  A. Decide now, if you can, to receive God's free gift.
  B. Follow through with baptism, which shows burial of the old life and the rising of a new life.
  C. Walk in the new life.

Monroe's scheme is flexible enough to combine attention and need steps (for what could be more gripping than a clear and relevant picture of the hearer's need?). We may present need and satisfaction in a number of sequences, treating particular aspects of need, each immediately followed by its mode of satisfaction. We can do the same with satisfaction and visualization.

A sermon designed to explain, inform, or convince will not necessarily take the last two steps—visualization and action. It will summarize the points covered, for we seek not action but understanding or belief. Review reinforces.

Another type of sermon that combines modes of structural development is what has been called the "plain style" sermon. James Cleland called his adaptation of it the "old expository" sermon. The essence of it is rather simple and natural. Elton Trueblood, the Quaker philosopher, reflected his own tradition of lay preaching when he described the simplicity of preaching. Lecturing to one of my classes, he told homiletics students that, first, the preacher must explain the text; then, tell what it means; and finally, apply it to the lives of the hearers.

We can amplify this brief description and pursue some specific types of development.

This is how such a sermon may look:

TEXT
INTRODUCTION

BODY:
  I. A nontechnical exegesis of the text *or* a narration of the text if it is the type that tells a story (historical incident, biography, parable, miracle). This is roughly an inductive approach that leads up to a central idea that is the thesis, proposition, affirmation—call it what you will. It is the *time-bound* truth, and the key word is *then*.
  II. A setting forth of the meaning or truth of that central idea. This may take the form of logical proofs, scriptural evidence, historical examples, or doctrinal statements and explanations. It is the *timeless* truth, and the key word is *always*.
  III. Application of the message of the sermon to the entire congregation, or to some individuals or groups within the congregation, or to the present age. Perhaps it can be applied to all three. It is the *timely* truth, and the key word is *now*.

CONCLUSION: The sermon may or may not need a separate conclusion.

The following sketch is an example of the "old expository" sermon. James T. Cleland, dean of the chapel at Duke University, preached it on the second Sunday of Advent, 1958, in the chapel.[25]

TEXT: Luke 4:16-30.
INTRODUCTION: (A description of the purpose of Advent as preparation for Christmas, not a time to damn the merchants downtown, to debunk Santa Claus, or to celebrate infancy.) "The newborn babe, wrapped in swaddling clothes and lying in a manger, is to be appreciated, understood, and adored only in the light of the church's interpretation of his whole earthly career."
"If we expect to use the preparation of Advent aright, we had better know who Jesus was, as this is shown through his own words."
  I. EXEGESIS (key word, *then*):
     "This incident . . . is either a transcript of Jesus' first public sermon and its outcome, or what the evangelist thought Jesus ought to have said at the opening of his ministry."
     A. Jesus openly asserts that he is uniquely related to God.
     B. Jesus pointed out that his message was good news—to the down-and-outs. Thus "it is a revelation of the character and will of God." (This is the central idea of the sermon.)
     C. This was effective preaching—it got a reaction. The people were angry and tried to throw him over a cliff.

II. EXPOSITION (key word, *always*):
"We may well rejoice that not all the hearers of this gospel, down the centuries, have reacted like the Nazarenes. Yet, lest we be too complacent, think of the history of the church, in its constituency and in its appreciation of good news for the poor."
   A. Consider Paul's description of the membership of the Corinthian church. 1 Corinthians 1:26-28.
   B. A century later Celsus pointed to the disreputable character of the converts.
   C. Not ignoring Constantine's making Christianity the official religion, recall St. Francis, Wesley, and General Booth and their efforts to reach the oppressed.
   D. "Christianity appeals not only to the poor but to the poor in spirit, to those who know they are captives to themselves or to the world, blind to the things of the soul and oppressed in mind." Remember Lord Shaftesbury, William Wilberforce, and Florence Nightingale and their expressions of the "social gospel."
   E. The persecution that Jesus received at Nazareth is repeated in different forms today. "This good news of the kingdom, incarnate in Jesus of Bethlehem, is not always what the church wants either to hear or to preach."
III. APPLICATION (key word, *now*):
   A. Many of us have responded affirmatively and have "seen and welcomed and—in some measure—live in the acceptable year of the Lord."
   B. "But have we allowed our response to become stereotyped, pedestrian, in a rut? . . . God is full of unexpected moments and so should His children be . . . The good folk may not like it . . . It offends both personal pride and social idolatry."
   C. "If we want a quiet, a normal, a conservative Christmas, let us not go too near the manger-cradle in Bethlehem . . . For, at a minimum estimate, there is a nuisance value in the incarnation, the nuisance value of one whose thoughts are not necessarily our thoughts, religious though we be."

The sermon needs structure, just as the human body needs it: to give the sermon form and to make movement possible. An occasional gelatinous sermon may not do any harm, but it surely will do little good.

12. The Primacy of Story

Story has been one of the most discussed items in preaching, and deservedly so. Story has characterized the Judeo-Christian tradition from the beginning. In truth, the entire Bible is one magnificent story. Within this larger story are many smaller ones. We find there primeval stories; stories of families, tribes, and nations; as well as stories of individuals. The most magnificent of all is the account of the Christ event, characterized by one writer as *The Greatest Story Ever Told.* Within that narrative we find miracle stories and parables, each with its own discrete integrity. Even in the epistles of Paul, abstract as they may sometimes seem, stories vibrating with life surge just beneath the surface.

The preacher who takes account of this narrative quality of the Christian faith and who proceeds homiletically from this fact is the preacher who will be heard. Children love stories and entreat their elders with, "Tell me a story, please! . . . Now tell me another story!" As long as we live, we never become immune to the charm of a well-told story. A noted psychologist, George W. Crane, took frequent opportunity in his newspaper column to argue the merits of the "anecdotal" style of sermon. As a much sought after public speaker himself and a sharp observer of human nature, he was convinced that the concrete instance could make an otherwise dull speech or sermon come to life.

Telling stories in the pulpit, however, ought not to be done just because they are in the Bible or because of their potential entertainment value. I suppose my first impression of the true value of the story in preaching came from something I read in one of Andrew W. Blackwood's books. He suggested that a preacher could make the doctrine of repentance, for example, more meaningful to a hearer through the story of Simon Peter's repentance than through an abstract discussion of repentance.

Describe to me someone in the process of repenting, and I will learn what repentance means!

Of course, stories well told possess other values too. They *are* interesting, but their entertainment value can be a plus and does not have to be a minus. Furthermore, they delineate truth from a variety of angles. What a variety of dramas can be found in the Bible itself!

Stories may be revelatory for those who listen. The hearer may discover the truth about herself or himself in relation to God and fellowman as the story unfolds. One discovers that one is a part of the story and understands the story from within it, not just as a disinterested observer. That is why Jesus would say, after he had spoken a parable, "He who has ears to hear let him hear!"

We must be cautious in our storytelling. A story may be trivial and not worth the telling. Even some stories in the Bible are not edifying in certain situations. The story of King David's sin with Bathsheba, for instance, may be told in such a way as to pander to an audience's prurient interests. Again, people can draw wrong inferences from our stories, seizing on some detail and missing our point, and we may be to blame for it. Also, the use of story may become too exclusive a method. Our Lord, recognized as *the* artist of the parable, sometimes used a more direct method of teaching. Whatever we may say in favor of an overall concrete approach to preaching, we should note that people need a systematic view of the Christian faith, that is, a way of putting together all the fragmentary and fleeting insights and feelings, engendered by stories, so that they make a more or less consistent whole.

With these caveats before us, it can be emphasized: A good story can be the whole of a sermon—just the story, nothing else! What H. Grady Davis has called "a dramatic continuity" can say everything that the preacher wants or needs to say. Consider any of these three biblical narratives: the prodigal son, Paul in the Areopagus, or Zacchaeus. Here one finds stories in three parts: (1.) situation (or exposition), in which a purpose emerges;

(2.) complication (or hindrance), in which fulfillment of the purpose is blocked or frustrated; and (3.) resolution (or illumination), in which the purpose is carried through to a satisfactory conclusion or finally abandoned.

But note! In the story of the prodigal son the apparent resolution (the great reception and festival of rejoicing) becomes the new situation as the story continues. For that new story there is a complication (the elder brother's churlish refusal to attend the party), but there is no resolution! So it is with other parables of Jesus: The resolution or application is left up to the one who hears—no spoon-feeding here! Either you get the message or you don't, depending on your willingness to recognize the truth when it tugs at your sleeve and says, "Here I am—look at me!"

There are, of course, other ways in which the story does its work. Not only may I tell the story and let its inner force make the application but I also may explicitly apply it to different life situations. Perhaps we expect too much of people when we assume they can always get our point or make a valid one of their own. Who will say that Martin Luther was wrong when he preached by simply explaining and applying the text as he went? Some preachers learn to do this with a biblical story and do it with color and appeal, so that the hearers do not have to feel they are being talked down to or spoon-fed. This, however, is as much an achievement of character as it is of homiletical formation, for egotism and arrogance must be kept to a minimum.

Using another method of applying the meaning of a story, the preacher may relate fully or summarize the story, distill a central, controlling idea, and then draw out the implications in one or several applications.

Up to this point we have been thinking mainly of a story as the basis of an entire sermon. Obviously a good story may be only a *part* of a sermon, though a vital part. A story may provide an example or an illustration of some truth. Henry Ward Beecher, the noted pulpit orator of the nineteenth century, was the consummate master of illustration. Supportive materials in remarkable variety appeared in his sermons, but he had stories mainly in mind when he listed the values of illustration: to clarify ideas, to help hearers to remember, to stimulate imagination, to provide for various hearers, to telescope or shortcut argument, to bridge difficult places by treating delicate issues indirectly, and to educate the people by showing them how to make illustrations and examples themselves.[1]

And now for a debatable matter! What about autobiographical stories—"confessional" preaching? Who can deny that "truth through personality," Phillips Brook's definition of preaching, has the ring of reality in it? Every saving relationship of life derives its "truth" through personality. The world is richer for *The Confessions* of Augustine, John Bunyan's *Grace Abounding*, and other such autobiographical works, including sermons that reveal the works of divine grace in human experience. Yet good taste and fitting humility must reign here, controlling subject matter, frequency of use, confidentiality, and various matters of like importance. Unfortunately, the preacher can give the impression that no truth is worth talking about that has not found its way into his or her own experience. An individual personality is a box too small for the vastnesses of God's truth.

Preachers who are reticent about speaking of their own private experiences—and there are many—can achieve the purpose of a personal story by citing a parallel instance. One preacher, hesitant perhaps to speak of his own emotional crisis as a young theological student, told of the despair and thoughts of suicide that plagued young William James. He got his message across effectively without having to make a "personal reference." The same preacher, however, speaking in a different situation years later, told his own experience in the first person.

The supreme value of the story lies in its intersection with *our* story, especially when God is at the intersection.

13. Introduction, Conclusion, and Title

The middle—or the body—of the sermon is its heart, but the introduction, the conclusion, and the title are important too, for different reasons.

They may or may not be the last parts of the sermon that we prepare. We might prepare the introduction last, assuming the logic of having something to introduce before introductions are made. Or, we might introduce a problem and work our way forward toward a solution. Or, why would it not be lawful to determine as the first order of homiletical business where we wish to come out, before preparing what precedes this? Of course, more often the conclusion is done last. In any case, the conclusion is a significant appendage to the main development of the sermon. And, finally, the sermon requires a title. We shall look at each of these—the introduction, the conclusion, and the title—separately in this chapter.

THE INTRODUCTION

The introduction presents the theme of the sermon or the question to which the sermon addresses itself. Very early the hearers need to know what the sermon is about. This does not have to occur in the very first sentence, though it may. Some preachers would like to pack as much as possible into the opening sentence. More likely, the theme will emerge later, perhaps at the last moment before the sermon moves into the main discussion. At that time, we can let the audience know where we are headed with the theme.

The introduction, however, is more than a place to state or reveal a fact to be learned. It prepares the hearers psychologically, not just intellectually, for the discussion that follows. They must become *interested* in what is to come—deeply involved, if possible, in the whole message—by seeing quite early that they have a personal stake in it. If there is any reason for the hearers to know that the message means anything personally at all—the fulfilling of a need or desire—this is the place for understanding that or, what is better, for feeling it. Many sermons of vital importance to individuals have been ignored or quickly forgotten because the preacher failed to link up the sermon with the hearer's life and to do that soon enough for the hearer to give it proper attention. The effectiveness of a sermon may be saved or lost in what is done to bring to consciousness the vital issues that are actually present but perhaps unrecognized in the sermon. Other means of gaining interest in a theme or a truth also are available and useful. Some subjects are only remotely vital though important, and appeal to the most compelling motives may not be possible or appropriate. Thus other factors of interest, such as conflict or humor, may have to be brought into play, not only in the introduction, but throughout the sermon.

Another use of the introduction is to relate text and theme. We may show that the text particularizes a general truth that has wider application. We will highlight that truth and then go on to apply it to other areas of experience. James S. Stewart did this in his sermon "Holy Alliances." The text is Mark 10:9: "What therefore God hath joined together, let not man put asunder." The preacher begins like this: "Let us take this deep saying of our Lord out of its original setting. As it stands here, it was spoken in answer to one particular question, the question of the Pharisees about marriage and divorce; but like so many of the Master's sayings, its application goes far beyond the original intention. The circumstances which first elicited this profound remark of Jesus by no means exhaust its significance. Indeed, what we have here is not simply a ruling on one isolated problem: it is a principle which can be seen running through the whole of life."[1] Then Stewart proceeds to discuss three "God-intended alliances": religion and character; faith and reason; and the human soul and Jesus.

Moreover, the introduction may enable the hearer to identify personally with the theme of the sermon. When the sermon has to do with me personally, why should I have to guess that it may be so or wait until the end to be told? Harry Emerson Fosdick argued that the application of the sermon ought to begin in the introduction and should not be tacked on at the end. His sermon "Are We Part of the Problem or the Answer?" is an example of what he meant. Here are some isolated sentences from the introduction:

Everywhere today the word *problem* confronts us.

God might have made this universe like Aladdin's palace, all complete for our lazy occupancy, no difficulty to face, nothing new to discover, nothing puzzling to solve, nothing required but to settle down and luxuriate. After even a few weeks of that, can you image anything more boring?

Willy-nilly, we are all in the thick of the world's game . . .

We have a traffic problem on our American highways . . . Well, you drive an automobile—are you a part of the problem or of the answer?

We have a family problem in this nation . . . Well, are we part of the problem or the answer?[2]

Then Fosdick proceeds to say that we are powerfully tempted to make exceptions of ourselves, that the difficulties are so great that one life seems to make little difference. Yet, one life can be so useful as to be positively inspiring.

Another purpose of the introduction is to gain the goodwill of the hearers. We cannot hope to accomplish much in the sermon if the people are against us. If we have known and served a congregation over a period of time and if we have found a place in the people's hearts, then we do not have to work for their goodwill. We already have that or we cannot hope to get it in the best introduction we can devise. If we are occasional preachers or preachers facing a particular audience for the first time, then we need to establish our *ethos*—our intellectual, spiritual, and human credentials. We may, therefore, use humor, some personal reference, an appreciative word for our hearers, or something we share in common with them. Perhaps the Apostle Paul often found it necessary to tell of his experience on the Damascus Road in order to get a hearing from audiences who were suspicious of him because of his preconversion persecutions of Christians. But it would not have been necessary to do this with the same people each time he addressed them.

CHARACTERISTICS

The introduction should be related to life. It should find people where they are and join with them in an adventure that may take them where they want or need to go. Some introductions get bogged down in a dry discussion of Greek grammar, of some technical theological issue, or of an archeological discovery, any of which could come alive if imaginatively related to living and breathing human beings. Many preachers have found their preaching revolutionized by simply highlighting a life situation in the introduction and then doing in the rest of the sermon what that situation demanded. This is not to say, however, that every sermon must be of the life-situation type. Yet whenever any introduction is touched with life, it will be better and more interesting for it.

The introduction should be anticipatory, that is, it should successfully point forward to the main discussion. It must decrease while the body of the sermon increases. If the introduction is too good, everything that follows will go downhill. We might use a powerful illustration far more effectively in the conclusion.

Normally the introduction should be brief. Brevity, however, is not necessary or desirable in every case. Fosdick's introductions varied in length according to his theme and purpose, and usually appropriately so, though one's impression is that they tended to be too long. George Buttrick, on the other hand, wrote short introductions of uniform length—one-half page was the pattern to which he consistently adhered.

STRATEGIES

Let the very first sentence be promising. I could have put this negatively: Do not kill the sermon with the opening sentence. Fosdick was widely quoted as saying to his homiletics students, "Tell all you know in the first sentence,"[3] so that the "big truth" would be highlighted early. Charles R. Brown, an effective preacher and teacher of preachers, said that five sentences of his sermons were always carefully prepared and memorized— the first sentence and the last four.[4] One preacher got into the habit of beginning his sermons, after he had announced his text, "This is a very significant verse." After a while, these opening words tended to trivialize every text he used. If indeed the texts were as significant as he said they were, why did he not begin with something like this: "The more I thought about this text, the more excited I became"? "This is surely too good to be true." "Where on earth can you hear such good news as this?" "With those words we walk into the Holy of Holies." Of course, these examples suggest that the preacher reads a text immediately before the sermon. This, however, is not necessary. One may introduce the text *and* the sermon at the same time, so that the text comes in the middle or at the end of the introduction.

Begin the sermon, if possible, on common ground with the hearers. If you are going to discuss later something about which the congregation may have little or inadequate knowledge, first talk about something the people know well, something to which they can relate the new information or understanding. This is one of the contributions of Herbart's educational theory: broaden the range of knowledge by beginning with the knowledge the learner already has; move from the known to the unknown. D. W. Cleverley Ford often used this principle in the very first sentence of his sermon. Here are several examples from his sermons:

• "It is very difficult, Moses. It is very difficult to describe God. We have been trying down through the ages."

• "That is what the onlookers said about the Apostles, 'They've been drinking!' "

• "I would like you to think for a moment this morning about a bank book, a deposit account bank book. Let us say it is yours. Let us say it represents all your dealings with your bank since you were twenty-one."[5]

Use a variety of beginnings. In the thirty-seven sermons in *The Twentieth Century Pulpit*, Vol. 1, each of which is by a noted preacher, the first sentences begin as follows: fourteen with statements, eight with references to the text, five with stories or anecdotes, two with quotations, one with a personal reference, and one with a definition.[6]

The sermons that began with statements showed, as a group, the least use of imagination, though there were exceptions. How could Fosdick's approach be improved on in his sermon "The Sacred and the Secular Are Inseparable"? "Human life can be differentiated into secular and sacred just as water can be analyzed into hydrogen and oxygen. Water, however, ought not to be served to us—first, two parts hydrogen and then one part oxygen; water ought to be taken as a whole."[7]

Let the introduction point to the text or point out from it. In other words, the focal Bible passage ought somehow to be effectively mixed into the introduction. A sermon does not reach its potential unless it leaves the hearers with a better understanding of some portion of scripture. Understanding is achieved when the sermon moves either along with the text or toward it. The journey begins in the introduction. If the text is a narrative incident or a longer story, we can summarize it by quickly drawing the picture with a few bold strokes. The subsequent references to the text will then be clear to the hearers. If the text is a type of literature needing explanation, we can paraphrase the text or, perhaps, focus on single words or phrases to be explained. This is no place, however, for tedious explanations—for squeezing the life out of an otherwise interesting story or for being so unimaginative as to make the hearers hate the priceless words of scripture.

The introduction can be instrumental in the understanding of the text even if the introduction does not contain a shred of scripture. In theory, the text may not be mentioned until the last moments of the sermon. In practice that is highly unlikely. The introduction will serve mainly to present the problem or difficulty to which the rest of the sermon gives the biblical answer.

Speakers and writers have long known that it is important early in a speech or an essay to define terms or to explain what is confusing. This ground-clearing work makes it possible, then, to get on with the main items on the agenda.

There is one more important way of making the introduction useful. We can enter into a "contract" with the congregation.[8] This is a more or less formal way of indicating where we intend to go with the sermon. It offers a helpful, clarifying point of reference as the people continue to listen. We may do this in various ways. Just before launching into the body of the sermon, we may raise the central question that the discussion that follows will answer: "What are some of the ways in which we can deal successfully with these fears?" Or, we may make a statement of the central idea or proposition of the sermon, to be followed by explanations, arguments, or applications: "God can make every event of our lives serve his high purposes." Or, we may state the main points to be developed: "I. God showed his love to the world by sending his Son; II. The purpose of this gift was to offer us eternal life; III. The gift is ours through faith," or, "I. The Measure of God's Love; II. The Purpose of God's Love; III. The Experience of God's Love."

Sometimes a too explicit contract might give away too much of what is to follow and thus remove the element of anticipation or surprise. Careful wording, however, can avoid that possibility.

A sermon given mainly to explanation or argument can only be helped by marking out the ground to be covered, or even by clear assertions of what is to be explained or supported.

THE CONCLUSION

Andrew W. Blackwood believed that, apart from the text, the conclusion is the most important part of the sermon.[9] There is where the hearer renders a verdict. There is where the conclusive work of the sermon gets done. This is mostly true, though there are exceptions, as we shall see.

To finish the sermon with a conclusion—a recognizable one— is simply a satisfactory way to bring the sermon to a close. It contributes to a sense of wholeness.

Moreover, there is in a well-planned and well-executed conclusion the opportunity to make the main point of the sermon *stick*. Clearly, in a sermon of twenty or thirty minutes duration, the main point of the sermon—the objective—could be lost among numerous ideas of lesser importance. While this is not likely to happen in a sermon that has been thoroughly arranged, it does happen in many cases. For their life, many of the hearers could not tell what the preacher wanted them to know, to believe, to feel, or to do. The conclusion gives the hearers a final opportunity to respond to the sermon.

But there may be no conclusion to the sermon at all—and for a good reason. If we have clearly stated the issue, if the hearer has had opportunity to reflect on the questions we have raised or to identify with the characters in an unfolding story, then the proper conclusion may be only the one that the hearer will give. This way of ending may seem abrupt to some hearers. They would like the sermon to be tied up in a neat bundle and handed to them, so that they can tuck it neatly away where it will bother no one. Or, to change the analogy, they might like to be spoon-fed the truth.

Scholars believe that Jesus often presented his message with a parable that, when originally spoken, added no application. The conclusion lay in the conscience of an honest listener. "He who has ears to hear, let him hear," said Jesus: That was all the conclusion that was required, and it was no conclusion at all. In the parable of the prodigal son and the elder brother, where is the conclusion if not in the minds and hearts of Pharisees and scribes of two thousand years ago and in the minds and hearts of self-righteous Christians of today?

CHARACTERISTICS

Ordinarily the conclusion should be brief. Conclusions that never seem to conclude are uniformly an abomination. The rambling conclusion irritates the hearer and erects or thickens barriers to communication. Almost as bad is the conclusion that is actually a series of possible conclusions, all of them well thought out and making good sense. Yet the exasperated hearer thinks, "He had a perfect place to stop minutes ago!"

While the conclusion need not take the congregation by surprise, the preacher does not have to give verbal or visual signals that the sermon is nearly done. Nothing psychologically is gained by saying or suggesting, "I'm almost through. Bear with me a little longer!"

One good way of holding down the length of the conclusion is never to introduce new material in it. It is too late to take up ideas there that have not been introduced before. This is the place to bring ideas that have been explored to a sharp and—if possible— *single* focus. There *may* be a distributed application, but there *must* be one dominant idea that has either pushed or drawn the sermon until "it stands forth in its final clarity."

Let the conclusion be phrased in simple words and the syntax be uncomplicated. The time for nice shading of words is past; that should have been done in the main discussion. The conclusion is the time for emphatic, unqualified statements or sharp, direct questions. Otherwise the sermon may wind up in a fog bank.

WAYS TO CONCLUDE

Some sermons can best end with a summary of the main points. This is especially true of sermons that have undertaken to impart knowledge or explain something. The same applies to sermons that argue for the acceptance of a thesis. For the latter, one might even briefly restate the main arguments. However, such recapitulation does not rule out the use of other materials in the conclusion. If we usually mix the sermon's objectives, that is, if we blend the informative, the convictional, the inspirational, and the persuasive, then we will no doubt wish to employ elements that touch the emotions and prick the will.

Often a story that exemplifies or illustrates in some graphic fashion what we have tried to say will provide the most desirable way to conclude. It may demonstrate precisely the action toward which we have been moving the hearers. It may bolster the courage for continuing to try to do the will of God. Or it may simply help to liberate a feeling of joyous gratitude. It would be a mistake, however, to assume that every sermon should end with a touching story. If all that has preceded the conclusion has been of an informative or reasoning nature, an emotion-arousing story would be out of place.

Furthermore, an appeal is the logical conclusion of a sermon with an evangelistic emphasis. Such a sermon may convey information, explain the doctrine of salvation, deal with personal need, offer the good news of forgiveness and eternal life, and then call for decision. Should a sense of need that has been aroused and a desire to appropriate what Christ offers be allowed to evaporate because no appeal for decision is given and no opportunity through prayer or public profession of faith is offered to conclude the matter? The very place where such an approach would tend to embarrass some parishioners is most likely the place where evangelistic appeal is most needed. William James said, "When a resolve or a fine glow or feeling is allowed to evaporate without bearing practical fruit, it is worse than a chance lost; it works so as positively to hinder future resolutions and emotions from taking the normal path of discharge."[10]

Sometimes what is needed in a sermon calling for decision of a different type is our personal declaration of our intent to do this thing. We then call upon the members of the congregation to join us in some momentous decision. This kind of conclusion will not often be appropriate or honestly possible. Yet when it is needed and we find the inner grace to commit ourselves for some worthy objective, then nothing could offer greater incentive to a sensitive people than to make this a community covenant.

What of the use of poetry as a way to conclude? It may be the most impressive way to bring the sermon to a close—occasionally. The old joke about a sermon consisting of three points and a poem should remain what it is—a joke. In the first place, the poetry should be appropriate to the mood and objective of the sermon. It must not be a mere bauble to make the sermon look pretty, if that were possible. Next, it should be clear in what it says, as clear as any prose statement that we might compose for the conclusion. Furthermore, it should be brief. A couplet or a quatrain is ordinarily enough. One might go longer with verse like George MacDonald's "Obedience," whose message is clear in a first reading. James S. Stewart effectively used six of the seven stanzas to conclude his sermon "Sacrifice and Song."[11] Also, well-known hymns might be quoted at greater length. But try that with Robert Browning or Dylan Thomas, and the sermon will end with a dull thud, thud, thud . . . . While some poetry is meaningful on reflection, beautiful in protracted contemplation, it nevertheless may make little sense with only one time through, which is all that is possible in a sermon.

THE TITLE

The sermon needs a name. If the church advertises the services of worship in the newspaper, has a bulletin board outside the church, mails out a bulletin, or distributes to the worshipers an order of service, a title for the sermon has a definite value. It can stimulate interest in the sermon and help the congregation to remember it.

Of course, many fine sermons have been preached without a title given to them and congregations have profited from hearing them. In fact, some theologians disdain titles, for they seem presumptuous. One said, "The attempt to find a title for a sermon means that one feels able to summarize what God wants to speak through the sermon text."[12] A minister friend said to me that he found the sermon title to be a bother and that he felt it was intended not for the preacher but for the congregation. If the preacher allows a clever title to determine the direction of the sermon, then the sermon may go astray from the text and from the central idea and the objective. For this reason, the title ought normally to be decided after the sermon has been prepared or after basic preparation, not before.

Notwithstanding objections, for the sake of the congregation that needs a peg on which to hang the preacher's message, the effort to formulate a memorable title is time well spent. For example, the title gives a focus for later reflection and discussion. Also, if the preacher later wishes to poll the congregation about the most helpful sermons they have heard, so that they can hear them again, the title will be useful.

It should be clear that the sermon title should not be misleading. For this reason, Billy Sunday's sermon on Naaman's dipping seven times in the River Jordan deserved a better title than "Seven Ducks in a Muddy Stream."

Moreover, the sermon title should not be sensational. An evangelist packed the house by announcing that on the next night he would preach on "What Two Old Maids Saw Through a Keyhole" and did not preach on that subject after all. Though the prurient deserved his betrayal, he lost credibility in the process.

Aside from the function of the title as an aid to memory, what can the title do?

It can focus on a need. Consider these titles of sermons by Harry Emerson Fosdick.[13] "The Power to See It Through," "When Life Reaches Its Depths," "Handling Life's Second Bests," "Handicapped Lives," and "Six Ways to Tell Right from Wrong."

It can create curiosity. David H. C. Read preached a sermon that was a Christmas fantasy. Its title: "Star Out of Orbit."[14]

Theodore Adams, while minister of the First Baptist Church in Richmond, Virginia, said,

You always want to be on the alert for timely topics and matters of special interest—books and movies and plays, as well as current events that call for special attention. I remember a certain editor . . . who deplored the fact that "the pulpit in the great old First Baptist Church in Richmond had certainly degenerated." The pastor was preaching on, of all things, "What Has Become of Little Boy Blue." . . . The sermon on Little Boy Blue did not come from any nursery rhyme. It came from that beautiful verse of Eugene Fields about a little boy and his toy soldiers and the eternal question, "What has become of Little Boy Blue since he kissed them and put them there?" The theme, of course, was the Christian doctrine of immortality, and Little Boy Blue helped introduce it.[15]

It can raise a question. George A. Buttrick asked these questions in his sermon titles:[16] "Has Christ Left Us?" and "Who Owns the Earth?" Halford E. Luccock asked:[17] "Religion—A Toy or a Power?" and "Restorers or Creators?"

Arthur John Gossip, in a remarkable and classic sermon, asked a question that first took its cue from a question in the text and then let the topic dictate the strategy of the entire sermon:[18] "But When Life Tumbles in, What Then?" Fosdick, in a cliff-hanging sermon, asked:[19] "How Believe in a Good God in a World Like This?"

It can make a statement. A sermon by Henry Ward Beecher used almost the very words of a phrase in his text: "The God of Comfort." The words imply that God is a God of comfort and that the preacher intended to talk about precisely that truth. Thomas Chalmers, likewise, implied a theme complete with subject and predicate in his celebrated sermon "The Expulsive Power of a New Affection."[20]

As noted previously, Buttrick raised a question concerning the whereabouts of the crucified, so as to seek and find the answer with the congregation. Chalmers Coe asserts the truth in the title "Christ is Alive!"[21]

In one sermon Fosdick implies a truth—that amid the various problems of our world we can be part of the problem or of the answer. But he made the statement indirectly—in the form of a question: "Are We Part of the Problem or of the Answer?" In another sermon he makes a statement flat out: "The Church Must Go Beyond Modernism."[22]

It can focus on the text. There may be no effort in particular cases to be striking. Buttrick sometimes simply pointed to the text:[23] "It Shall Come Back," "God's Ways and Man's Ways," "Judge Not," and "Babel and Pentecost."

James Cleland did the same, but not so simply: "Jonah: A Very Minor Prophet." Paul Scherer used the very words of scripture in one title:[24] "They That Wait for the Lord."

It can suggest a theme. William Ellery Channing preached a sermon titled:[25] "The Character of Christ." Billy Sunday preached on "Heaven." Karl Barth preached on "Repentance."

Such sermon titles, suggesting a general theme, may suffice in particular cases, but as compared with most of the other titles cited here, they lack color, vitality, and imagination. Perhaps Channing, Sunday, and Barth did not need better titles for their sermons, since their personalities commanded attention. But most preachers could use the additional help to gain the interest of the people, aside from the other considerable values of an attractive title.

14. The Factors of Attention and Interest

How does the preacher get a congregation to listen throughout a sermon? The most obvious way might seem to be to load the sermon with human interest stories or with humor. We have all heard speeches and sermons that kept us enthralled by the sheer drama or humor of what was said. And the stories, jokes, or witticisms were all fitting and relevant! But we have also heard speeches and sermons whose stories and humor were farfetched and for various reasons inappropriate. Stories and jokes as such cannot guarantee the kind of attention and interest that produce the results at which a sermon should aim. The presence or absence of certain qualities, regardless of the type of prose, captures attention and keeps it alive.[1]

MATTERS OF VITAL INTEREST

Suppose someone made one of these statements and then commented on it. Would you not listen to every word that was said?

• "The land your home sits on is going to be bought up for a new expressway."
• "I have just come from the hospital—your husband is in intensive care."
• "The Bureau of Missing Heirs called while you were out. This is what they said."
• "I'm with the Internal Revenue Service, and I have a message for you."
• "You are under consideration for president of the company, and I was asked to talk with you about it."

•"We've been friends a long time. I have a reliable tip that can make us both rich."

•"The report from the lab is not good. Let me give you my considered medical opinion on what you will have to do."

These statements and their explanations would not rate high on a spiritual scale, yet they do indicate some of the vital concerns that will engage the attention of most of us.

The most involving vital interests are universal—or nearly so. They are morally positive or neutral; they have religious implications that are personal and societal. Stated negatively as problems, they could include guilt, fear, disappointment, loneliness, anger, failure, frustration, discouragement, inferiority feelings, compulsions, and so on. These problems may be called universal, not because they trouble everyone at the same time but because they can happen to anyone and do happen to most of us sooner or later. It would be a mistake to assume that each of these problems would be of the same degree of interest to all hearers or indeed of any interest whatsoever to some of them. Furthermore, it would also be a mistake to assume that every sermon that dealt with a matter of vital concern would hold the hearer's attention. To begin with, the need might be stated so vaguely that the hearers could not get a clear focus on it. But even if the need were stated clearly and related explicitly to the hearers, they might lose interest in what we were saying because we took the discussion into a jungle of abstractions. On the other hand, a sermon might be of intense interest to one type of hearer for the very reason that we did not treat a problem in a simplistic way but went boldly and honestly into its complexities. In *The Twentieth Century Pulpit*, Volumes 1 and 2, comprising sixty-four sermons by pulpit masters of this century, none of the sermons fails to deal with at least one matter of vital concern. Yet some sermons are far more interesting than others—and not because the concerns of the most interesting ones are more vital! The key is in how the vital issue is handled, how the preacher understands the audience and addresses it, how much credibilty the preacher brings to the sermon and maintains in the discussion. From the hearers' side, a great deal depends on how much they know, what they like, and how upset they are at the moment or how eager they are to learn something new.

THE FAMILIAR

Diplomats and others who negotiate the vital interests of those they represent have long known the value of "common ground." A good place to begin is with what we have in common. Birds of a feather tend to flock together, whether the "feather" be theological, social, ethical, financial, artistic, or gustatory. The educational philosophy of Johann Friedrich Herbart holds that in classroom instruction the teacher should begin with something the pupil knows and then go on to relate to that the new information or experience. What is familiar may be some ordinary experience, some area of special knowledge, or a well-known historical incident (in preaching, this might be a story from the Bible).[2]

One preacher who has made frequent use of this approach is D. W. Cleverley Ford. Here are several examples from his sermons (pages 172–73):

• "You'd be bored to tears if I read through the whole of the genealogy with which St. Matthew's gospel begins. But suppose your *own* name was in the list! Or the name of someone you knew!"

• "I wonder if you've even been misunderstood? I wonder if you've tried hard to make yourself plain, and your hearers have derived the wrong impression?"

• "I wonder if you have any enemies; personal enemies, I mean people who are 'up against you'?"

• "That's what you do when you've finished some task. You sit down and survey your handiwork. And that's what the soldiers did at Calvary. They crucified Jesus; they cast lots for his clothes, and then they sat down to watch him there. That was their Good Friday."[3]

We can overdo the familiar, of course. We can make too much of the obvious; we can dwell on it too long. In the words of Shakespeare:

To gild refined gold, to paint the lily,
To throw a perfume on the violet,
To smooth the ice, or add another hue
Unto the rainbow, or with taper-light
To seek the beauteous eye of heaven to garnish
Is wasteful and ridiculous excess.[4]

Furthermore, the preacher needs to be careful not to tell the same old stories the same old way. Even the oft-told stories of the Bible need a dash of surprising application or apt allusion to make their very familiarity do its best work. John Fry did this in his sermon on Bartimaeus. Referring to the blind beggar's "super-wailing," he said, "This was an impertinent wailing. Uppity. A breach of the unspoken contract between beggars and beggees: namely, that beggars be demure, their faces to the ground, not overdoing it, otherwise beggees will be offended, stick their noses in the air and put their camels in low, and take off."[5] This is precisely the quality that makes so delightful and refreshing even the very familiar biblical character sketches in Frederick Buechner's *Peculiar Treasures*.[6]

THE UNUSUAL

By the unusual I mean "the new, the strange, the rare, the unfamiliar, the unique."[7] What can be unusual in a sermon whose main business is to tell "the old, old story"?

The preacher may treat a well-known text in an unusual way. Biblical texts are the coin of the homiletical realm, but some of them are worn so smooth by repeated use that the people can hardly see God's image and superscription on them. "The surprise-package" sermon described by Halford Luccock offers one different approach. He suggests that this surprise-package sermon is to be used sparingly, though its occasional employment is useful. What he had in mind was starting, for example, with the text "It is more blessed to give than to receive," and after properly acknowledging the truth of that statement, going on to affirm how good it is to receive. Then the sermon would deal with the grace or art of receiving.[8] When approaching texts in this way, the preacher should be careful to avoid the reputation of a preacher who was too, too clever with the scriptures and won the nickname Dr. Tickletext.

One of the most breathtaking sermons I have heard (on tape) is Harry Emerson Fosdick's "How Believe in a Good God in a World Like This?" What is unusual about this sermon is its ruthless honesty. Fosdick says, "The first effect of Christian faith in a God of love is not to solve this problem but to state it in its most difficult form."[9] As he proceeds to state the problem, he lays it out in precisely the terms in which one would confront it in the most agnostic philosopher. Then he gives the Christian response. The result is high drama.

Moreover, the form of the sermon may elicit unusual interest and attention. The sermon may take the form of a dramatic monologue (Frederick Speakman's "What Pilate Said One Midnight"),[10] a dialogue (Ralph H. Lightbody and William D. Thompson's "If I Should Die"),[11] or even a prayer (Walter J. Burghardt's "Do We Deserve Peace?").[12] It should be noted, however, that some preachers who are most skilled in the use of unusual sermonic forms recommend their use no oftener than every two months or so. If the unusual becomes habitual, it is no longer unusual.

MYSTERY

The sense of mystery has wide and continuing appeal. Note the considerable interest in so-called mystery stories. We like to be able to solve puzzles or at least to know how a particular puzzle is solved. Many are drawn to astrology, numerology, palm reading, and the like. And let us face it—some of the fascination of the book of Revelation lies in its near inscrutable symbolism. If we do not know the key to it, we like to know someone who thinks he or she knows the key to the interpretation of things to come. Also, it should be noted that the allegorical interpretation of scripture has intrigued both interpreter and hearer. In brief, some people love the Bible more for what is hidden than for what is clear and plain for all who have eyes to see and ears to hear.

However, the preachers who are sincere students of the Bible do not need to appeal to morbid curiosity to arouse interest in their sermons. There are in the Bible, of course, many things hard to understand that we must explain, some mysteries (at least from the standpoint of our hearers) that we must explore and clear up. For that, we do not have to profess any occult insight, special revelation, or gnostic powers. If we live with the scriptures and love them, if we are faithful in bringing to our people what hard study and divine guidance have imparted, then our illumination of dark passages of the Bible will excite unusual attention to what we say.

SUSPENSE

A contemporary novelist had a character explain how he kept his audience attentive while he was making a speech: The speaker precariously balanced himself on the edge of the platform, so that the audience would keep watching to see if he would fall off. The preacher needs no such tricks.

Yet there is a sermonic strategy that does utilize suspense. Harry A. Overstreet describes it in his *Influencing Human Behavior* and calls it "the chase technique."[13] The speaker sets out in quest of a solution to a problem of vital concern to the listeners. The speaker considers with them a possible solution, shows its inadequacies, and goes on to consider a second possibility and a third and a fourth in the same way, continuing until the right solution has been found. Depending on the initial interest in the problem and the skill of the preacher in pursuing the solution, this method can maintain high interest. But if the issue is a trivial one and if the preacher has no excitement about the task, then the quality of suspense will be absent.(cf. p. 154.)

A preacher challenged the usual popular interpretation of Romans 8:28: "And we know that all things work together for good to them that love God." He said that it is not true that all things work together for good, and we know that. Further, he said that all things do not work out for the good even of those who love God. Needless to say, in that congregation there was rapt attention, heightened by the fact that this was a visiting preacher and, as was generally believed, a prospective pastor. At the right moment, the preacher presented the clarifying truth of the text as it appears in the New English Bible translation.

CONFLICT

The principle of antagonism, the interplay of opposites, is the basis of drama. Conflict, whether actual or potential, is the raw material of an interesting story. Indeed, we say that the unity of a dramatic incident consists of situation, complication, and resolution. It is all there in the Bible: chaos and order, light and darkness, God and Satan, good and evil, summer and winter, plenty and famine, heaven and hell, Pharisee and publican, unproductive soil and good soil, the house built on the rock and the house built on the sand, and so on.

Someone has observed that everyone will stop to watch a dogfight. There is a "dogfight technique" in sermon building:[14] The preacher chooses an "enemy" and goes after it. I say "it," for it is error rather than persons that we attack—if we attack anything. Perhaps it would be more entertaining and exciting if some person were at the center of our target, but it would not for that reason be more Christian. Polemics, that is, going on the warpath for God, is rarely a necessity in preaching.

However, apologetics is a frequent necessity. We must often make a good defense for our faith. As 1 Peter 3:15 puts it, "Be always ready with your defence whenever you are called to account for the hope that is in you, but make that defence with modesty and respect."

In his *Preaching and the Contemporary Mind*, Merrill Abbey has advocated that the preacher challenge the axioms of modern man—those half-truths and falsehoods that become popularly axiomatic by frequent repetition and by congruence with our passions and predilections.[15] Immediately Fosdick's sermon, "The Means Determine the End," comes to mind.[16]

My colleague, Clyde Francisco, often said to students in our team-taught course in biblical preaching, "The ideas in your sermon are good, but the sermon lacks tension." It was this quality of tension in his own preaching and teaching that made him in wide demand as a speaker. If the tension was not in the text itself, the tension between the text and the hearer received full attention.

The best battles for stimulating and sustaining interest are not those long ago and far away. They are the battles close to home—conflicts in the family, at the office, at school, in the community, between friends. However, we can so describe the struggles recorded in the Bible that our hearers will be utterly absorbed. Why? Because these struggles are so much like their own.

HUMOR

Humor is one of the most valuable means at our disposal for gaining and keeping attention and interest. What William Zinsser said about writers, we can say about preachers by substituting "preacher" for "writer": "Humor is the secret weapon of the [preacher]. It is secret because so few [preachers] realize that is is often their best tool—and sometimes their only tool—for making an important point."[17] No other means can so quickly break the ice, relax inhibitions, and create an attitude of expectancy.

It has been observed that a speaker can make a serious point more effectively after a light moment in the speech. Humor is serious business—but delightfully serious. Comedy writer Abe Burrows said in an interview, "I claim with comedy we make much more serious points than we do with anything that's supposed to be serious. See, a laugh is one of the most profound things that can happen to a human being. When you make a man laugh, you have evidently hit him right where he lives—deep. You've done something universal. You've moved him in an area that he probably didn't even dare think about, and he laughs explosively."[18]

Unfortunately, some people have assumed that the pulpit is not the place for humor. I say unfortunately, for if preachers believe and follow this, they reject a natural and wholesome way of dealing with life as it is—and making their hearers like it at the same time. If the hearers have qualms about humor, they miss many a soul-restoring opportunity to laugh at themselves and surmount many of their troubles.

In truth, humor breathes the very atmosphere of the gospel; the gospel breathes the very atmosphere of humor. This does not mean that they are one and the same. Yet Frederick Buechner has dared suggest that some of Jesus' parables are a kind of "holy joke."[19] There is at least enough humor in the teachings of Jesus that Elton Trueblood wrote an entire book on *The Humor of Christ*.

To be sure, some humor—or attempted humor—in the pulpit is in poor taste. It may be dragged in by the heels and serve no purpose except to get a laugh. It may be worn threadbare through much telling. It may tend to downgrade some individual or group or reinforce prejudice against them. In such cases, the so-called humor is out of place.

There are many humorous devices that the preacher may find useful. *Exaggeration* often emphasizes a point. Jesus compared the entry of a rich man into the kingdom of heaven to a camel going through the eye of a needle. One preacher who was a guest for several days in the home of an affluent lady described his confusion as to whether he should use the exquisite hand towels in the bathroom. He said, "I didn't get dry for a week!"

Reversal is the technique of the O. Henry short story and of many a humorous incident. Jesus' parable of the laborers in the vineyard is followed by the statement "The last will be first, and the first, last" (Matt. 20:16). While that parable is not at all funny, it does illustrate the principle. When my brother was in his teens, my mother once said to him as we were finishing a meal, "You haven't eaten any turnip greens!" He answered, "I don't like them." Mother said, "I don't like them either, but I'm eating them anyway." Then he said, "Well, you just don't have enough willpower."

Fractured quotations sometimes convey a subtle message or give occasion to correct an error. One man said, "A lie is an abomination unto the Lord, but a very present help in time of trouble."

Witty definitions can serve positively or negatively. Ambrose Bierce's *Devil's Dictionary* is well known for its cynical but often embarrassingly true definitions. His definition of a Christian may indeed be true of some of us: "One who believes that the New Testament is a divinely inspired book admirably suited to the spiritual needs of his neighbor."[20] Someone defined a camel as an animal that looks like it was put together by a committee. Abraham Lincoln said, "Tact is the ability to describe others as they see themselves."[21] H. I. Phillips defined oratory this way: "The art of making deep noises from the chest sound like important messages from the brain."[22] Another defined a preacher as someone who talks in another person's sleep.

An example of *understatement* (and double meaning at the same time) was the story told by a Maine congressman. A woman was "interviewed in the hospital after her husband had confessed to police that he had been putting traces of arsenic in her jar of instant coffee. The reporters asked, 'How do you feel about your husband now?' 'Oh,' she said, 'he makes me sick.'"[23]

Another example was the annual budget day sermon of a certain minister. The congregation has just approved a budget of a half-million dollars. The preacher says in the course of his sermon, "The budget committee chairman has led us to adopt a very ambitious budget. He should set for us an example in stewardship. If he doesn't drop a nickel in the collection plate every Sunday, we all know we will never reach our goal."

Another source of humor is the *puncturing of pomposities*. An example is a parody of the lines by the poet Alexander Pope.[24] It was said of a popular nineteenth century clergyman that his approach to a vice was (1) to denounce it, (2) then to show its possible merits, and (3) at last to embrace it and practice it himself.

One of the most consistently interesting preachers I have known kept his congregation with him partly because of his *humorous asides*. He would be talking, let us say, about the miraculous catch of fish that the disciples pulled in by letting down their nets on the other side of the boat at the Lord's command. Then he would turn his head and say something like "Jim, we'll have to remember that on the lake tomorrow." Another preacher told a story about a millionaire. He interrupted his story by saying, "Now I don't know many millionaires, but those I know I pray for every day!" It was good for a chuckle and he went on with his story. When Gerald Kennedy was bishop of the Los Angeles area, he said in a sermon that Hawaii was in his jurisdiction and that once a year he had to go there—"as one of the sacrifices I make for the church!"

The *pun*, while it is not the most useful humorous device, occasionally brings a smile to a congregation. Though puns can be found in the Bible, they are for that reason not recommended for frequent use. Too often they call attention to the cleverness of the punster. But they have their place. H. W. Fowler says, "Puns are good, bad, and indifferent, and only those who lack the wit to make them are unaware of the fact."[25]

Little *stories about children* can sometimes help a preacher who has no talent for any other kind of humor. The following story can both illustrate a point and charm the congregation. As is well known, some denominations do not have infant baptism or christening. In such churches it is normal for a child of ten or twelve to make a profession of faith and be baptized by immersion. Occasionally a child much younger will want to be baptized. After the minister had baptized a candidate, he came to the front of the baptistry and said to the congregation, as was his custom, "See, here is water. What hinders you to be baptized?" One six year old answered in a loud voice, "My mother!"

When I was in college I went to hear the renowned E. Stanley Jones, the missionary-statesman who had served in India for many years. He spoke to an audience of five thousand on Sunday afternoon. Probably all of these people had attended their own church services that morning. Jones spoke for about an hour, but the audience was attentive to the end. I observed, however, that at several points he dropped in a story to rest and refresh us. I definitely recall that at least some of his humor was something said by a small child. Such humor—if indeed it is humorous—can hardly fail preachers who think they have no talent for humor. Thoughts of the congregation will turn to the child and away from the comic talents of the preacher or the lack of them. Preachers should be careful, of course, not to feature their own children in these stories, nor should they ever embarrass anyone else's children.

One-liner *topical allusions* can often spice up a sermon. Brylcreme hair dressing had an advertising slogan: "A little dab will do you." A preacher said, "The religion of too many people is like Brylcreme—a little dab will do you."

Sometimes *a series* will brighten the sermon. One veteran preacher-professor spoke to seminarians on the value of beginning to prepare for retirement while yet students. He gave a number of suggestions. Among them was this: "Learn to appreciate great music. Listen often to Brahms, Beethoven, Mozart, and Dolly Parton." The room rocked with laughter, but the students got the serious point too.

THE CONCRETE

Concreteness appeals to everyone, intellectual or not. While abstract thinking may be for a small percentage of us, the appreciation and use of the concrete is for all of us. Most of our thinking relates to pictures, hence the proverb, "One picture is worth a thousand words."

Dale Carnegie reported that one of his speech classes carried on an experiment in concreteness. As a special exercise, it was decided that every student speaker would make sure that every sentence in his speech would have in it "a fact or a proper noun, a figure, or a date."[26] That was, of course, a difficult but useful assignment. We can only imagine the increase in the interest quotient of sermons that attempted this in only half the sentences.

Narrative sermons or sermons that use narrative incidents within them offer the best possibilities for use of the concrete. One of my own sermons was on Zacchaeus, the quisling tax collector who climbed a tree to see Jesus passing by and to his astonishment found that he was to be Jesus' host. I made a studied effort to establish the feeling of reality about the story. I did this, first, by portraying emotions with which the hearer could easily identify: revulsion against a traitor; snobbery and compromise; desire for approval; love of money and luxurious living; a sense of rejection and loneliness; nostalgia; guilt feelings; longings to be better persons; hope for a new life.

Second, the words and phrases tended to ground the narrative in reality: Zacchaeus, Jews, Jericho, quisling, spy, churches, fanatic, officials, balsam trees, wilderness of Judea, Mediterranean Sea, money, Dead Sea, Jordan River, Herod the Great, Pompeii, a million dollars, gardens, fountains, walls, children, a song, legal power, Pharisee, aqueduct, cold water, twenty-third Psalm, lavish meal, fertile valley, sharp, astringent pain, faces, eyes, Egypt, Babylon, Jewish law.

Third, there was indirect appeal to the senses of the listener:[27]

- *Visual* appeal: "You could look to the south and see the dreadful but beautiful Dead Sea, and to the east, the Jordan River."
- *Auditory* appeal: "The sound of carefree laughter, the haunting refrain of a song heard in childhood . . ."
- *Motor* appeal: "He ran on ahead of the crowd and scrambled up a sycamore tree."

• *Tactual* appeal: "The tired, hungry travelers bathe hands and face and feet with the cold water."

• *Gustatory* appeal: "Perhaps the others were too busy eating the delightfully seasoned food—mouth-watering enough for a king—and talking among themselves . . ."

• *Olfactory* appeal: "Zacchaeus awoke every morning to smell the fragrance of the balsam trees."

• *Thermic* appeal: ". . . high, windswept, often-cold Jerusalem."[28]

15. The Ethics of Motivation

Should preachers try to persuade people to adopt their beliefs and their style of life? This is the problem.

One preacher was thoroughly convinced that everyone had to accept Jesus Christ as a personal Savior in order to find salvation. Few in the mainstream of Christian belief would find fault with his opinion. But this man said that he would wave a magic wand over men and women, boys and girls, if that would make them Christians. He implied that he would use almost anything he could lay his hands on to get the job done.

The history books are full of stories of how some people have tried to compel other to accept their way of faith and life. Threats of the torch, prison, exile, and the rack have been used to convert men for "the glory of God"! Other methods—more "civilized," more "spiritual," and subtler—have been just as effective. For example, lurid pictures of hell have harrowed tender emotions; exaggerated images of an angry God have misused normal guilt feelings; fear of being cast out of the Christian community to die has compelled grudging obedience.

Yet, here is a fact to face squarely: You don't make many important decisions without someone else's help. You may be glad to accept a certain belief or course of action. When you hear about it for the first time, it sounds like good news, and you can't turn it down. Perhaps some current of enthusiasm, like electricity, galvanizes you into faith and obedience. On the other hand, you may defend yourself at the outset against something definitely good for you but later on accept it. Why? Because someone is interested and patient enough to show you why it is good to accept or bad to reject it. You receive encouragement and moral support in making the right decision. In brief, you are persuaded.

A growing child learns by the interplay of both forces—example and persuasion. As long as we live, these forces continue to shape our beliefs, our loves, our tastes, and our habits. Each individual adds his or her own ingredient to the crucible of decision making; however, no decision is ever made that does not have other ingredients as a part of the final product.

Preachers are uniquely privileged. Their influence touches individuals in all walks of life and at every stage of their development. As concerned persons, we are strategically located in the dynamics of our parishioners' decision making. But as representatives of God, especially, we exert a crucial influence. Behind us stands the massive weight of Christian history and tradition, and above us the power of the living God. Can we avoid having positive influence on others, unless we are unworthy representatives of the church and her Lord? Yet some preachers—good, intelligent, dedicated servants of God—are less effective for God than others who are no better, no more intelligent, and no more dedicated. Why should this be so? Ought this be so?

The basic question, then, is: May we preachers use the art of persuasion to help us gain acceptance for our message?

PREACHERS AS COMMUNICATORS FOR GOD

Let us accept as true the Judeo-Christian assertion: God reveals himself to humankind; he communicates with people. If we grant this, then we can go on to make several statements.

1. God uses us to communicate with others like us. We transport God; we make his purpose known; we speak his message. The Bible takes for granted the reality of the God who reveals himself. There is an impressive list of those who have served as God's communicators: his angels (who may have been human beings made into special messengers), his prophets, his Son (the Word made flesh), his apostles, his pastors and teachers, and his unordained witnesses.

Again and again they have said what he wanted said so that people might know him, obey him, and love him. "How shall they hear without a preacher? And how shall they preach, except they be sent? . . . So then faith cometh by hearing, and hearing by the word of God" (Rom. 10:14-15, 17).

2. God uses the messengers' humanity in the communication process. The way God says things to us corresponds with the ways we hear, think, believe, feel, and act. Human beings communicate with one another by sound, by reasoned argument, by emotion, and by action. Why would God not use these means to get something across?

3. God uses persons called and dedicated to the preaching task to speak for him—"worthy" individuals who have had experience with God. This does not exclude the laity; they may speak God's authentic message as truly as the ordained.

4. God-called persons may make their efforts to communicate God's message more effective by their manner of communication. If they analyze the means by which people are led to belief and action, if they mobilize the shapeless motivations lying dormant in their hearers, if they at least clear away the negative, prejudicial factors that stand in the way of belief and action, then those otherwise deaf may be caused to hear and heed.

These are sweeping assertions. Are they really true? Will they stand up under closer scrutiny? They need to be examined more closely. Are there exceptions or extensions?

1. Within the range of our experience and knowledge, God does communicate with us through others like us. But we cannot say that this is God's exclusive method. We must allow for the significant roles of intuition, rational thought, dreams, visions, and auditions. The seer, the prophet, the philosopher, and the mystic have all learned certain things about God through the ways peculiarly open to them. Still,

private meditation, original thought, and spontaneous action do not exclude the contribution made by person-to-person contact.

2. While our very humanity is caught up in our message and becomes a part of it, this humanity can present obstacles to communication of the truth of the message. The gospel signifies joy, but the preacher may be a confirmed pessimist. Our manner may be offensive, conveying the impression that God is "a bundle of thunderstorms." Our thought may be abstract, our sermon structure obscure, our grammar faulty. In other words, our humanity may get the best of us. If we succeed in speaking for God it has to be, at least in part, despite our humanity, as well as because of it.

3. Though God actually uses good people to communicate his truth, he is not bound by their moral and spiritual limitations. In the Apostle Paul's time, some preached Christ from envy and strife, from "contention, not sincerely." Paul asked, "What then? notwithstanding, every way, whether in pretense, or in truth, Christ is preached; and I therein do rejoice, yea, and will rejoice" (Phil. 1:15, 16, 18).

4. While we may communicate more effectively because we have acquired persuasive skills, we may wrongly assume that good ends justify questionable means. To some, psychology signifies manipulation and exploitation. Communication becomes Machiavellian. However, appealing to certain motives—such as fear, desire for approval, and the like—may be a necessary means of putting people in touch with reality. In preaching, fear can destroy and kill, but it can also build and heal.

IMPLICATIONS FOR PREACHING

What does this imply?

It should be self-evident that the normal means of effective communication must be used. You must express your thoughts in language; you must speak audibly; you must use words (and concepts) that your listeners understand. Your words must not say one thing and your manner another. Whatever goes beyond these concerns gets into the realms of rhetoric and theology.

Karl Barth raised questions as to how far we are justified in trying to make hearers favorable to our message. For example, he recognized no "point of contact" that would make it possible for a preacher to render a person receptive to the Word of God. So, as he saw it, the traditional use of the "introduction" of the message to gain the goodwill of the hearer is wrong. Yet Barth himself did in his preaching—perhaps without design—what he did not allow in theory. However, Barth would not have quarreled with studied efforts to use "the normal means" to bring the Word of God to expression in preaching. How much further may one go?

You may also need to use extraordinary measures to make it possible for the Word of God to be heard. Admittedly, you may usurp the prerogatives of God in this area. Unless God is involved—radically involved—in the communication process, the effort is useless. But cannot God choose to employ your knowledge of the behavioral sciences and a practical application of this knowledge to do at least a part of his work?

William Sargant made this almost shocking observation: Conversion takes place only when a deep disruption of personality patterns takes place. Something strongly akin to "brainwashing" may therefore be necessary.[1] In certain cases, only the terrors of hell, death, insanity, or alienation have been sufficient to make some people aware of their need of God and the sufficiency of God to conquer their condemnation.

Psychologist Fritz Kunkel argued that we should anticipate our crises and go through them in imagination, so that we shall be prepared for the actual event.[2] Isn't it the task of the preacher to bring hearers face to face with reality, confronting them with what is current, though hidden, and what is yet to come? This can be done constructively if it is done in the context of the love and forgiveness of God, remembering, as Peter Brunner put it, that every sermon should sound the note of absolution[3] and that the people of our time should not be forced to set faith against reason.

Never forget that you yourself are under judgment. God is searching your heart, to see if there is any wicked way in you. "My brethren," says the epistle of James, "be not many masters, knowing that we shall receive the greater condemnation" (3:1). Life offers no greater privilege than that of occupying a position from which one can influence others for good—and no greater peril. The blind may lead the blind and both fall into the ditch.

To remember that we are easily self-deceived about our own motives is a safeguard. A surgeon may perform a questionable operation because it is "good preventive medicine." A minister may use a questionable method to gain assent to a belief or course of action because it is "for the glory of God." Yet, in both cases, other motives may be more decisive.

The future may so dominate our thinking and living that we may be tempted to resort to any available means—ethical or not—to achieve a future coup for God and humankind that will justify, in the end, whatever we may do in order to achieve it. But judgment is now. Neither future failure nor future success can determine the moral quality of present behavior. "The means determine the end." It is nowhere truer than in preaching.

Moreover, never forget that God has ways of achieving his ends that often embarrass our strenuous human efforts. "For my thoughts are not your thoughts, neither are your ways my ways, saith the Lord" (Isaiah 55:8).

We do not need to run ahead of God; in fact, it is dangerous to run ahead of him. When I was a small boy, another boy slightly older proudly showed me the setting hen with her nest of eggs soon to be hatched. The longer he talked, the more excited and impatient he became. It was impossible to wait for nature's time. He helped nature along—in the wrong way—and the chicks in the prematurely cracked shells died. A pastor wisely cautioned a young evangelist working zealously with a group of children in a revival meeting, "Don't pull them too green, Pete!"

NECESSITY FOR PERSUASIVE METHODS

All of this leads up to a needed caveat: Don't permit your fear of doing the wrong thing to cause you to do nothing to bring people to faith and obedience.

As a boy, I used to listen regularly to a radio comedian who played the role of a salesman. He was the world's lowest low-pressure salesman. Knocking at a prospective customer's door, he invariably muttered, "There's nobody to home here, I hope, I hope, I hope!" This approach may easily become the *modus operandi* of a well-educated, cultured, open-minded minister who fears to intrude on the privacy and sanctity of another personality. Though we are personally ethical by the best community standards, we may be so permissive that we have nothing but weakness to offer the guilty and bewildered. We are responsible not only when we do the wrong thing but also when we fail to do the right thing. Half-heartedness can spell the difference. No wonder the living Christ said to a congregation of self-satisfied, well-to-do Christians: "I know thy works, that thou art neither cold nor hot: I would thou wert cold or hot. So then because thou art lukewarm, and neither cold nor hot, I will spew thee out of my mouth" (Rev. 3:15-16).

As individuals and groups we are subjected to all sorts of forces. We are influenced one way or another. It is inevitable. Though we recognize that we may be self-deceived as to our motives and wrong in our beliefs, we nevertheless set our example, give our advice, and sometimes win our way with a bit of persuasion. Such is life: parents, teachers, friends, husbands, and wives do this all the time. It is not only inevitable, it is necessary.

However, this calls for serious, careful, and prayerful thought. You, as a minister, must be as certain as possible that what you attempt to lead others to believe or to do is right and true. Then you may go ahead with lawful and responsible methods of persuasion.

Augustine, author of the first formal defense of the use of rhetoric in preaching, saw rhetoric as a lawful weapon that proponents of truth could not afford to ignore while proponents of error used it so effectively in the cause of falsehood.[4] As Christians, we believe that Jesus is "the way, the truth, and the life." The prologue to the fourth gospel tells us that Jesus Christ, the enfleshed Word of God, corresponds to the structure of reality. Jesus Christ recapitulates, in a fullness, the personal expression of that reality. Thus, if other persons can be persuaded to believe in him and obey him, they can come close to what every human life is intended to become.

A preacher, a teacher of preachers, spoke of his reaction against the anti-intellectual, emotional preaching on which he was brought up. He became an "intellectual" preacher. Later, he saw that he had omitted an essential ingredient in convincing, persuasive proclamation. Without diminishing his commitment to facts and reason, he committed himself also to emotion. He was no longer content merely to cite facts and make arguments. In a burst of emphasis, he said, "Now I give my preaching everything I've got!" What is wrong with that—if he first yields himself to God?

16. The Forms of Development and Support

As preachers, our effectiveness in ministry may be determined largely by our use of what is popularly called illustration. Preachers who illustrate, we are told, get a large and faithful audience; preachers who never illustrate can hardly keep an audience that circumstances have given them. All speakers who have made a lasting impression, who have taught the multitudes, who have convinced the inquiring and the skeptics, who have inspired the dispirited, and who have challenged men and women to noble action—all such speakers, preachers, or whatnot, have made large use of a wide variety of the forms of development and support. This includes illustration, which properly speaking is but one of many such forms.

We think immediately of Jesus' use of parables, figures of speech, and examples. If for no other reason, he could be called the Master Teacher. One of the greatest expositors in the history of the church, John Chrysostom, lifted images and instances from everyday life to illuminate his sermons. The traveling friars of the medieval church embodied their messages in stories. Charles Haddon Spurgeon, who preached for four fruitful decades in the nineteenth century to congregations numbering in the thousands, often made his points and made them stick with homely examples. His contemporary, Henry Ward Beecher, was always on the lookout for examples and illustrations, acknowledging, "I use fifty now to one in the early years of my ministry."[1] Perhaps no preacher of the twentieth century has furnished his sermons with a wider variety of choice material to develop and support his sermonic ideas than Harry Emerson Fosdick. At the same time, we remember that every Sunday in churches of low visibility, the good news of Jesus Christ comes to expression, changing lives and instilling hope, through the same kinds of resources used by Chrysostom, Spurgeon, Beecher, and Fosdick.

We can fairly well forecast the kind of hearing we will regularly receive by taking the measure of the care and attention we give to the way we present our ideas.

AMPLIFICATION OF IDEAS

Usually one idea forms the core of the sermon. But that one idea is not the sermon itself. We have to amplify it to get it understood, believed, felt, or acted upon. We shall discuss four primary methods of development of thought: definition, explanation, restatement, and argument.

DEFINITION

Our first business is to make sure that the terms we use are understood. This often calls for definition. We may tell what a term means by simply using a synonym or at most by putting our definition in one clear sentence, or we may use the entire sermon to define a word or an idea. We may define logically or rhetorically. That is, we may put a word in its proper classification and compare it to other words in the same classification; or we may use examples, comparisons, contrasts, and so on to make clear what we want to be understood.

EXPLANATION

Definition shades into explanation when we define words *rhetorically*. However, explanation has to do not just with words but also with processes, events, speeches, writings and the like. A definition can tell us what sanctification is, but that is not enough. Definition often makes explanation possible, for we can go on from the definition to a fuller understanding of the term through the process of explanation.

Explanation itself makes use of several of the forms of support that we shall later explore in some detail. The process of explanation may require restatement, examples of various kinds, comparisons, and even testimony.

Explanation answers the questions: who, what, when, where, why, and how. The title of the Ring Lardner story "Shut up! She Explained" is actually a contradiction in terms, for explanation opens up and proceeds to unfold, unpack, reveal, or do whatever else is needed to help the hearers to gain information or understanding. Of course, explanations can be banal, for who needs explanation of the obvious? In any case, needed or not, they can be patronizing, condescending; they can suggest attitudes of superiority in the preacher. Usually, however, we make our mistakes in the opposite direction. We charge on ahead, assuming that our hearers know more about some matters than they actually do. Why should an intelligent scientist who has never made a special study of theology or philosophy be expected to know our field any more than we should be expected to know his?

RESTATEMENT

Restatement may be an important element in explanation, but it is simply one of the forms of support for an assertion. Restatement does not add to the meaning of an assertion; it repeats that meaning, usually in different words. It holds an idea before the eye of the mind until that idea can be clearly seen.[2] Or it brings conviction by the intensity of repetition. Or it cumulatively engages the emotions. Or it moves to action by the persistence of its repeated challenge.

To be sure, restatement can be boring. It is designed only to serve a high purpose, never to fill up time or pad an outline. That purpose is to bring the thought being presented closer to the hearer than a mere hit-and-run approach could accomplish.

Arthur Edward Phillips has suggested a special use of restatement: for presenting an undemonstrable proposition. The example he cites is from a sermon by Alexander Maclaren in which the preacher asserts:

The dead and the living are not names of two classes which exclude each other. Much rather, there are none who are dead. The dead are the living who have died. Whilst they were dying they lived, and after they were dead they lived more fully. All live unto God. God is not the God of the dead, but of the living. Oh, how solemnly sometimes that thought comes up before us, that all those past generations which have stormed across this earth of ours, and then have fallen into still forgetfulness, live yet.

Somewhere, at this very instant, they now verily are. We say they were—they have been. There are no have beens. Life is life forever. To be is eternal being. Every man that has died is at this instant in the full possession of all his faculties, in the intensest exercise of all his capacities, standing somewhere in God's great universe ringed with the sense of God's presence, and feeling in every fibre of his being that life which comes after death is not less real, but more real—not less great, but more great—not less full and intense, but more full and intense than the mingled life which, lived here on earth, was a center of life surrounded with a crust and circumference of mortality. The dead are the living. They lived whilst they died, and after they die they live on forever.[3]

This is valuable as an example of a particular use, but also as an extended example of restatement as such.

A close look at the sermons of George A. Buttrick will show that he often used restatement following his topic sentences. In one sermon he asserted, "Our modern anxiety is modern only in its form, for anxiety is as old as human nature." His next two sentences say the same thing, but in different words: "The atomic bomb has not *caused* our fear-anxiety; it has only *awakened* it to give it new occasion. Men have always been anxious, even though some ages seem to have been more anxious then others." In the same sermon, he asserted, "This Light by which we know our darkness must presumably shine on us, at least from time to time, or the light of life will utterly go out." Buttrick restated the idea in this way: "Faith in God must know God's visitation, nay, must come from God's visitation, or faith will languish. Faith in any area of man's life is first a beckoning and then the valor of response."[4] Sir Walter Raleigh, commenting on style, said, "In writing, a thing three times said, and each time said badly, may be of more effect than that terse, full and final expression which the doctors rightly commend."[5]

We can use restatement also as a kind of symphonic refrain in several fitting places in the sermon. Here we will use the same words again and again until they sing their way into mind and heart. For this, we may use the words of the text, a line or two of poetry, or an epigrammatic statement of our own. Unfortunately, I have heard this done in a shocking way with a scripture text. The preacher's sermon rambled along, as he pursued his own fancies and opinions, which he sought to legitimate by now and then repeating his text. But there was no connection between that and the preacher's statements, except an arbitrary one. It was an embarrassing performance.

Rightly done, restatement has important usage, but we must see to it that we do not simply reiterate ideas already made clear and impressive.

ARGUMENT

Often a statement needs more than the illumination and impressiveness that definition, explanation, and restatement can give: evidence is required. What are our reasons for asserting a particular thing? What is our proof?

In sermons, we are expected to quote scripture. We may cite the church fathers. It is likely also that we shall look to some contemporary authority (to be discussed later in this chapter as "testimony"). However, we may choose to pursue a rigidly logical line of argument, proving that what we say follows the canons of reason with the exactness of a syllogism. Or, we may adduce experience—our own or that of others—to prove our point. Or, we may rely on thoroughgoing studies or investigations of the matter at hand and cite their evidence. As I argue an item, I may point to known causes for an existing condition, or I may point to consequences that are likely to follow a thought, an act, a habit, or a quality of character.

We would like to believe that regeneration, faith, and the teachings of scripture are sufficient to solve every problem. Why should it not be enough simply to "take God at his word"? We cannot argue anyone into the kingdom of God or keep anyone there by disputation! True, but the Bible itself says, "Come now, let us argue it out, says the Lord . . ." (Isa. 1:18). We are told that the Apostle Paul, soon after his conversion, "was proclaiming Jesus publicly in the synagogues . . ." He "grew more and more forceful, and silenced the Jews of Damascus with his cogent proofs that Jesus was the Messiah" (Acts 9:20, 22). Before and after faith we sometimes have to make a good argument for our faith. Traumas— personal, family, and national—demand at least an attempt to deal honestly with the burning questions they provoke. As Gilbert Highet has stated it, "The sufferers ask, 'Why?' They ask, 'What am I to do?' They ask, 'How can I bear this?' Sometimes they make violent threats which they themselves know to be wrong, *which they want someone to overcome by persuasion*.[6]

This is a challenge to the personal counselor, but it also marks out a large part of the preacher's homiletical territory. Fosdick noted that when the old preachers were at their best, they appealed to the major motives, such as fear, love, gratitude, self-preservation, and altruism. He saw in these very motives the sources of human action, and he himself used them with remarkable effect. To him, preaching was "wrestling with individuals over questions of life and death."[7]

Paul Tillich provides a striking example of the supportive use of argument. The sermon is on "The Riddle of Inequality." He has been saying that each of us must consider the increase or loss of what was given to us, as a matter of our own responsibility. But he says that we cannot apply it to others:

We cannot tell somebody who comes to us in great distress about himself—"Make use of what was given you," for he may have come to us precisely because he is unable to do so! And we cannot tell those in despair because of what they are—"Be something else," for the inability to get rid of oneself is the exact meaning of despair. We cannot tell those who failed to conquer the destructive influences of their surroundings and thence were driven into crime and misery—"You should have been stronger," for it was just this strength of which they were deprived by heritage or environment.[8]

SUPPORT OF IDEAS

We have just examined definition, explanation, restatement, and argument as primary methods of development of thought. Examples, illustrations, and testimony, while they must be considered separately, serve the development of thought in supportive capacities. Each of the primary methods will often make use of these forms of support which we now discuss in greater detail.

EXAMPLES

To begin with, an example is an actual instance of what we are talking about; sometimes, we might say, a case. We shall examine three types of example: (1) general, (2) specific, and (3) hypothetical.

The *general example* shows what the assertion or topic sentence contains. It gives us the heart of the assertion concretely. However, it will not specify names, dates, times, places, and incidents. When we use general examples, we speak of such things as, let us say, a family, a time of beginnings, a great city. We do not say what family, what year, or what city. Our main interest is simply to convey the idea of our assertion more fully. The general example "is that form of support that presents to the listener a detail or details of the idea expressed in the original assertion. It shows a part or parts, a group or groups, included in the statement itself. It does not, however, individualize."[9] General example is useful in achieving any of the ends of a sermon—understanding, belief, feeling, or persuasion.

Eduard Schweizer says that we as Christians live on the basis of what has already happened in Jesus Christ and also on the basis of what is to come. Then he particularizes that: "A person with Paul's perspective lives not only in anticipation of the meeting he will attend tomorrow evening, the book he will read this afternoon, the examination he will stand in the spring, the trip he will take next summer, his wedding this year, or the surgery he will undergo next month. He lives toward the day when God will be all in all."[10]

James S. Stewart speaks of the barriers Christ came "to level to the dust." Then he gives general examples: "racial barriers, class barriers, barriers of sect, denomination and government, of taste and temperament."[11]

Theodore Parker Ferris asserts that God's kingdom is greater than any empire that man will ever build. He then gives these general examples: "It includes all living creatures, all nations, all cultures, all classes, all races."[12]

The *specific example* does what the adjective suggests—it specifies with names, dates, times, places, and incidents.[13] It speaks not of a family, but of the Jones family; not of a time of beginnings, but of July 4, 1776; not of a great city, but of London. The general example has the advantages of being more comprehensive and of being more impressive in some ways, but the specific example lends more of a sense of reality and therefore of credibility.

This form of support requires accurate data and demands more of us than, let us say, restatement or general example. We cannot depend simply on our memory to provide us with this material. A good personal library with standard reference resources, an uncomplicated filing system, and wide reading will make specific examples readily available. It does help, too, if one is blessed with a sticky memory.

Carlyle Marney uses well his knowledge of church history:

Does it come as a surprise to you? The modern fight against prejudice began at least eight hundred years ago. Have you heard of our spiritual kinsmen, the Waldensians, of the twelfth century, fleeing to the Alps to multiply their free gospel of free worship high in the mountain valleys?

Or have you heard of John of Paris and of Marsilius of Padua . . .?

You likely know of Dante Alighieri and his *Divine Comedy*, but in 1311 he was also proclaiming a people's peace . . . .
The predawn thunderings of John Wyclif were not silenced even when his long dead body was exhumed for burying.
And so on![14]

The third type of example is the *hypothetical*. It is not an actual instance, but it may serve as well as one. It brings reality to the imagination of the hearer. If the example rings true to life and experience, it can serve any of the several objectives of the sermon.

Some preachers deplore their limited experience—"Nothing exciting ever happens to me that I could make into an illustration!" Or, "I have not read enough yet to have a wide range of material to draw from." The hypothetical example offers a way of exemplifying an idea for which we do not have an appropriate specific instance, whether historical or personal.

Perhaps no preacher has used this method more effectively than did Phillips Brooks. He seldom used anecdotes or specific examples, unless they came from the Bible. But he could build his sermon with half a dozen cases, as Andrew W. Blackwood called them, showing how a principle drawn from the scriptures worked in the lives of people.[15]

In his famous sermon "The Candle of The Lord," Brooks says, "What shall we make of some man rich in attainments and in generous desires, well educated, well behaved, who has trained himself to be a light and help to other men, and who, now that his training is complete, stands in the midst of his fellow-men completely dark and helpless? There are plenty of such men. We have all known them who have seen how men grow up. Their brethren stand around them expecting light from them, but no light comes." In another sermon, he gives a series of brief hypothetical examples:

Suppose a man is wrestling with his passions. Some miserable dissipation which he never hates and despises so much as just when he is ready to yield to it, is haunting him all the time . . . . And in his weakness he looks round for help. Where shall he find it? It seems to lie close by him, in the very structure of the body in which the lust is raging. There are the laws of health. Shall not they be his safeguard? . . . Or take another case, and see a man tempted to dishonesty in some dealings with his fellow-men. Where shall he turn for strength to his integrity? Let him picture to himself the disgrace that must come if he is found out, the loss of reputation and of his fellow-men's esteem. . . . Or yet again when a man is tempted to cruelty or quarrelsomeness he may resist because he considers that, after all, the discomfort of a quarrel is greater than the satisfaction of a grudge indulged. Or one who feels the weakness of indolence creeping over him may put himself into the midst of the most active and energetic men he knows and get the contagion of their energy and be kept alive and awake by very shame. All these are perfectly legitimate helpers for the man beset by his temptation. The fear of pain, the fear of disgrace, the fear of discomfort, and the shame that comes with the loftiest companionship—we may have to appeal to them all for support in the hours, which come so often in our lives, when we are very weak.[16]

These hypothetical examples can be constructed out of bits and pieces of personal experience and observation. They may be composites of the characters and personalities of many people. Yet they must not be used as thinly veiled true stories designed to lecture the individuals who inspired them. The pulpit must not become a pillory. Nevertheless, one lawful purpose of these examples is to enable an individual to identify with characters described and analyzed, while never having to think that the preacher is holding him or her up to ridicule. The treatment should be sufficiently indirect so that the hearers will not become defensive but, it is hoped, will gain insight into their way of living and make free decisions pleasing to God. Hence, what is called for on the part of the preacher is exercise of good taste, sensitivity to the feelings and needs of others, and growing insight into human behavior.

ILLUSTRATIONS

The term *illustration*, while popularly used to include examples, will not be so used here. As I use the term, an illustration is a comparison of one thing with another. It is not an instance, example, or case of what the sermon is discussing.

The first type of illustration is the *explicit comparison*, that is, the simile and the analogy.

The *simile* is a brief comparison, indicating a similarity between two things in only one respect. Similes occur frequently in poetry; the Bible makes extensive use of them. I have discovered, however, that they are not often found in sermons, where greater use could be made of them. As we turn to the Bible these similes come to mind:

• Like as a father pitieth his children, so the Lord pitieth them that fear him (Ps. 103:13).
• Though your sins be as scarlet, they shall be as white as snow (Isa. 1:18).
• The ungodly . . . are like the chaff which the wind driveth away (Ps. 1:4).
• The words of the Lord are pure words: as silver tried in a furnace of earth, purified seven times (Ps. 12:6).
• They shall mount up with wings as eagles (Isa. 40:31).

To this day I remember a simile from a Baptist Hour radio sermon by Fred F. Brown, which I heard when a college student. He quoted a description of the pilgrims' landing in Plymouth, "wading in water that froze on their garments until they rang like armor."[17] Perhaps this description was a slight exaggeration, but the comparison was memorable.

John Killinger describes the feeling of the people on Thor Heyerdahl's little raft during a great storm, "when the sea would heave and pitch like a great liquid serpent." Peter Marshall describes what Simon Peter sees after his Master has been arrested: "Only once in a while could the lights of the procession be seen through the trees—like giant fireflies." Frederick Buechner tells us that on Christmas Eve in St. Peter's Basilica "singing would break out like brush fires."[18]

As you may have noticed, all the contemporary similes are from descriptive passages in sermons. And that is a proper use of them. But why can we not use them as the Bible often does—to make moral and religious comparisons? "Fears are like termites eating away the inner structure of our peace and security." "The grace of God breaks through our gloom like the cheering sun on a dark, cloudy day."

Analogies—extended comparisons—we find in sermons more often. Leslie Weatherhead tries to help us understand how God guards his universe: "Let us imagine that you are bringing up little children. You do not pad the walls with eiderdowns and put foam rubber on the floor. Your little boy can meet with quite a nasty accident on the edge of the fender, perhaps, or the table leg. But you do not leave razor blades about, or saucers of sulphuric acid."[19] John Stott helps us to understand the different functions of faith and reason with this analogy:

Let's imagine that God is like a beautiful garden totally enclosed by a very high wall. Two men are determined to scale the wall and discover God. One man is called Reason and the other Faith. Reason, a rather stolid, matter-of-fact fellow, manages by herculean effort to climb slowly and cautiously a short distance up the wall, where he gets stuck. Faith, a nimble and imaginative creature, is wildly impatient with Reason's laborious progress. He takes a flying leap into midair, trembles for a few moments near the top, precariously suspended in space, and then crashes painfully to the ground. Dismayed by their failure to scale the wall independently, Reason and Faith resolve to cooperate. Reason plants himself at the foot of the wall, with both feet firmly on the ground. Then Faith climbs onto his shoulders, and from this vantage point springs neatly over the wall. God, you see, is apprehended by faith, but the faith which apprehends Him is grounded upon reason.[20]

The second type of illustration is the *implied comparison*, that is, the metaphor and the allegory.

A *metaphor* is a figure of speech in which a word or phrase that denotes one object is used for another, to imply the comparison between the two objects. Our language is full of metaphors, dead and alive. Words used in the most abstract statement have their origin is some concrete term, a picture of something. We can do nothing about dead metaphors but use them. The live ones have to be lassoed and corralled, then used. Metaphor, as well as simile, is the language of poetry. Though sermons make altogether too little use of simile, they use metaphors in abundance. The importance of metaphor is so widely recognized that many public speakers, in an effort to be colorful, sometimes mix them—with ludicrous results.

If Jesus had been using a simile, he would have said, "Ye are like salt." But he spoke a metaphor, saying, "Ye are the salt of the earth." The simile says flat out that one thing is like something else; the metaphor clearly implies that the thing is like something, but does not say so.

Buechner uses picturesque metaphors: "The singing would billow up into the great Michelangelo dome. . . . What sense anybody might have had in its being a holy time and a holy place was swallowed up by the sheer spectacle of it. . . . The moral and spiritual struggle . . . has exploded into the open with force enough to shake history itself no less than our private inner histories."[21] Marshall uses metaphors in profusion: "the silence was pierced," "the trumpet of the dawn," "the familiar bugle of the farmyard," "intoxicated with the lure of the city," "There swept over Peter the realization," "the icy fear that gripped his heart," "Her faith might have been born, a fire kindled by the spark the winds of strange circumstance had blown from the altar fires in the heart of the Son of God."[22]

Neither Buechner nor Marshall mixed his metaphors, certainly not in an offensive or ludicrous way. Bergen Evans has remarked that mixing metaphors is not necessarily bad unless the mixture is bad. Nobody cringes when the half-crazed Hamlet speaks of taking up arms against a sea of troubles, though there is a clash of images. But it is quite a different matter when someone under no great stress says, as the Welfare Secretary lamented, "People come to us to save their bacon when the baby has already gone down with the bathwater."[23] Similarly, "The floodgates of sectarian controversy were opened, and the apple of discord . . .

was thrown into the midst of the House of Commons."[24] Another, "The new measure took a firm foot-hold in the eye of the public."[25]

Charles W. Ferguson has proposed that we liven up our speech by deliberately learning to think and speak in images. He suggested that one focus attention for, say, one day a week on some particular profession or trade and use the terms common to it. "In his reflections let him pick his images from this vocabulary, and let him by this process see how many can be carried over into common speech and writing."[26]

The *allegory* is "an extended or continued metaphor," according to the *Oxford English Dictionary*. One of the best-known examples of the allegory is John Bunyan's *Pilgrim's Progress*. It tells a more important story while narrating the events in the pilgrimage of a man from The City of Destruction to The Celestial City. The underlying intention is to chronicle the spiritual struggles and victories of a Christian in the varied experiences of life. Such a form of development and support might be used occasionally—perhaps only rarely—but if done well it could have dramatic effect.

A third type of illustration is the *story*, which may be an anecdote, a parable, or a fable.

Perhaps we would best define *anecdote* as an undocumented—even undocumentable—incident, a piece of gossip. It is supposed to be true, but it is not necessarily true. Abraham Lincoln said, "They say I tell a great many stories. I reckon I do, but I have found in the course of a long experience that common people . . . are more easily informed through the medium of a broad illustration than in any other way, and as to what the hypercritical few may think, I don't care."[27]

In the anecdote the point is the thing, not the authenticity. However, it behooves the preacher, the herald of truth, to introduce an anecdote in such a way as to be relieved of responsibility for the factuality of the story. One could begin, "I am told that . . ."; "The story is told of . . ."; "It may be just a story, but . . ."; or "Have you heard the one about . . . ?"

The *parable* is a story that explains something or reveals something. In the very telling of it in a particular context, a point is made. In the case of Jesus' parables, they were realistic, yet there was in them something of a surprise, a divine reversal. Buechner dared suggest, as noted earlier, that they might even be thought of as a kind of "holy joke."[28]

The parable has this in common with the hypothetical example: It may be fictional, but it must possess verisimilitude—likeness to truth. There is no reason why the preacher today should not construct parables that reveal spiritual truth or make a point. Søren Kierkegaard used telling parables in his written "sermons," wherein he pursued his conviction that truth can best be communicated indirectly. And there is nothing like the parable to do just that. A good parable told in a certain setting does not have to be smothered with interpretation to be noticed. Henry Grady Davis notes that even though Jesus did not explain his parables, his enemies got his point and killed him for it.[29]

The fable is a story in which animals or inanimate objects talk. By comparison with other stories, fables have a limited usefulness, but the enduring value of Aesop's fables proves that they have an honorable place as a means of illustration.

TESTIMONY

Another important supportive form is *testimony*. Although this would not exclude personal testimony of the preacher, it is mainly the testimony of an outside person. We are familiar with testimonials by highly visible and respected persons, who tell us why they use a certain commercial product or why they participate in certain activities that are being promoted by this or that person or group. Their names have a magic that carries over to the product or activity.

To be sure, sermonic testimony should serve a worthy purpose. The purpose we recognize immediately is that of authority: The testimony of another person may lend authority to the preacher's word. This is especially true when the person is someone who is well known and highly respected, and who gives informed testimony on a subject. Yet an anonymous person whom experience has given a right to speak can provide us with an authoritative word: "A man who grew up in Jerusalem told me that. . . ."

If we are using testimony from "authorities," we must make sure that our congregation regards them as authorities. They may in truth be authorities, yet if that is not the perception of them held by the people to whom we speak, their testimony can be counterproductive. This calls for audience analysis. But there is another angle to consider. It may be that our quotations from persons toward whom the congregation holds unwarranted prejudice will show that they are right at least in some matters and perhaps deepen understanding of them and lead to genuine appreciation.

Another use of testimony is for corroboration or illustration. The person quoted may be no more an authority on the subject than the preacher, yet his or her word adds luster to the discussion. That is why we quote a line or couplet from a poem. To put it another way, the person quoted may state the matter in striking, memorable words that make the discussion easily portable.

If we are using testimony for corroboration or illustration, we would do well to ask, "Does this person put the matter any better than I can do it?" "Is the quotation terse enough to add vigor, or is it beautiful enough to add feeling?" We might interrupt our own flow of thought with testimony from another, and then it would be better to omit what would not add to the impression being made but would definitely take away from it. At any rate, too frequent quotation irritates many listeners. It does not impress perceptive persons, who know that quotations on any subject can be cheaply garnered. Furthermore, when the preacher does quote, the longer the quotations, the less impressive the effect. As to the beauty of the quotation, that is a matter of personal taste. It can be more easily overdone than underdone.

Is testimony necessary at all? That is determined by your purpose for the sermon. If your objective is mainly to expound a text, then you do not have to go outside the text itself for supportive testimony. The text is your authority: It provides the central idea of the sermon and the testimony. You do not even need to get support from other parts of the Bible, especially to balance up the one-sidedness of the text. Remember the words of Eduard Schweizer: "A too well-balanced sermon does not really convey its message."[30]

17. Style

Every person has a style. This style is completely the property of the person who possesses it, though it may be slavishly imitative of another person or, conversely, imitative of the style of numerous persons. The person of whom we speak, therefore, may be characteristically an impersonator, and that is his or her style. Obviously there are styles we prefer, just as there are persons whom we like better than others. Buffon, the French stylist, has been often quoted as saying, "Style is the man himself." Precisely so! Your style may be that of an actor or it may be something more original.

However, the person who is untouched by the persons he has known and admired and the varied experiences through which he has passed could be the dullest person imaginable. Individuals may be indeed persons of integrity, yet reflect in their style bits and pieces of all that they have seen and heard and at the same time maintain their own integrity. What is different here? Such an individual has maintained a central integrity of character and purpose that has permitted and encouraged assimilation of experience, rather than mere reflection of experience.

Buffon was right: Our style is what we are, be that good or bad. There are ways, however, in which we can improve our style, that is, ways in which we can improve the persons we are and in so doing make ourselves and what we have to offer more desirable.

We shall look, first of all, at the qualities of style that affect hearers positively. Then we shall consider several methods that may be used to improve style.

CLEAR STYLE

Of first importance is clarity. We must make sure that our hearers understand, as far as that depends upon us who speak, what we are trying to say. Clarity of expression determines clarity of understanding.

WORDS

We begin our quest for clarity by choosing the right words. Some people disdain simple language, for it seems to hide their education. Others grow so accustomed to the technical vocabulary that they and their peers use that, without knowing it, they go on and on talking to laypeople in a language these people do not understand. Preachers can be guilty on both accounts. It is more likely that our wide reading in many fields tends to distance us from the language of our people. They no doubt understand most of it, though we could enable them to understand more.

If our aim is to reach the largest number of people most effectively, then we will choose words that will most quickly and surely convey our meaning. This means that the words we use in preaching will favor the Anglo-Saxon part of our language, rather than the Romance, the part derived from the Latin. Anglo-Saxon is everyday speech, usually the little words. Latin is the language of the ecclesiastical establishment, of the law, of the academy. Anglo-Saxon is spoken English; Latin, as it has filtered into our language, is technical and usually written English. The distinction is not absolute, as we shall see. Compare these examples of words with roughly the same meaning:

Anglo-Saxon	*Latin*
get	acquire
greathearted	magnanimous
better (v.)	ameliorate
opening	fenestration
foreshadow	adumbrate
nightly	nocturnal
daily	diurnal

Many necessary words are of Latin origin. We could struggle to find ways of expressing in Anglo-Saxon what these words say, but why should we try? We need and understand these

English words from the Latin: *beauty, company, destroy, develop, example, flame, humor, interest, language, measure, nation, operation, pleasure, quality, relation, science, tendency, voice,* and thousands of others. H. W. Fowler, in his *Dictionary of Modern English Usage,* gives good advice to preachers as well as writers: "Any writer who becomes aware that the Saxon or native English element in what he writes is small will do well to take the fact as a danger-signal. But the way to act on that signal is not to translate his Romance words into Saxon ones; it is to avoid abstract and roundabout and bookish phrasing whenever the nature of the thing to be said does not require it."[1]

Fowler put the matter succinctly in these five rules: (1) Prefer the familiar word to the farfetched; (2) Prefer the concrete word to the abstract; (3) Prefer the single word to the circumlocution; (4) Prefer the short word to the long; and (5) Prefer the Saxon word to the Romance. He added, "These rules are given in order of merit; the last is also the least."[2]

SENTENCES

To make sense, words must be put in proper order; that is, they must be made into sentences—uncomplicated sentences. The English sentence is capable of amazing variety. You can begin an English sentence awkwardly and somehow always manage to fight your way out of the tangles and arrive safely, though exhausted, at the period. This capability of our language, however, does not ensure clarity. Rudolf Flesch commends the short sentence for its contribution to clarity. He discovered that we can measure ease and difficulty in reading and understanding by counting the number of words in the average sentence length. This is his table:

Average Sentence Length in Words

Very easy	8 or less
Easy	11
Fairly easy	14
Standard	17

Fairly difficult	21
Difficult	25
Very difficult	29 or more

Flesch says, "Count two sentences where there are two, even if there is no period between them but only a semicolon or colon."[3]

Just as writers can train themselves to write in shorter sentences, so can extemporary speakers train themselves to speak in shorter sentences.

Nevertheless, a sentence does not have to be short to be understandable. Long sentences can be as clear and understandable as short ones. H. Grady Davis has made a convincing case for the use of the longer sentence. We find numerous examples in the Bible and in modern literature of the effective long sentence. In each case, we discover that the longer sentence simply amplifies a shorter basic structure embedded within the longer one. Also, certain connecting words make it easy to see the relation of the different parts of the sentence. Furthermore, parallel construction characterizes the form of the sentence.[4]

ENUMERATION AND TRANSITIONS

A further aid to clarity is the careful use of enumeration and transitions. We are well acquainted with the words *first, second,* and *third* in the development of speeches and sermons. These words offer the hearer considerable help when the speaker intends to explain something, give information, or present arguments. It is a heavy-handed way of getting out the message and perhaps, in certain cases, the most effective way. Still, injudicious use of enumeration confuses the hearer. When the speaker uses enumeration within a series of numbers, the hearer can easily get lost in the thicket. The speaker who is sensitive to audience reaction can, however, manage even a series within a series. Here is a speaker who has just named five items, numbering them one after another, under the second main point of her speech. She can say, "As I have discussed my second point,

I have listed five things that have to do with that point. Now let us go on. In the third place, . . ." This may appear tedious; however, in the interest of understanding and belief it is necessary. Inspirational and celebrative messages seldom require extensive enumeration. In fact, this may hinder the flow of thought and feeling.

In all kinds of messages, transitional words, phrases, and even sentences are required. These may be statements or questions. They help us move from one of the main divisions to the next, from one paragraph to the next, and even from one sentence to the next. As to "links" between divisions, Paul B. Bull has said,

> The reason why we should take great care in passing from one division of our subject to another, and prepare the phrases of transition, is to save a mental shock. We have taken much pains to secure the attention of our audience. We are hoping to instruct, to please, and to move or persuade. The preacher must try to hold their attention without a break as he passes from one division to the next. A bad link or phrase of transition gives a severe jolt to the mind which may quite distract the attention. A good link carries on the attention without jar or distress, as in a well-laid railway line the train passes smoothly over the points from one pair of lines to the next.[5]

Consider this example from a sermon on Matthew's account of the stilling of the storm. A transitional question (the "contract") concludes the introduction of the sermon: "In what ways are we Christians, church people, a ship of fools, though it be fools for Christ's sake?" Here are the main points illustrating the principle of transition:

    I. To begin with, if we take our discipleship seriously we have to renounce the usual securities.

    II. The fact is, instead of enjoying security with its cozy comforts and its time-honored guidelines, we are flung out into the storms that threaten our very existence.

    III. Our old securities fail us, our new uncharted experiences threaten to overwhelm us, and then we discover our true security.[6]

We have a cornucopia of phrases and words available as we move from thought to thought:

> If . . . then, . . .
> Neither . . . nor . . .
> Both . . . and . . .
> For these reasons, . . .
> On the one hand, ... On the other hand, . . .
> This means . . . . It means also . . .
> I do not mean to imply . . .
> Also, . . .
> Again, ... Therefore, . . .
> Further, ... Finally, . . .
> Furthermore, ... So, . . .
> Still, ... Then, . . .
> Yet, ... Of course, . . .
> Nevertheless, ... Naturally, . . .
> Moreover, ... Turn now from . . .
> But . . . . For one thing, . . .
> However, ... In spite of all, . . .
> Consequently, ... The upshot of all this . . .
> As a result, ... I repeat: . . .
> What we are saying now . . . . Let us at the start . . .
> What this comes down to . . . . Another . . .
> Or, ... Indeed, . . .
> One . . .The other . . . Well, . . .
> Of course, ... Once more, . . .
> To be sure, ... To begin with, . . .
> Next, ... Beyond that, . . .

PLEASING STYLE

Next, consider the need for a pleasing quality in the style. When the preacher's style grates on the nerves of the listener, the message gets a poor hearing. This does not mean, however, that the style has to be soporific to be pleasing.

Charles Spurgeon regularly packed about five thousand people into his church twice on Sunday, yet he did not take his congregation for granted. When he felt that his style was becoming too smooth, he read Thomas Carlyle, whose angular style helped Spurgeon to put new life into his sermons.

GRAMMAR

What troubles many as they listen to sermons is the preacher's faulty grammar. It is true, grammatical standards change. What was once considered incorrect may now be acceptable even in formal speech. But the pulpit is hardly the place to lead a grammatical rebellion. Preachers should aim at correctness, availing themselves of reliable English grammars and of the regular services of friendly critics who will help them clean up their mistakes. This effort to speak correctly should not, however, become the preoccupation of a preacher while in the pulpit; it should be carried out mainly in the study and in everyday conversation, so that the preacher will have to give only marginal attention to it during the delivery of the sermon.

Here are some common errors that should be quickly and permanently corrected:

• Incorrect: They invited my wife and I to the party.
• Correct: They invited my wife and me to the party.

(The pronoun *I* is the object of the action of the verb and takes the objective case. You would never say, "They invited I." Putting "my wife" in front of the pronoun does not change the case.)

• Incorrect: One of the men were in the accident.
• Correct: One of the men was in the accident.

(Subject and verb must agree. You are talking about *one*. This determines the number of the verb. One *was*, not one *were*.)

• Incorrect: (Past) I laid down for a nap.
• Correct: (Past) I lay down for a nap.

(I laid down the book, and it lay there for a week. Next time, I'll let it lie there until school starts. These are correct sentences.)

Strunk and White, in their *Elements of Style*, point to an elementary principle of composition that can contribute to the pleasure of listening: "In summaries, keep to one tense." Some exceptions may be made to this rule, yet the value of generally adhering to it should be obvious. Sticking to one tense avoids "the appearance of uncertainty and irresolution."[7]

The preacher who gives regular and persistent attention to grammar will gain in self-confidence and will extend his or her usefulness within a widening circle of hearers.

VARIETY IN SENTENCE FORM

Another stylistic quality that audiences find pleasing is variety. I refer here to variety of arrangement and of types of sentences. As you read sermons, you will often see statement after statement, unrelieved by a different form of sentence. Note the different ways in which you can rephrase a statement:

Statement: The true believer will endure to the end.

Exclamation: Imagine one who truly loves Christ giving up the struggle!

Exhortation: Let us, then, resist every temptation to quit.

Command: Keep up the fight, friends, keep it up against every difficulty.

Question: Who of us does not want to be found faithful to our Lord at the very end?[8]

While an oral style, especially when extemporaneous, can be undisciplined and turgid, it can also demonstrate remarkable variety. Extempory speakers who are in touch with their own feelings and those of the audience can produce a kaleidoscope of stylistic variety. A rush of feeling about an issue naturally dictates an exclamation or an exhortation; audience reaction suggests a command or a question. Also, preachers can learn to write in the study in a style that resonates with the imagined preaching situation.

CONCRETENESS

It would be an unusual audience that did not find a concrete style more pleasing than an abstract one. Ralph Waldo Emerson remains a much-read writer because he used language that you can see and hear, taste and feel. His advice on eloquence included this: "Condense some daily experience into a glowing symbol, and an audience is electrified. They feel as if they already possessed some new right and power over a fact which they can detach, and so completely master in thought. It is a wonderful aid to the memory, which carries away the image and never loses it. . . . Put the argument into a concrete shape, into an image—some hard phrase, round and solid as a ball, which they can see and handle and carry home with them— and the cause is half won."[9]

The preacher must exercise care in the use of concrete words and images. We can use too many images, for the hearer may not be able to shift quickly from one image to another. A poem with a profusion of images might offer no problem to a reader who can pause and savor and perhaps reread the lines. An oral presentation of the same poem, however, would overwhelm a listener. The same is true of a sermon. Paul Scherer once said, "We have to school ourselves rigidly in the fine art of being understood. You will allow me to speak feelingly, being cursed myself with what some people say is a sort of knack for words and phrases, and liking them so well that I have been known more than once to lay a sentence down on an altar to the picturesque and without more ado cut its throat."[10]

V. A. Ketcham called the seven principal kinds of imagery "the seven doors to the mind,"[11] since some persons respond more readily to one type of imagery and others to another type. I have illustrated these types by quotations from a narrative sermon on Zacchaeus in chapter 14.

Though Professor Scherer rightly admonished us about the "fine art of being understood" and promptly used an image that requires too much reflection to understand at once, an image in one of his sermons that I recall from my seminary days stands out in stark clarity: "We can't see how or why God deals with us as He does: any more than a spaniel in a living-room can grasp the mysterious movements of his master's˙thought."[12] Such concreteness helps the hearer remember powerful ideas that would otherwise be quickly forgotten.

EFFECTIVE STYLE

Now let us consider the qualities that make style effective. The style must be clear and should be pleasing. Our ultimate goal, of course, is that our style be effective, that is, accomplish something.

There is no question that *speaking in the first person singular* engages attention. The thoughts, feelings, and experiences of the preacher are important to the hearer. To be sure, the preacher's opinions may be trivial, the feelings inconsequential, and the experiences boring. Also, the preacher may be an obvious egotist and exhibitionist. Yet significant first-person revelations, hints, and narratives, when used judiciously, command attention. I would not personally state the case in relation to preaching so sweepingly as Rudolf Flesch has stated it for writing. Yet he makes an important point:

That is the great paradox of writing—the thing about it that you have to understand before you can make a decent job of it. If you want to convey information, you must first show the reader the extent of your ignorance before you began to learn. If you want to describe an adventure, you must first confess that you were afraid of the danger before you went into it. If you want to write about health, your point of view must be that of someone who has known sickness; if your subject is beauty, you must be familiar with ugliness; if it is money, you must first tell your reader that your own financial troubles are just as bad as his.[13]

An important element of this first-person effort is that of engaging the hearer in a kind of dialogue. No one in the congregation has to say a word, but an invisible current of exchange will be going on all the time. Not recitation, but engagement characterizes the sermon. This rapport is what John A. Broadus called "sympathy." He said, "Everybody who can speak effectively knows that the power of speaking depends very largely upon the way it is heard, upon sympathy which one succeeds in gaining from those he addresses. If I were asked what is the first thing in effective preaching, I should say sympathy; and what is the second thing, I should say sympathy; and what is the third thing, I should say sympathy."[14] The concept of "truth through personality" operates with singular force as the witness of the preacher molds the style of the sermon.

Effective style is always *appropriate to the subject matter, the audience, and the occasion.* Cicero distinguished three styles—the plain, the middle, and the grand. Or, the subdued, for teaching; the temperate, to give pleasure; and the majestic, to persuade. Augustine followed Cicero:

Although our teacher should speak of great things, he should not always speak about them in the grand manner, but in a subdued manner when he condemns or praises something. But when something is to be done and he is speaking to those who ought to do it but do not wish to do it, then those great things should be spoken in the grand manner in a way appropriate to the persuasion of their minds. And sometimes concerning one and the same important thing, he speaks in a subdued manner if he teaches, in a moderate manner if he is praising it, and in a grand manner if he is moving an adverse mind to conversion.[15]

Of course, God is the final judge of whether we preach in the best and most effective way, but our audience judges us too. Whether we do what is fitting for that audience may, therefore, determine how it looks to God. If the people turn away from what we say, it may be not because they are dolts or skeptics, but because we have been insensitive to what is appropriate.

Effective style is *honest.* The preacher brings truth—that is our business. Exaggeration, such as the heaping up of superlatives, destroys credibility. Playful exaggeration is a fruitful source of humor; dishonest or careless exaggeration produces mistrust.

Effective style *reflects the mood intended in the choice of words.* When I was in high school, our English teacher told us of a nationwide radio broadcast that had unexpectedly injurious consequences. For an hour the listeners heard sad songs and melancholy poetry. Wailing winds and driving rain in the background complemented the words of the songs and poems. As a result, a number of people committed suicide and others suffered nervous breakdowns. Gorham Munson, in *The Written Word*, says, "It is impossible to read a list of melancholy words without experiencing a tinge of melancholy, and it is impossible to read a list of gay words without experiencing a lift of spirit."[16] Here are some of the words he lists in each category:

Melancholy	*Gaity*
somber	mirth
sad	joy
lonesome	pleasure
dreary	dance
aging	laughter
tears	chuckle
drizzle	cheery
fall of leaves	dawn
howling of a dog	sunlight
sighing	bright
tomb	dog wagging its tail
nevermore	hallelujah

Our word choice may reveal whether we have inwardly received the gospel as good news or as bad news.

Effective style *favors the indicative mode.* People generally associate preaching with exhortation. "Do this. . . . Do that." "Let us. . . ." "We should. . . . We ought. . . . We must. . . ." These imperatives or their cousins are the hortatory stock in trade of the stereotyped preacher! However, a sermon can be effective without using one of these hortatory terms. In fact, we may improve a particular sermon by recasting our phraseology, so that what we have to say appears in the indicative mode. Theodore Parker Ferris made this suggestion: "Go through a sermon and cross out every *ought*, and *must*, and *should*, and *let us*. You may be shocked to find that there isn't much left and you may have to dig more deeply than you have ever dug before in order to replace those moral imperatives with religious indicatives. Remember that the Gospel is good news. If, when, you read one of your sermons, there is not good news in it, then it is not a Christian sermon and it had better not be preached."[17]

When I first read this advice, I found it in a library copy of Ferris's *Go Tell the People*. I was amused to discover that a seminarian had gone through one of Ferris's sermons in the book and had underlined with red pencil each instance in which author had used an imperative expression, of which there were several. However, Ferris had acknowledged that some imperatives are appropriate if not necessary. We find biblical precedents for it. Notwithstanding, the entire ethical structure of Judeo-Christian faith rests upon bedrock indicatives concerning what God has done, is doing, and will do. The Ten Commandments are prefaced by the words, "I am the Lord your God, who brought you out of the land of Egypt, out of the house of bondage" (Exod. 20:2). The ethical demands of the Sermon on the Mount are prefaced by the affirmations of the Beatitudes: "Blessed are you," says Jesus again and again (see Matthew 5:3-12).

By and large, it is much better to say "What a joy it is to serve a God who has gone to the last extreme to redeem us" than to say "We ought to serve God; he has done so much for us." Paul Scherer put it well: "The Great Commandment is sometimes quoted as if it were the sum total of religion. It is nothing of the sort. It is the sum total of the Law and the Prophets. Without the gospel in front of it, it is nothing but an imperative without any visible means of support. The imperative must have it indicative. 'God so loved the world': therefore, 'thou shalt love the Lord thy God, and thy neighbor as thyself.'"[18]

Effective style uses *skillful repetiton*, whether it is a kind of symphonic refrain or a repetitive form like rhythmic parallelism. We may find it helpful, in some cases, to repeat our text or a portion of it at significant points in the sermon. To repeat the words "God says, I will never fail you nor forsake you" can have a cumulatively impressive effect. In the same way, a line or two from a poem or a hymn may be useful. More especially, you can regularly phrase your own words to achieve such a purpose.

Franklin Delano Roosevelt liked the poetry of Walt Whitman and often reflected in his speaking style the power of Whitman's rhythmic parallelism. It is not difficult to see how the varied rhythm of Whitman's "I Sit and Look Out" could be extrapolated for either a political speech or a sermon.

I sit and look out upon all the sorrows of the world, and upon all
 oppression and shame,
I hear secret convulsive sobs from young men at anguish with themselves, remorseful after deeds done,
I see in low life the mother misused by her children, dying, neglected,
 gaunt, desperate,
I see the wife misused by her husband, I see the treacherous seducer
 of young women,
I mark the ranklings of jealousy and unrequited love attempted to be
 hid, I see these sights on the earth,
I see the workings of battle, pestilence, tyranny, I see martyrs and
 prisoners,
I observe a famine at sea, I observe the sailors casting lots who shall
 be kill'd to preserve the lives of the rest,
I observe the slights and degradations cast by arrogant persons upon
 laborers, the poor, and upon negroes, and the like;
All these—all meanness and agony without end I sitting look out upon,
See, hear, and am silent.[19]

Albert Edward Phillips has cited the importance of the principle of what he calls "cumulation," the heaping up of "a succes-
sion of statements on the same point":

By the use of cumulation the speaker can give the listener the necessary
time and expend upon him the necessary energy. Each detail or

illustration works in time, and each has a given power which adds to the total force. Thus to say that Edison has been of inestimable benefit to mankind may make a slight impression, but, when working through time and force by means of cumulation, we are told that, among other things, he invented the phonograph, the mimeograph, the electric pen and the kinetescope; that he conceived and perfected the electric lighting station with its incandescent lamp, and thereby revolutionized our lighting methods; that he invented and perfected the process for the extraction of iron ore by electricity, and has brought to perfection a storage battery; and that, incidentally, he has taken out several hundred patents covering other useful inventions—when we hear all this the idea that Edison has been a great benefit to mankind becomes a profound conviction that can never be effaced.[20]

Effective style is *economical*. It does not waste words. Effective style may employ many words, but always with a purpose. Nouns and verbs, not adjectives and adverbs, carry the weight of the sentences. Whenever we omit an adverb or an adjective without changing our meaning, the sentence will likely be the better for it. Most of the quotations that ring in the memory and find their way into anthologies have a crisp, epigrammatic quality.

METHODS FOR IMPROVEMENT OF STYLE

The improvement of style is a lifetime project. Our general education contributes to it, but the lessons learned in school need to be supplemented as well as implemented. How can we do this?

Wide reading will enrich style immeasurably. Reading will furnish the mind with images, words, and phrases that become readily available to the preacher when writing or speaking. It gives a sureness of touch, vitality, and freshness. Speed-reading has its place, but that is not what is comtemplated here. We must savor and digest language, and that takes time.

Writing helps us to see what we do and to improve it. It affords opportunity to explore different ways of saying the same thing— different and more effective words, different and more effective sentence structure. We will find valuable help in a thesaurus and a dictionary. A reliable grammar is indispensable. A book of readings by various authors, which gives examples of different styles for study and imitation, may prove invaluable. Compilations of a wide variety of sermons should help with the preacher's specific task. With these aids available, consider the following pointed suggestions.

Write the way you talk. Oral style does not come easy to the studious preacher. We consciously or unconsciously let our writing fall into the style of the textbooks we have used or the technical works that we regularly read. We can overcome this suffocating habit by simply putting our thoughts into the kind of language that our friends would understand and like to see in earnest and lively conversation or in letters. I would agree with Jacques Barzun that the advice to write as we speak is "absurd" if we mean by that the "vague, clumsy, confused, and wordy" speech so characteristic of courtroom dialogue.[21] However, there is a quality in the simplicity of word choice and directness of style of a good conversationalist that points the way for the preacher.

Imitate for practice the most effective preachers. Some preachers know how to begin a sermon and gain attention immediately. Others know how to narrate with gripping drama a biblical story. Still others are skilled at making a difficult subject clear. These and other aspects of the sermonic task can often be taught better by example than by mere rules of rhetoric or homiletics. Adela Rogers St. Johns, author of best-selling novels and of hundreds of short stories, listed more than eighty literary works of various types, saying that these books were indispensable to her own writing. She said, "I do not travel anywhere without at least some of them—and usually all of them." She explains:

To ignore them would be as though an architect said, "I will never look at a house or building that has ever been put up." Or as though a musician refused to go to a concert to hear Mozart and Beethoven. Or an electrician refused to recognize or utilize the words of Edison. . . . These writers over the years, many of them inspired as anybody can be, have ironed out some of the stresses and strains, they have discarded the impossibles, they have established certain patterns just as Mozart established them in the world of music. They hold high the torches of their spirit and their work. Why should we refuse to see by that light?[22]

Harry Emerson Fosdick has been regarded by liberals and conservatives alike as the foremost preacher of the first half of the twentieth century. In his autobiography, *The Living of These Days*, he lets us in on one important source of his effectiveness:

I . . . began to see how much the old preachers had to teach us. At their best they did achieve results. Their sermons were appeals to the jury, and they got decisions. They knew where the great motives were and appealed to them with conclusive power. I began studying sermons of men like Phillips Brooks—not merely reading them but analyzing sentence by sentence the steps they took toward working in the auditors the miracles they often did achieve—and I concluded that while we modern preachers talk about psychology much more than our predecessors, we commonly use it a good deal less.[23]

Write freely, then revise. Our education sharpens our critical faculties and often, in the same experience, paralyzes our creativity. Some of us cannot think of anything to put down when we face a blank sheet of paper. It is as if we were about to write a masterpiece for posterity. Paul Scherer made a simple but wise suggestion: "May I counsel you not to write the original draft in ink? There seems to be less finality about it when you do it in pencil, and as a result the words come more smoothly. You are free to express your mind without restraint if you are aware the while that it is all going to be worked over again anyhow. Especially will you find it easier to get started."[24]

Peter Elbow has written two books exploring the means of maximizing the possibilities of "freewriting." He describes freewriting as "the easiest way to get words on paper and the best all-around practice in writing" that he knows. "To do a freewriting exercise, simply force yourself to write without stopping for ten minutes." He states the value of this approach: "Freewriting for ten minutes is a good way to warm up when you sit down to write something. You won't waste so much time getting started when you turn to your real writing task and you won't have to struggle so hard to find words."[25]

Many preachers are using word processors, which are excellent for such purposes. Revision is easy. Whatever the method of writing freely, revision is necessary. The critical and analytical faculties must be put to work after the fact, so as to bring forth a true, orderly, and impressive product.

Speaking, recording, and then criticizing and revising offers some preachers the best help. Charles Haddon Spurgeon improved his style by revising the galley proofs of the shorthand transcriptions of his sermons as he actually preached them. Since he was an extemporaneous preacher and did not normally write manuscripts, he labored over these transcripts until they pleased him. He said that he would never let anything go into print the way he spoke it. Such an approach could hardly fail to be a learning experience while it met editorial requirements. The ubiquity of recording devices puts this method of improving style within every preacher's reach.

V. THE DELIVERY OF SERMONS

18. The Mastery of the Message

Outstanding preachers have used various methods of sermon delivery and, despite the drawbacks of each method, have been effective. Clarence Edward Macartney wrote a complete manuscript for his sermons but preached without notes. Charles Haddon Spurgeon and W. E. Sangster did not write manuscripts and preached from brief notes. John A. Broadus did not ordinarily write manuscripts but prepared carefully and preached without notes. Thomas Guthrie memorized his sermons. Thomas Chalmers wrote a full manuscript and was called a "fell reader." George Buttrick took his manuscript into the pulpit with topic sentences underlined and used that as a "road map."

Harry Emerson Fosdick said that he had at one time or another used all the methods.[1] He was convinced in his later years that he could be just as effective reading from a full manuscript as using other methods. That he was effective there is no question. However, those who had heard him speak without a manuscript probably felt that this extemporaneous method was much the better method for Fosdick, whatever he believed about it personally.[2]

Too much is at stake for preachers to be self-deceived about their delivery. Therefore, what follows is intended as a guide for exploration and self-discovery, not as an exclusive rule for every preacher.

PREACHING WITHOUT NOTES

Preaching without notes has strong support. To begin with, this is the kind of preaching that the people who listen like best. It suggests to them a direct conversation—that the speaker is talking out of a heart-to-heart feeling. And it is true that there is a kind of electricity that flows between speaker and hearer. They are thinking together, looking each other in the eye, so that the speaker can read from the hearer's face agreement, disagreement, questions, and excitement. This is a powerful stimulus to further creativity. The celebrated orator of antiquity, Cicero, observed, "In delivery, next to the voice in effectiveness is the countenance and this is ruled over by the eyes."[3]

A more contemporary writer, M. Bautain, considered the matter from a different angle: "On the very occasions when it should seem you would have most need of them, [your notes] are totally worthless. In the most fervid moments of extemporaneous speaking, when light teems, and the sacred fire burns, when the mind is hurried along upon the tide of thoughts, and the tongue, obedient to its impulse, accommodates itself in a wonderful manner to its operations and lavishes the treasures of expression, everything should proceed from within. The mind's glance is bent inwards, absorbed by the subject and its ideas"[4] Perhaps more important—to some hearers, at least—is the feeling that swirls among the hearers, as that is set in motion by the speaker when an issue is momentous, when the speaker and the hearers both have a vital stake in the subject. Then any method of communication will suffice. However, this condition does not exist every day or every week. We have to use what will be for us and our audience the most effective method under the circumstances.

When we are looking at the congregation, we can see the beginning of inattention and say to ourselves, "What can I do to get John Smith interested again?" A sharply worded question, an analogy with special appeal to Smith, or in an informal setting, calling John Smith's name can bring him to attention again. Preachers who are buried in their notes can hardly bring off this lively dialogue and will have to take their chances otherwise.

Of course, this method of speaking can seem so offhand and impromptu that some hearers will not take it seriously. They may be, in particular cases, justified. Some speakers have such a facility with words that they could go on for hours speaking fluently but saying nothing of substance or significance. The best speakers are not necessarily those born with the gift of gab. One preacher, who preached without notes and recognized the necessity of having something to say, carefully wrote a manuscript for his sermons, believing that for him that was the best way to prepare for the pulpit. He acknowledged that this was perhaps the most difficult method of preaching: Preaching without notes was no shortcut.

It is not necessary, however, to write a full manuscript in order to speak acceptably without notes. John A. Broadus believed that one could speak most effectively by normally giving the bulk of the time available for preparation to the thought, not to the phraseology of the sermon. He noted that there is writing in which the preacher writes without adequate thought, in contrast to extemporaneous preaching, in which the preacher speaks on the basis of careful thought but couches the thought in the language available at the moment. Of course, for special reasons the preacher may need to work out the exact wording of a sentence, perhaps a definition. This can be done with great care without losing the freedom of the extemporaneous style.

How can the preacher use this method?

Of first importance is the necessity of having an orderly sequence of thought. It would be difficult to remember a sermon that made no connected sense logically or psychologically. Broadus put it well:

If the different topics and subdivisions, details and illustrations, are arranged according to their natural sequence and connection, there need be little anxiety about recalling, for each point will suggest what is to follow. Thus, too, the necessity of putting things together so that they can be remembered, will compel a man to find out the true relations and natural order of his thoughts, when he might otherwise shrink from the task. Instead of presenting a mere conglomeration of ideas, it is better if we be forced to have them in solution in the mind, that they may crystallize according to their own law. There may be exceptions in peculiar subjects; but, in general, a discourse which cannot be easily remembered has been ill-arranged, and details which do not readily present themselves were better omitted.[5]

R. S. Storrs, an outstanding pulpit orator of the nineteenth century, recommended a method for fixing in mind the basic sequence of thought. The preacher should rewrite the outline of the sermon again and again—twenty times if necessary—until each successive point or movement of thought would be present before the preacher when needed as the sermon is preached. This rewriting is not a copying from page to page; it is a true rewriting, in which the preacher recreates the ideas, perhaps in different words, each time the outline is rewritten. In this way, the preacher will not struggle from point to point, but will be freely carried along with the flow of thought.[6]

Ralph W. Sockman, of whom Fosdick said, "In his first student sermon, [he] exhibited such mature ability and skill that I told the class he acted as though he had twenty years of experience behind him,"[7] wrote out his sermons, but preached them without notes—*except for his quotations*. He always read his quotations. It was important to him not only to *be* exact when quoting someone but also to *seem* exact. His broadcasted and printed sermons were a conflation of the manuscript he wrote before he preached and the transcript of the sermon as actually delivered.[8]

My own practice in sermon delivery has varied according to need and circumstances. While I have used other methods often, I chose during an interim pastorate of some ten weeks to preach without any notes whatsoever. Each week I preached the same sermon twice on Sunday morning, a different sermon on Sunday evening, and led a Bible study on Wednesday evening. It was a demanding task, and occasionally I omitted an illustration or an idea. But I felt that the extra effort proved worthwhile. As I reflect on that experience and others, I would make these suggestions for learning a sermon, so as to be able to present it without manuscript or notes.

1. Get the overall structure of the sermon clearly in mind. This can be done by noting the main ideas in the devel-

opment, speaking them over, and making logical transition from one idea to another. What this amounts to is simply summarizing for yourself the main points one after the other, while trying to see how they belong to each other and how they may be best fitted together.

2. Elaborate this very brief outline somewhat—expand, amplify. Fill in detail here and there as you can easily recall it. This will help reinforce the natural sequence of the main points.

3. Practice speaking over paragraphs, points, or "blocks of thought" in all details until each such section is thoroughly worked through. If a particular section is, for example, an illustration, master all the details, until you can say it accurately and with whatever feeling is appropriate.

4. Get a key word or phrase for each section, and rehearse the entire sermon, referring only to these words or phrases. The purpose is to link the content of each section to the word or phrase for easy recall. Refer to your notes as necessary for this early rehearsal.

5. Picturize this outline mnemonically. This procedure is unnecessary for some whose power of recall works acceptably or even better without such a quasi-mechanical aid. However, the ancient orators and many other speakers have used mnemonics to learn their speeches. When Cicero rehearsed his orations, he went from one room to another in his house as he developed each phase of his speech. Then, when he delivered the oration before an audience, he mentally walked from one room to another in his house and the setting helped him recall what he had rehearsed there.[9] Similarly, you can place each of the key words or phrases of your sermon, which you link to concrete images, in a familiar mental setting and in imagination walk from place to place in sequence, easily recalling what comes next in the sermon.

6. Referring only to key words and phrases, mnemonically or otherwise, rehearse the entire sermon several times. You

will learn better and remember longer the *ideas* of the sermon if you do not attempt to repeat it in the same words. Try each time to recreate the feeling.

7. Rewrite a brief outline of the sermon as many times as needed to fix the message thoroughly in mind, not attempting to put the ideas in the same words when you rewrite.

PREACHING WITH NOTES

Of course, speaking without manuscript or notes is the ideal method of preaching. For various reasons, we may choose, at least part of the time, a less demanding method.

Rather than spend the time necessary to write a manuscript, some preachers, like Broadus, prefer to use their available time in production of the ideas of the sermon. And this has much to commend it—provided that the preacher has already worked through the normal problems of grammatical correctness and proper diction, so that extemporaneous expression falls into a fitting style. Also, the preacher can save time by not attempting to learn even brief notes.

If you plan to preach with notes, then put them in a form that is most useful to you when you stand in the pulpit. For purposes of clarifying thought and having an intelligible record of that thought, a full-sentence, formal outline will be helpful as a preliminary step. However, you may reduce this larger outline to mere words and phrases, which will be sufficient to recall any part of the sermon you may wish to present. Sometimes even a grotesque form of the pulpit outline will make it easy either to remember or to pick up with a quick glance during delivery.

VERBATIM MEMORIZATION

The method of preaching memoritor does not command much approval among public speakers. Memory is important, obviously, and memory is a large part of the most acceptable methods of public speaking. However, for most people memorizing verbatim is so time consuming and places such unnecessary pressure on the speaker that memorization receives low marks. Yet some individuals have a remarkable ability to memorize and to reproduce naturally what they have learned. It would be presumptuous to say that these persons should not memorize word for word what they wish to say.

READING FROM MANUSCRIPT

Sir Winston Churchill learned quite early a method of speaking that was effective without requiring either memorization or slavish reading of a manuscript. His love of the English language is well known, as is his ability to use that language with electrifying effect. For a time, Churchill memorized his speeches and impressed his colleagues in Parliament with the power of these "impromptu" efforts. However, he once broke down and could not recover his train of thought. Thereafter, he developed a method of speaking that did not require word-for-word memorization nor the reading of a manuscript. He prepared a full manuscript, but he lifted out words and phrases in sufficient quantity to preserve his style and to enable him to reproduce his manuscript virtually *in toto*. Since every word was not typed out on the page, he had to create as he went along, and that gave him an unusual amount of freedom and naturalness. When he spoke, it sounded more like extemporaneous speech than like reading.[10]

There are times when a preacher may feel it necessary to use a full manuscript. Some formal occasions seem to demand it. And then, there are some preachers who for their own reasons wish to have a complete manuscript before them. If this is your practice, then do everything possible to gain and maintain rapport with your hearers. It will help to underline key words or phrases and use them to move you along in the sermon, just as you would use a brief outline. If you should forget what you wish to say, the words are there before you to be read if necessary. Such a use of the manuscript does not have to enslave you to mere reading if you sternly resist the temptation to reproduce the exact words on the page. A further suggestion may prove helpful—type your manuscript to look more like poetry on the page than prose. Let each new sentence begin flush with the left margin. Indent to set off certain clauses, phrases, or even individual words. Give the manuscript a graphic personality that will help you pick up whole paragraphs with a glance. This was the method of Peter Marshall, who was able to use a manuscript so skillfully that some hearers did not realize that he had the full text of his sermon before him.[11]

ADVANTAGES AND DISADVANTAGES OF VARIOUS METHODS

What are the advantages and disadvantages of the different methods of learning and delivering a sermon?

If *preaching without notes* is done well, the hearers almost universally prefer it. It sounds more natural than other methods. The preacher maintains a kind of dialogue with the audience. Creativity during actual delivery is possible. However, the preacher may rely on glibness rather than on thought. The preacher may get carried away in the excitement of delivery and say things unintended or omit significant points.

If *preaching with notes* is done well, most hearers will not object. A high degree of directness and naturalness is possible. The preacher can make important statements and give quotations with exactness. This method can save the preacher from rambling. However, the preacher can bury his or her face in even brief notes and sever eye contact with the audience. Overall, precision and elegance of style do not come easily.

With *verbatim memorization*, the preacher can say what he or she intends to say and say it with exactness and elegance. If it is done well, the hearers may possibly be impressed and moved as with no other method. Memorization of manuscripts requires almost inevitably a clear, orderly structure and abundant use of concrete material, both of which impress an audience. However, too much time may be required to learn a manuscript by heart. Because of the possibility of forgetting, this method may lay too much stress on the preacher. Also, the preacher may forget important points. This method may be no better than slavish reading, for the preacher may be glassy-eyed and detached from the congregation while "reading the sermon off the back of his mind."

By *reading from a manuscript*, the preacher can say all that was intended, exactly and elegantly. If done well, a high degree of audience rapport is possible, since freedom from the anxiety of forgetting may allow concern for the audience as well as concern for the thought of the message. However, many preachers who use a full manuscript use it poorly. Reading usually stifles potential emotional elements in the sermon. The time required to write a full manuscript could be more profitably spent on other aspects of the homiletical or pastoral tasks.

As Christians, we believe that God calls people with different levels of ability and varying gifts. Each of us has to fulfill his or her calling in the preaching ministry according to the measure of those abilities and gifts. We must recognize that the measure of our effectiveness has a definite relation to the way we exercise those abilities and gifts. No preacher should quickly settle into a pattern of sermon delivery without exploring the different possibilities, so as to determine which method of delivery will maximize one's effectiveness. Sir William Osler was recognized as one of the most outstanding physicians of his time and received worldwide acclaim. Yet, he thought of himself as a one-talent person. However, he deliberately used that one talent to the fullest advantage and thus made his mark, citing Jesus' parable of the talents as his inspiration.[12] Likewise, preachers can often accomplish more than they at first imagined possible—if they are faithful.

19. The Use of Voice and Body

Aside from character and reputation, voice and body language are the preacher's most important assets for proclamation of the gospel. Yet voice and body reflect character and enhance or diminish reputation.

THE VOICE

There are practical reasons for a preacher's giving attention to the voice. In his unusually helpful book, *Training the Speaking Voice*, Virgil A. Anderson states the case well: "The transmitting and exchange of information are primarily functions in the biological world, the cohesive force in every human culture, and the dominant influence in the personal life of every one of us. While communication may take many forms, naturally it is human communication that concerns us most; and within this form, there is little doubt that oral communication is by far the most immediate to our everyday lives."[1]

The voice may divert attention. Vocal peculiarities, harshness, or insufficient volume can cause the message to go unheard— figuratively and literally. An evangelist, who had probably ruined his voice by misuse, repeatedly reminded his hearers that he was not angry as he spoke, but that he had no control over the harshness of his voice. His reminders helped, but his harsh voice nevertheless tended to convey a negative message.

The voice may be so abused as to threaten the preacher's future as a public speaker. My speech teacher in seminary, Inman Johnson, used to warn students with some humor that if they did not care for their voice, they would end up selling insurance. It was a timely warning. While we were young we could correct vocal faults that sooner or later would produce serious problems.

There are several factors that relate to desirable voice production:

PITCH:

We think of the voice as in the upper, middle, or lower register. Where we find a problem is in the misplacement of the pitch of the voice, not in its being naturally too high or too low. We can usually find our optimum pitch by identifying the highest note and the lowest note on the scale that we can reach with ease and then striking the note precisely between the two. This may be difficult, however, for someone who, perhaps for psychological reasons, has long spoken in an unnaturally pitched voice. I heard of a male theology student who spoke in a feminine, falsetto voice and who could see that was a formidable problem for his aspirations as a minister. A speech therapist learned that the student had affected his falsetto as a defense, from the time his classmates had laughed at him as an adolescent when his voice was changing. The therapist, by using special electronic equipment, enabled him to hear his true voice, and he was liberated. Sometimes it may be just as important for another person to get his voice out of "the mosquito barrel," as one speech teacher put it. The too deep voice may sound too much like "the voice of God" and may need to explore the notes of the upper end of its range. The goal is flexibility, and it is not too important whether the voice is naturally deep or high.

QUALITY:

What we seek is a pleasing quality of voice. Ideally the voice will be free of raspiness, hoarseness, breathiness, thinness, or too much or too little nasality. However, dramatic presentations sometimes call for sounding a strident note to emphasize a point. The sounding of an alarm always departs from the ordinary. The preacher must be careful to learn how to use these vocal variations in such a way as not to damage the voice. Improper use of the voice may not only grate on the listeners' nerves but it may also in time produce nodes on the vocal cords.

ARTICULATION:

This has to do with the way we carve out our vowels and consonants. Sounds may be (1) omitted, as in *guvmen* (government); (2) distorted, as in *faht* (fight); (3) substituted for, as in *gineration* (generation); improperly voiced like *lives* or *words* (*livz*, *wordz*—the final s should be sounded as a z); or (4) added, as in *idear* (idea).[2] We may slur our words so that we are often misunderstood by persons close to us and not understood at all by those at a distance. Preachers with comparatively weak voices are often heard with ease because they articulate their words clearly. The cure for faulty articulation, however, is not a fussy, fastidious overpreciseness that calls attention to the speaker's lingual, dental, and labial dexterity, but a natural and correct boldness of attack when enunciating words and phrases.

PRONUNCIATION:

This has to do with the stress we place on the syllables in a word or the sound we give to a particular vowel or consonant. These pronunciations may be considered correct one place and incorrect another. Thus there is regional pronunciation and there is national pronunciation. Also, pronunciations may differ in the same region and both or all be considered correct. This, however, should not suggest that "anything goes." The preacher should attempt to learn and use pronunciation that is standard in the country where he or she serves, unless there are compelling reasons for using regional speech. We must recognize, of course, that cultured regional speech often has a charm and power beyond the region where it was born.

RATE OF UTTERANCE:

There is no norm for rate of delivery in effective speaking. The average for American platform speech is about 120 words per minute. The most interesting delivery will vary between slow and rapid. Some phrases or sentences are appropriately delivered at a fast pace, and others very deliberately. Narrative flows rapidly, but argument sometimes crawls along. The preacher who is too slow puts us to sleep; the preacher who is too fast exhausts us.

PHRASING:

Words in a sentence normally group themselves according to meaning, and in this way they convey the true meaning of the speaker. Some speakers impose a pattern on their sentences, a pattern as rigid, let us say, as iambic pentameter. However, this tends to confuse and impede meaning. The speech becomes singsong.

Pausing is related to phrasing. The pauses give the units of thought their discrete integrity. Within each thought unit, one word is usually emphasized. However, the emphatic word does not always come at the same place in each thought unit. For example, emphasis might come on the *last* word—or the *first*. The arrangement of words and the demands of meaning will determine what words are to be stressed.

VOLUME:

Volume should always be appropriate to setting and subject. The speaker will attempt to speak with enough volume to be heard by all persons present. In many cases, of course, amplification is necessary, either to make hearing possible or to save the speaker's voice. Some speakers, to the contrary, need to be toned down: The room is too small for the amount of volume they like to use. Many speakers have discovered that by proper attention to articulation a large expenditure of volume is unnecessary.

When the speaker is using his or her voice properly and when the meaning of the message is being properly reflected in the delivery, volume will vary from soft to loud. At some points in a sermon, a stentorian tone may herald an important proclamation; at other points, a whisper will suffice. Henry Ward

Beecher, perhaps the greatest pulpit orator of the nineteenth century, spoke wisely: "You may fire an audience with a loud voice, but if you wish to draw them into sympathy and to win them by persuasion, and are near enough for them to feel your magnetism and see your eye, so that you need not have to strain your voice, you must talk to them as a father would talk to his child. You will draw them, and will gain their assent to your propositions, when you could do it in no other way, and certainly not by shouting."[3]

Using the services of a *vocal coach* may be a way of making steady progress in voice improvement. It is too late for most seminarians to get experience in dramatics; it is not too late for them to get a personal tutor. Often preachers in mid-career need such help. When Phillips Brooks preached in Westminster Abbey for the first time, his voice failed him. Upon returning to Boston, he began to work with a voice teacher to correct the bad speaking habits that had caused his difficulties. He continued these lessons for years. His biographer wrote: "Under her guidance he learned to use and control his voice so well that at his later preaching in Westminster Abbey he could be heard clearly by everyone."[4] Beecher gave this advice:

If you desire to have your voice at its best, and to make the best use of it, you must go into a drill which will become so familiar that it ceases to be a matter of thought, and the voice takes care of itself. This ought to be done under the best instructors, if you have the opportunity; if not, then study the best books and faithfully *practice* their directions. . . . You do not understand the truth of anything until it has so far sunk into you that you have almost forgotten where you got it. No man knows how to play a piano who stops and says, "Let me see, that is B, and that is D," and so on. When a man has learned and mastered his instrument thoroughly, he does not stop to think which keys he must strike, but his fingers glide from one to the other mechanically, automatically, almost involuntarily. This subtle power comes out only when he has subdued his instrument and forgotten himself, conscious of nothing but the ideas and harmonies which he wished to express.[5]

Many preachers can improve their voices with proper attention. Learning new vocal habits and unlearning old ones often open up new effectiveness in speaking.

I have noted that a number of my students with *experience* in dramatics have excelled as preachers, though play-acting could have an air of unreality that carries over into preaching. But these students seem to have a learned and practiced ability to express with freedom the emotion that fits the thought of the sermon. Also, the advice of capable directors has no doubt helped them to slough off many of their worst vocal faults.

THE BODY

Not only the voice but also the body communicates truth. Body language reveals the soul. In truth, the entire body in action can enhance immeasurably the effectiveness of what the voice is saying. Charles R. Brown dramatized the importance of getting the total person into the sermonic picture. In one of his Yale lectures on preaching he said:

The ideal pulpit is one where the preacher is not barricaded behind heavy wooden breastworks which allow the people to see nothing of him except what may appear above the top button of his waistcoat. This pulpit where I am standing now is an abomination. I should be almost ready to give two hours of extra credits to any adventurous divinity student who might steal in some dark night and carry it off as Samson did the gates of Gaza. Let the whole man stand out and speak! The man's attitude and bearing in the declaring of some vital truth may become as eloquent as the words themselves.[6]

There is an eloquence of the body that includes approach to the congregation; posture; movement of legs, arms, and head; as well as changes of facial expression. This body language is of two kinds: the expressive or spontaneous and the descriptive. Expressive movement is response to feeling; it has emotional ties to what is being spoken. Descriptive movement is more cerebral; it describes size, direction, shape, and process.

There are several desirable qualities of body language, especially gestures. Gestures should be *natural*. This does not mean that the use of gestures will be at first comfortable. When speakers first begin to put more action into their speaking, they may feel painfully inhibited and the whole process may seem highly unnatural. Practice, however, will take care of the discomfort, and the speaker will have to give attention to several factors that contribute to naturalness. For one thing, timing must be right. A gesture is ludicrous if it does not slightly anticipate the corresponding spoken word or appear simultaneously. Also, there must not be too many gestures. Constant movement detracts from the spoken word. Moreover, gestures must be congruent with what the speaker is saying. To talk about God's love with a bitter scowl cancels the words.

Gestures should be *graceful*. They should not be angular, wild, or too small. Preachers can develop graceful movement by practicing in private, perhaps before a mirror. With no one watching, one can let the arms swing freely and sweep in flowing movements. Reciting poetry or reading literature that suggests various emotional changes of pace will provide occasion for practice.

Gestures should be *varied*. Hearers are understandably irritated when a speaker constantly punctuates statements with a jabbing finger, moves an arm up and down, up and down like a mechanical man, or does any other one gesture without variation. Even gestures that we would deem graceful can become tiring unless they are relieved by other types of movement.

Charles Haddon Spurgeon, England's most popular preacher of his day, concluded a piece of advice to young preachers with these wise words: "Do not allow my criticism upon various grotesque postures and movements to haunt you in the pulpit; better perpetrate them all than be in fear, for this would make you cramped and awkward. Dash at it whether you blunder or no. A few mistakes in this matter will not be half so bad as being nervous. It may be that what would be eccentric in another may be most proper in *you*; therefore take no man's dictum as applicable in every case, or to your own."[7]

ELECTRONIC AIDS

Electronic assistance is imperative in many situations. The voice must be amplified so that all members of the congregation can hear without strain, and, just as important, so that the preacher can speak without difficulty. This is an essential accommodation to the hard-of-hearing and to the size and acoustical qualities of the sanctuary or auditorium. Several practical suggestions may prove helpful.

Any permanent installation of a public address system should be carefully engineered so as to yield to the peculiarities of the room. The sound should be more or less evenly distributed, so that the speakers will not overwhelm the hearers. An unnatural magnification of sound can change the perception of the character of the message as well as the perception of the attitude of the messenger. It can raise the listeners' defenses by the sheer harshness of the tone. Special devices made available to the hard-of-hearing will obviate the need to increase excessively the volume throughout the auditorium or sanctuary. A stationary microphone or microphones are standard equipment; however, a lavaliere or wireless clip-on microphone is ideal additional equipment and will allow the preacher to move about naturally and as special circumstances require.

RADIO AND TELEVISION SPEAKING

Many religious programs on radio and television simply listen in or look in unimaginatively on a service of worship. These programs largely ignore the listening or viewing audience. Sometimes ministers make a special effort to help the people in the radio or television audience to feel that they truly participate in what is taking place. One pastor meets the viewing audience in the church vestibule and opens the door to the sanctuary, inviting these viewers to join the service in progress. Also, this pastor picks up a movable microphone during the offertory and, while seated, speaks directly and quietly to the viewing audience only. The most effective preaching in these settings will happen when the speaker takes note of both audiences and requires a producer to use the various technical means to maximum advantage.

The preacher who speaks basically in a conversational manner will best engage the attention and interest of a radio or television audience. The sermons will seem to be person-to-person dialogue and thus the audience cannot easily ignore them. Elevated, declamatory speaking is rather easy to ignore after a while. Attention lags and the words wash over the listener unimpeded. This is not true in all cases—stirring oratory from a master will always command attention, whether it is heard in church or on radio or television. However, the eye-to-eye, heart-to-heart manner normally promises the most attentive and reponsive audience.

Some of the most effective radio and television preaching has put aside the usual Sunday morning service format and has used innovative means to proclaim the gospel and to teach the scriptures. While preaching has its most congenial and most effective setting in the traditional service, the extra-church, unconventional, nontraditional approaches deserve study and experimentation. For many churches and their preachers, these different approaches offer extraordinary opportunities for a refreshing kind of evangelism. For example, television is a more intimate medium than the large service of worship and can maximize nonsermonic means of proclamation, teaching, and witnessing. The talkshow format, music programs especially adapted to television, documentaries highlighting the work of local churches, or the "fireside chat" can extend the ministry of the churches in particular cases much better than the televising of a conventional service of worship. In theory, a thirty-second spot on radio or television may be more effective than a thirty-minute sermon. Why? The medium, the message, and the audience are more compatible. Even though traditional services and sermons require the greater part of a preacher's time and energies, the possibilities and promise of electronic means of evangelism and Christian nurture should be explored. Using these means, the sermon may sometimes have to decrease in visibility, while other media of communication increase.

20. The Preacher's Personality

Spiritual formation stands at the top of the list of personal achievements essential to lasting effectiveness in ministry. This is nowhere more true than in the preaching aspect of ministry. If genuine commitment of life to God is lacking and if those disciplines through which this commitment is channeled are lacking, then the results will show up in the pulpit. The preacher may have brilliant intellect, superior speaking gifts, and a radiant, friendly bearing, yet fail to speak for God with the conviction and compassion that authentic preaching requires. The Apostle Paul said that he buffeted his body and brought it under subjection, lest having preached to others he himself might be rejected.

What I am pointing to here is not a species of playing God. No preacher can honestly claim perfection of motive or behavior, yet he or she may become a finely tuned instrument through which God can play his own music.

At the foundational level, this demands attention to what the ancient rhetoricians called *ethos*, character. Who is going to listen long—or at all—to a speaker who does not command the hearers' confidence? The speaker must be intelligent, of good character, and of goodwill toward the hearers. These are qualities that are to be expected of anyone who wants to be believed, trusted, and followed. There are still deeper qualities to be desired and sought, but intelligence, good character, and goodwill should be almost taken for granted.

BIBLE READING AND PRAYER

The route to spiritual formation follows well-known landmarks. We can begin with developing an appetite for the Holy Scriptures. This presents no problem for persons who live under the stresses of persecution for their faith, who are denied ready access to a personal copy of the Bible. They know a constant famine, not necessarily for bread, but for a knowledge of the Word of God. Critical study of the scriptures is an essential part of the professional training of ministers. Seminaries see to it that ministers in training get a knowledge of the facts of the Old and New Testaments, understanding of how the scriptures came into existence and then were handed down to us, and skills for interpreting the meaning of these words for present day congregations. Yet, the same seminaries cannot guarantee that these students come to love devotionally the scriptures they study technically. They can suggest, encourage, and hope that students reach the next and higher level. Markus Barth has likened this achievement to a conversation. Just as one in love eagerly awaits a letter from the beloved and reads and rereads it when it arrives, even listening for messages between the lines, so the reader of the Bible, realizing that it is God's love message, will take it eagerly to heart.[1]

The preacher who wants to reach this level of understanding, feeling, and devotion can take effective initiative to see that it happens. The most easily available means is private reading and meditation. For this purpose, focus in on a small portion of scripture. See it as a whole, considering it in its setting, but then savor each sentence, each phrase, each word. Apply it to your life in every possible way. Question it; argue with it; listen to it. Just as Jacob wrestled with the night-visitor until the visitor blessed him, so we should struggle with a text until it blesses us. It is a mistake to assume that a strong and deepening love relationship is characterized by serenity and sweetness. There may be stormy sessions and bitter quarrels—but they are ingredients of love.

An outstanding Old Testament scholar, Hans Lietzmann, has graphically stated the matter:

When, having studied and grasped a text, I arrive at something, then a dialogue replaces the monologue of the biblical author. I begin to speak, breaking in on the conversation with questions and answers, with my doubts and my faith; and *the biblical text ceases to be a discourse belonging to a determined time*; the text becomes a message resounding through history, which must answer the countless questions hurled by a humanity tormented by a growing anguish. It is a message that reaches me and places me in the presence of God.[2]

Counsel has been given to preachers not to let the production of an upcoming sermon intrude into the time of devotional reading of the Bible or into the practice of devotional meditation. I would agree that this should not be done with a sermon in mind. One should read and meditate on a regular basis without a view to the possible homiletical uses of what one thinks, feels, and discovers. However, it would seem that no hours would be more productive for the pulpit than those hours of devotional reading and meditation. Sermons would be struck off incidentally. Yet it should be emphasized that the preacher's approach to reading and meditation should be no different from that of any serious Christian whose devotions would never reach the pulpit.

Of course, prayer will be intimately related to this. Reading of the Bible and meditating on its meaning open a pathway to prayer. It would be impossible to hear God speaking through the pages of the Bible without being drawn or pushed toward prayer. As we read and meditate, we shall be drawn or compelled to different types of prayer. Praise, confession, thanksgiving, petition, intercession, and dedication—all of these forms will sooner or later channel our prayers. If we are sensitive to what we read, if we have hearts opened to what God would like to say to us, our thoughts will turn to these kinds of prayer. Prayer is a learning process, while it is everything else that prayer is supposed to be and to do.

CHARACTER

As the preacher is developing some skills and disciplines in prayer, corresponding qualities of character may be achieved. If this should happen in a self-conscious way, that is, if one should become more and more pleased with one's righteousness, then it is doubtful that much spiritual progress has been made. Of all people, those who pray ought to recognize their personal human vulnerability and solidarity with sinners. There is such a thing as a healthy sense of sin and shortcoming. And there is such a thing as a morbid preoccupation with sin and failure. In the former, one does not take spiritual attainments for granted but continues the path of growth, alert at all times to the reality of temptation and sin. In the latter, one tends to focus on the temptations themselves, on one's unworthiness, perhaps even despising oneself.

In any case, we have to take our human condition seriously, and by "we" I mean "we Christians." This has both promise and peril. The promise is that of a deep and abiding understanding of human frailty. If we truly believe that God has loved us despite our sin, and that he continues to love us even when we fall short of his glory, then we can see other people as we believe God sees us and love and care for them with something of the same love that God has shown to us. The word of the psalmist becomes real: "Like as a father pitieth his children, so the Lord pitieth them that fear him. For he knoweth our frame, he remembereth that we are dust."

The peril is that we will defend and tolerate temptations that need to be resisted and sins that need to be eradicated. The preacher may lower the standards of Christian life to such a level that anyone can qualify as a Christian. At the same time, the preacher may be cutting the nerve of motivation for higher and nobler living. The heresy of antinomianism has been with the church from the earliest days. In recent decades, we have seen one after another of the landmarks of morality fall, often with an effort to absorb the aberration into the Christian ethic and to comfort those who practice these abominations with assurance of divine approval. It seems right to some to assume that a crusading spirit against social oppression covers a multitude of other sins. Yet the law of sowing and reaping goes on, and the blanket absolution of everyday sins of the flesh, so freely bestowed, cannot nullify the reaping after the sowing is done. There is no doubt that the great social sins of greed, exploitation, injustice, and oppression are the greatest sins, but the sins of the flesh are still sins. Both varieties are destructive of the values we seek. Unfortunately the preacher participates too. Like Isaiah, he must confess, "I am a man of unclean lips, and I dwell in the midst of a people of unclean lips." Whoever gets a view of God in his majesty and holiness will have to say something similar.

The preacher, therefore, can despair of helping anyone else because of personal problems. Simon Peter, in the presence of Jesus, cried, "Depart from me, Lord, for I am a sinful man." Yet the preacher's temptations and doubts, far from disqualifying for ministry, may actually enhance ability to serve. The preacher will be more understanding, more willing to go out of the way to help, and better acquainted with resources for dealing with particular problems. From the side of the person being helped, the "sinner" will feel more trusting and open, knowing that he or she is not talking to an angel, but with a real human being of "like passions with us." As Henri Nouwen puts it,

No minister can save anyone. He can only offer himself as a guide to fearful people. Yet, paradoxically, it is precisely in this guidance that the first signs of hope become visible. This is so because a shared pain is no longer paralyzing but mobilizing, when understood as a way to liberation. When we become aware that we do not have to escape our pains, but that we can mobilize them into a common search for life, those very pains are transformed from expressions of despair into signs of hope.[3]

This does not mean that we have to exhibit our wounds in a tasteless and unproductive manner. Preachers who talk constantly about their own weaknesses and problems may have only weakness to offer others, not inspiring strength. Certainly, there should be a healthy measure of recovery in the life of the person who undertakes to bring health to others. Theodor Bovet writes, "The pastor is completely understanding; no sexual deviation shocks him, no crime makes him blanch; he feels himself in no way superior to the meanest and most depraved villain who ever walked the earth. But his understanding has nothing whatever to do with weakness or indulgence; it leads in a straight line to conversion: 'Neither do I condemn thee; go, and sin no more' (John 8:11)."[4]

TYPES OF TASKS

Four qualities draw bold guidelines for the preacher's goals and disciplines: caring, working, believing, and obeying.

The primary quality that should characterize the preacher is the quality of *caring*. This is the word that Elton Trueblood suggests should translate *agapé* in the New Testament, which is of course translated as "charity" or "love." It is the very essence of the nature of God, for "God is love." We see intimations of the quality in the attitude of a parent toward a child. People do care for their own children, whether the parents be pagan or Christian. When we are consciously gripped by the caring—the love—of God, our caring is more and more extended toward other people. God's caring becomes the pattern of our own behavior. "We know that we have passed out of death into life because we love the brethren." The Apostle Paul went so far as to say of his feelings toward unbelieving Israel, "I could wish myself accursed from Christ for the sake of my brethren." How could one say such things? "We love because he first loved us." Many are the ways and degrees in which this caring may be expressed. We see this quality clearly expressed when doctors and nurses minister faithfully and tenderly to a patient. However, it may be just as real, though not so obvious, in what the administrator of the hospital does. Likewise, the preacher may have a ministry that is more or less personal. Caring may be mostly for people *en masse*. Or it may be mostly one to one.

In any event, the preacher has to be a caring person. Though love can be expressed remotely even as an absent loved one can love across the miles and across the years, caring is learned up close. Loving the person up close, whether in a family situation or otherwise, can become a paradigm for all caring. Being loved by God in Christ can become the motivation for all caring. Caring is both taught and learned. We see it, and we know what it is. We begin to practice it in little ways, and gradually it becomes a part of our lives. Many ministers would find their personal life transformed, their depression lifted, and their ministry given a new surge of success by turning from self-pity to a persistent effort to care for people where their hurt is deep, caring for them in imaginative and concrete ways, ways as simple as giving a drink of cold water in the name of Christ.

Another quality for the goals and disciplines of the preacher is that of *working*. A ten-year-old boy was asked what he wanted to be when he grew up. He replied, "A preacher." "Why do you want to be a preacher?" Not being able to think of a better answer offhand, he answered, "Because it's easy!" He was wrong, of course, but perhaps he had seen enough or failed to see enough, so that he really spoke what he perceived to be the truth. While preachers must never seem so busy that people are afraid to approach them and "waste their time" with a marriage about to break up or with a moral problem eating away at the vitals, preachers must be busy. Sermon preparation, visitation and counseling, and church administration are usually considered, by most members, as the preacher's main tasks.

The editor of a denominational publication asked professors of homiletics at several theological seminaries to tell in a brief statement what they believed a preacher could do immediately to improve his preaching, that is, "to make his preaching more effective." My answer was, "Quit wasting your time." I thought of my own efforts to get my life organized efficiently, yet with enough room for those values that bring satisfaction to oneself and pleasure to others. I had in mind also the exasperated question of a minister's wife: "Why are preachers the most unselfdisciplined people in the world?"

In my response I pointed out that the preacher's problem is not lack of time; it is the inefficient use of the time available. We need prompt, regular, persistent movement toward realistic goals. With such a *modus operandi*, better and more effective preaching will result, and we will not have to sacrifice any reasonable amount of time essential for personal and other professional needs.

We must establish priorities. The "rent-paying" activities are of first importance. The congregation expects certain things of us, and unless we do them faithfully, outside revivals, community and denominational work, and golf will get us into difficulty, and rightly so. Most churches put effective preaching at the top of the list of expectations. To meet this and the secondary expectations, it would seem that these are things that we ought to do:

1. Set up and keep up a daily quiet time for reflection and planning. Long-range personal and professional goals should be decided, written down, and looked at *regularly*. Short-range goals should reflect and be consistent with those of longer range.

2. Before going to bed at night, make two lists: what has to be done and what is desirable but not urgent. The next day, draw a line through each item as it is done. The first list could include each phase of sermon preparation to be completed within the time allotted.

3. Seek a definite, inviolate time for sermon preparation. Get up a few hours before the telephone starts ringing; work late, after the telephone stops ringing; or, find a place to work during the day, which, if possible, is away from home or church, where you can be reached only in an emergency.[5] Clearly, my assumption is that most ineffective preaching is a result of too little time spent in preparation. More time allowed will help only if it is used intelligently and critically and with deepening gratitude for the privilege of proclaiming the Word of God.

Procrastination is a psychological game we play. We gorge our lives with meaningless rituals and with matters of secondary importance to avoid doing what is urgent and truly important. Here are some thoughts to put into the hopper of decision making on working:

• The necessary will have to be done sooner or later. So, why not now?
• The necessary may require slow and patient maturing. So, why not plan ahead?
• The necessary is often staggering in the aggregate. So, why not break it down into manageable bits and accomplish it a little at a time on a regular schedule?
• The necessary is sometimes unpredictable. So, why not stay far enough ahead to leave room for what you cannot anticipate?

Goal setting is an important part of the process. Quite early in his ministerial career, George A. Buttrick saw the value of aiming at a definite target. Two commitments stand out. He determined to read two significant books each week. In a year, this meant that he had read a total of one hundred books! He also determined to make thirty-five pastoral calls per week. When he was out of town he could not, of course, meet his quota, but he would catch up when he returned. His long and fruitful ministry is evidence that these commitments paid off. Sir William Osler, a noted physician, had filled chairs in four universities, had written a successful book, and had received various impressive honors, yet he considered himself a man of slender abilities. However, he attributed whatever success he achieved to the fact that he lived "in day-tight compartments." He commented, "One day must tell another, one week certify another, one month bear witness to another of the same story, and you will acquire a habit by which the one-talent man will earn a high interest and by which the ten-talent man may at least save his capital."[6]

In a panel discussion at Harvard, B. F. Skinner gave his advice to would-be writers, which applies to preachers as well. The writer, he said, should have a set place and a set time to do writing. Skinner said that he was pleased if he could produce a hundred words of publishable material each day. He observed that if one writes only one hundred words each day, in two or three years enough material will have been completed for a book.

A third quality for the preacher is *believing*. Like caring, this is a quality not entirely in the control of the preacher. We can decide to work and then work, but we cannot decide to believe and then believe—at least not so easily. In the ministry, there is a place for those with doubts about some things all the time, even about all things some of the time. Such is the human condition.

Many of the great servants of God have been people who have known great doubts and survived them. Many have walked through the valley of the shadow of death perhaps with anxiety or terror or panic. Many came through chastened, but they came through. Now they can say, because of the depth of personal experience, "Even though I walk through a valley dark as death I fear no evil, for thou art with me" (Ps. 23:4).

One of the classic sermons of Christendom is Frederick W. Robertson's sermon "The Loneliness of Christ." After a penetrating description of our Lord's loneliness and the temper of that solitude, Robertson said, "Let life be a life of faith. Do not go timorously about, inquiring what others think, what others believe, and what others say. It seems the easiest, it is the most difficult thing in life, to do this—believe in God."[7] These words must have been wrung from painful personal experience, which Robertson described in a lecture to working men: "It is an awful moment when the soul begins to find that the props on which it has blindly rested so long are, many of them, rotten, and begins to suspect them all."[8]

Over all, the preacher has to be a person of faith. That is indispensable. However, it is not the preacher's business, so R. E. C. Browne tells us, to make people believe *what* he believes, but *that* he believes. Christianity is caught, not taught.[9]

By temperament and unusual experience, some preachers have received special ministries. Their doubts equip them to serve people whom less troubled preachers would never understand. Some things widely accepted ought to be doubted by all and perhaps rejected. Other things commonly doubted merit consideration by all and perhaps acceptance. In any event, we follow Christ "feet first, not head first." Buttrick puts it well: "'If any man walk in the day, he stumbleth not, because he seeth the light of this world.' But he must 'walk,' not merely cogitate. So walking, he may arrive at last like Thomas—Thomas dour and aloof and melancholy in doubt, and chosen to be an apostle—who, more stubborn in love than he was stubborn in unbelief, followed; and who, following in a blind courage which yet knew Christ was Christlike, knelt down in joy at the end of the road confessing, 'My Lord and my God.'"[10]

A fourth quality for the preacher is *behaving*. The moral and ethical life of preachers greatly determines how they are heard. When we violate a commonly accepted code of behavior for Christians, our influence for good is immediately diminished. The cynical will rejoice, for that only confirms what they always believed and used to allay their own guilt feelings. But the faithful or those striving for a handhold on good character will be scandalized; sometimes their faith will be shaken—irreparably. Yet God brings good out of evil even by the hardest, and some few may grow in their own souls as they establish their faith on a more solid and realistic foundation.

To live a disciplined moral life is not necessarily easier for the preacher than for the average person. Of course, the preacher has an added deterrent in the matter of publicity. Everything wrong that we do is magnified by our position and is dealt with more severely. We have to consider economic and professional consequences. Besides, we know that our spiritual "fine-tuning" gained through years of formation—our meditation, prayer, worship, and obedience—will go out of focus, that we can easily become, even without damaging publicity, a sad case of "the blind leading the blind." The Apostle Paul knew the hazards. He said, "For my part, I run with a clear goal before me; I am like a boxer who does not beat the air; I bruise my own body and make it know its master, for fear that after preaching to others I should find myself rejected" (1 Cor. 9:26-27).

It is important for the preacher to know that essentially there are no new temptations. If we live in a time of relaxed moral standards, we will be more tolerant of the behavior of those among whom we live and work. Yet we would be fools to indulge ourselves for the same reason or to abandon the age-old moral sanctions. Antinomianism has always been knocking at the door of the church. And it has often been invited in and even celebrated in the name of Christian freedom or personal fulfillment. Alexander Pope said it well:

Vice is a monster of so frightful mien,
As to be hated needs but to be seen;
Yet seen too oft, familiar with her face,
We first endure, then pity, then embrace.[11]

Peer pressure can affect the preacher's lifestyle—dangerously. The question for the preacher is this: Who are my peers? Do call and ordination, to say nothing of common Christian prudence, mean anything special? "With all these witnesses to faith around us like a cloud, we must throw off every encumbrance, every sin to which we cling, and run with resolution the race for which we are entered, our eyes fixed on Jesus, on whom faith depends from start to finish" (Heb. 12:1-2a).

Every preacher needs a confidant, a spiritual director. Problems related to caring, working, believing, and behaving will inevitably emerge. It is highly unlikely that we are at the same time sufficiently mature, resourceful, and objective to handle these problems adequately. When we are tempted to say, "I can handle this without anybody's help but the Lord's," we may mean that we are prepared to bulldoze our way through the situation regardless of ethical and practical considerations—an obvious ego disorder. It may be a way of attempting to bend God to our will. We are never so far along in our spiritual progress and professional competency as not to need human help. "Confession," said Paul Tournier, "is the necessary and sufficient gateway to any spiritual action."[12] The ancient wisdom of James is still relevant: "Confess your sins to one another, and pray for one another, that you may be healed. The prayer of a righteous man has great power in its effects" (James 5:16). Even if it is not a matter of "sin," we need to see the other side of contemplated actions, which we so easily conceal from ourselves. I remember with gratitude a conversation with Dean Hugh Peterson, when I was a seminary student and about to make an important vocational decision. He raised a question about the practical wisdom of what I was about to do. I protested, "I feel that this is what God wants me to do." Dr. Peterson added, "And it's what you want to do!" He was right, and I had to consider and weigh his observation. I did what I was contemplating, but his counterpoint to my point was essential in my decision making.[13]

For the more stubborn needs, the choice of a confidant or spiritual director can be decisive. St. Francis de Sales has been quoted as saying that "one ought to choose one's confessor from among a thousand, and even ten thousand."[14] John Bunyan made a bad choice when he was troubled over the thought that he might have committed "the sin against the Holy Ghost." He told this "ancient Christian" all about himself, that he was afraid that he had committed the unpardonable sin. His "confessor" told him that he though so too. Bunyan wrote, "Here, therefore, I had but cold comfort; but, talking a little more with him, I found him, though a good man, a stranger to much combat with the devil."[15] Bunyan continues with page after page of description of his misery, misery that could have had a quick end if only his counselor had known the dark paths that a soul in its ignorance could take.

Occasionally problems pile up that are of such a nature as to require professional help beyond the competency of our usual resources. Sometimes we wrongly attribute certain problems to our lack of faith or to some disobedience. It may be something rooted in a physical or psychic illness beyond our immediate control. Help is available, and it is God's gift, just as the skill of a surgeon when more than prayer is needed.

Although this chapter on the preacher's personality has come last in the book, its concern is not least in importance. The most carefully crafted techniques and the most sublime artistic achievements in preaching may fail to do God's intended work—if the preacher does not really care about people and work faithfully for their good, or does not believe and live by the message preached. In such a case even an unassailable hermeneutic and a complete knowledge of the scriptures would fall flat. Therefore, the age-old concern about the kind of person the preacher actually is—or is on the way to becoming—has validity today. Through this means the preacher may serve as a reliable instrument of God and dare believe as the Apostle Paul, without pride or arrogance and with wonder and gratitude, "Christ lives in me" (Gal. 2:20).

NOTES

Chapter 1: The Nature of Preaching

1. Cf. Walter Eichrodt, *Theology of the Old Testament*, vol. 2, trans. J.A. Baker (Philadelphia: Westminster Press, 1967), pp. 69-78.
2. Gerhard Kittel, ed., *Theological Dictionary of the New Testament*, vol. 22, trans. Geoffrey W. Bromiley (Grand Rapids, Mich.: Wm. B. Eerdmans Publishing Company, 1964), p. 710; Walter Lüthi and Eduard Thurneysen, *Preaching, Confession, The Lord's Supper*, trans. Francis J. Brooke, III (Richmond, Va.: John Knox Press, 1960), p. 222.
3. H. H. Rowley, *The Servant of the Lord and Other Essays on the Old Testament* (London: Lutterworth Press, 1952), p. 120.
4. Ibid., p. 119.
5. Phillips Brooks, *On Preaching* (New York: Seabury Press, 1964), p. 8.
6. Alfonso M. Nebreda, *Kerygma in Crisis?* (Chicago: Loyola University Press, 1965), p. viii.
7. Charles Haddon Spurgeon, *Lectures to My Students*, Second Series (London: Passmore and Alabaster, 1877), p. 185.
8. Cf. Melvin L. DeFleur and Otto N. Larsen, *The Flow of Information: An Experiment in Mass Communication* (New York: Harper & Row, 1958), pp. 22-23.
9. From "Karl Barth on the Christian Church Today," a television interview with Vernon Sproxton, reported in *The Listener*, 19 Feb. 1961.
10. Helmut Thielicke, *How Modern Should Theology Be?*, trans. H. George Anderson (Philadelphia: Fortress Press, 1969), p. 12
11. John Baillie, *Invitation to Pilgrimage* (New York: Charles Scribner's Sons, 1945), p. 91.
12. Karl Barth, *Church Dogmatics*, vol. 2, part 2 (Edinburgh: T. & T. Clark, 1957), p. 557.
13. Dale Moody, *The Word of Truth* (Grand Rapids, Mich.: Wm. B. Eerdmans Publishing Company, 1981), pp. 299-302.
14. Ibid., p. 300.
15. Spurgeon, *Lectures*, p. 181.
16. Davis Collier Woolley, ed., *Baptist Advance* (Nashville, Tenn.: Broadman Press, 1964), pp. 425, 426.

Chapter 2: The Preacher's Authority

1. Charles Haddon Spurgeon, *Lectures to My Students*, Second Series (London: Passmore and Alabaster, 1877), p. 74.

2. R. E. C. Browne, *The Ministry of the Word* (Philadelphia: Fortress Press, 1976), p. 36.
3. Ibid., p. 40.

Chapter 3: The Cultural Context

1. Carl Rogers, *Counseling and Psychotherapy* (Boston: Houghton Mifflin Company, 1942), p. 286.
2. See James A. Pike, *A New Look in Preaching* (New York: Charles Scribner's Sons, 1961), p. 37.
3. Paul Tillich, *Theology of Culture* (London: Oxford University Press, 1959), p. 204.
4. Ibid., p. 207.

Chapter 4: The Worship Context

1. William Temple, *The Hope of a New World* (New York: Macmillan Company, 1943), pp. 26-27, 114.
2. Justin Martyr, *The First Apology*.
3. Yngve Brilioth, *A Brief History of Preaching* (Philadelphia: Fortress Press, 1965), p. 8.
4. Karl Barth, *The Preaching of the Gospel* (Philadelphia: Westminster Press, 1963), pp. 78-80.
5. Raymond Abba, *Principles of Christian Worship* (New York: Oxford University Press, 1957), pp. 11-12.
6. Josef A. Jungmann, *Public Worship*, trans. Clifford Howell (Collegeville, Minn.: Liturgical Press, n.d.), p. 179.
7. George M. Gibson, *The Story of the Christian Year* (New York: Abingdon-Cokesbury Press, 1945), pp. 75-78.
8. Paul E. Scherer, *For We Have This Treasure* (New York: Harper & Brothers, Publishers, 1944), p. 160.
9. Hans P. Ehrenberg, ed., *Luther Speaks* (London: Lutterworth Press, 1947), p. 50.
10. Roy Pearson, *The Preacher: His Purpose and Practice* (Philadelphia: Westminster Press, 1962), p. 126.
11. P. T. Forsyth, *Positive Preaching and the Modern Mind* (London: Independent Press, 1907), pp. 66, 64.
12. Johan Huizinga, *Homo Ludens: A Study of the Play Element in Culture* (Boston: Beacon Press, 1955), pp. 14-16.
13. Karl Rahner, ed., *The Renewal of Preaching*, Vol. 23 *Concilium* (New York: Paulist Press, 1968), p. 62. Cf. Paul W. Hoon, *The Integrity of Worship* (Nashville, Tenn.: Abingdon Press, 1971), pp. 25, 48, 107-108, 145, 147, 166-168. Cf. Richard Paquier, *Dynamics of Worship*, trans. Donald Macleod (Philadelphia: Fortress Press, 1967), pp. 53-54.

14. Yngve Brilioth, *Landmarks in the History of Preaching* (London: S.P.C.K., 1950), p. 18.
15. Cf. Rahner, *Renewal*, p. 55.
16. Walter M. Abbott, ed., *The Documents of Vatican II* (New York: Corpus Books, 1966), p. 35.
17. Eduard Schweizer, *Divine Service in the New Testament and Today* (Montreal: Presbyterian College, 1970), p. 15.
18. Ferdinand Hahn, *The Worship of the Early Church*, trans. David E. Green (Philadelphia: Fortress Press, 1973), pp. 104-105.
19. Abbott, *Vatican II*, pp. 3-4.
20. John Killinger, *Leave It to the Spirit* (New York: Harper & Row Publishers, 1971), p. xiii.
21. David Randolph, *God's Party* (Nashville, Tenn.: Abingdon Press, 1975, pp. 111, 110-121, 49-60.
22. Geoffrey Wainwright, *Doxology: The Praise of God in Worship, Doctrine, and Life* (New York: Oxford University Press, 1980), pp. 324-325.

Chapter 5: The Sharing of Meaning

1. Harry Guntrip, *Psychology for Ministers and Social Workers*, 3rd ed. (London: George Allen and Unwin, 1971), p. 69.
2. Quoted in *The Tie*, a publication of The Southern Baptist Theological Seminary, Louisville, Ky., April 1945, p. 3.
3. *The Merchant of Venice*, act 3, sc. 1, lines 61-70.
4. Don M. Aycock, ed., *Preaching with Purpose and Power* (Macon, Ga.: Mercer University Press, 1982), p. 54.

Chapter 6: The Text

1. Cf. Karl Rahner, *Encyclopedia of Theology* (New York: Seabury Press, 1975), pp. 127-128.
2. Claus Westermann, ed., *Essays in Old Testament Hermeneutics* (Richmond, Va.: John Knox Press, 1963), p. 36.
3. G. W. H. Lampe and K. J. Woollcombe, *Essays on Typology* (Naperville, Ill.: Alec R. Allenson, 1957), p. 38.
4. Krister Stendahl, "Biblical Theology," *The Interpreter's Dictionary of the Bible*, vol. 4, ed. George A. Buttrick (Nashville, Tenn.: Abingdon Press, 1962), 431.
5. Gerhard Ebeling, *Word and Faith* (Philadelphia: Fortress Press, 1963), pp. 330-331.
6. Karl Barth, *Deliverance to the Captives* (New York: Harper & Brothers, 1961), p. 29.
7. Cf. James Sanders, "Hermeneutics," *The Interpreter's Dictionary of the Bible*, supplementary vol., ed. Keith Krim (Nashville, Tenn.: Abingdon Press,

1976), p. 405; and *God Has a Story Too* (Philadelphia: Fortress Press, 1979), pp. 17-19.

8. Erik Routley, *Into a Far Country* (London: Independent Press, 1962), p. 22.
9. Some of these questions were suggested in classroom lectures of Professor Paul Scherer, by James Black in his *Mystery of Preaching*, by Harry Emerson Fosdick in a symposium by Charles McGlon, "How I Prepare My Sermons," and by Halford Luccock in his *In the Minister's Workshop*. This list and an example of its use can be found in slightly different form in my *Guide to Biblical Preaching* (Nashville, Tenn.: Abingdon Press, 1976), pp. 48-58.
10. Westermann, *Essays*, p. 36.

Chapter 7:   The Emergent Truth

1. Austin Phelps, *The Theory of Preaching* (New York: Charles Scribner's Sons, 1911), pp. 310-311.
2. Henry Grady Davis, *Design for Preaching* (Philadelphia: Muhlenberg Press, 1958).
3. Cf. Eduard Schweizer, *God's Inescapable Nearness*, ed. and trans. James W. Cox (Waco: Word Books, 1971), p. 17.
4. Joseph Sittler, *The Ecology of Faith* (Philadelphia: Muhlenberg Press, 1961), pp. 28-29.
5. Henry Grady Davis, *Design for Preaching*, pp. 141-145.
6. Austin Phelps, *The Theory of Preaching* (New York: Charles Scribner's Sons, 1911), pp. 311, 312, 316, 331, 360.
7. James W. Cox, ed., *The Twentieth Century Pulpit*, vol. 1 (Nashville, Tenn.: Abingdon Press, 1978), pp. 9, 57, 75, 89, 154, 167.
8. James W. Cox, ed., *The Twentieth Century Pulpit*, vol. 2 (Nashville: Abingdon Press, 1981), pp. 165, 172, 194, 27.

Chapter 8:   The Aim

1. See Paul W. Hoon, *The Integrity of Worship* (Nashville, Tenn.: Abingdon Press, 1971), pp. 149-191.
2. Herbert H. Farmer, *The Servant of the Word* (Philadelphia: Fortress Press, 1942), p. 6.
3. Charles Reynolds Brown, *The Art of Preaching* (New York: The Macmillan Company, 1922), p. 181.
4. Walther E. Eichrodt, *Theology of the Old Testament*, vol. 2, trans. J. A. Baker (Philadelphia: Westminster Press, 1961), p. 38.
5. William Temple in Samuel M. Shoemaker, *How To Become a Christian* (New York: Harper & Brothers, 1953), pp. 77-78.
6. William James, *Talks to Teachers* (1899; reprinted ed., New York: Dover Publications, 1962), pp. 34-35.

7. John A. Broadus, *On the Preparation and Delivery of Sermons*, rev. and ed. Jesse Burton Weatherspoon (New York: Harper & Brothers, 1944), pp. 145, 151.

8. Dietrich Ritschl, *A Theology of Proclamation* (Richmond, Va.: John Knox Press, 1960), pp. 139-140.

9. Leander Keck, *The Bible in the Pulpit* (Nashville, Tenn.: Abingdon Press, 1978), p. 55.

10. Fred B. Craddock, *As One Without Authority* (Nashville, Tenn.: Abingdon Press, 1979).

11. Donald G. Miller, *The Way to Biblical Preaching* (New York: Abingdon Press, 1957), p. 55

12. Walter Bülck, *Praktische Theologie* (Heidelberg: Quelle und Meyer, 1949), pp. 91-92.

13. Ronald Knox, "The Window in the Wall," in *The Twentieth Century Pulpit*, vol. 1, ed. James W. Cox (Nashville Tenn.: Abingdon Press, 1978) pp. 124-128.

14. James Stewart, *The Gates of New Life* (New York: Charles Scribner's Sons, 1940), pp. 102-111.

15. Karl Barth, *Church Dogmatics*, vol. 4, part 2 (Edinburgh: T. & T. Clark, 1958), p. 218.

16. Harry Emerson Fosdick, *The Three Meanings: Prayer, Faith, Service* (New York: Association Press, 1942).

17. John Dewey, *How We Think* (Boston: D. C. Heath and Company, 1910).

18. Frank C. Laubach, *Prayer: The Mightiest Force in the World* (New York: Fleming H. Revell Company, 1946), pp. 40-50.

19. Gordon W. Ireson, *How Shall They Hear?* (London: S.P.C.K., 1958), p. 99.

20. Peter Brunner, *Worship in the Name of Jesus* (St. Louis, Mo.: Concordia Publishing House, 1968), pp. 132-136.

21. Harry Emerson Fosdick, *The Hope of the World* (New York: Harper & Brothers, 1933), p. 201.

22. Eduard Schweizer, *God's Inescapable Nearness*, trans. James W. Cox (Waco, Tx.: Word Books, 1971), p. 71.

23. Henry Grady Davis, *Design for Preaching* (Philadelphia: Fortress Press, 1958), pp. 213, 214.

24. Wayne Oates, *The Revelation of God in Human Suffering* (Philadelphia: Westminster Press, 1959), p. 11.

25. Robert J. McCracken in the Edgar Young Mullins Lectures on Preaching, The Southern Baptist Theological Seminary, Louisville, Ky., 1955.

26. Harry Emerson Fosdick, "What Is the Matter with Preaching," *Harper's Magazine*, July 1928.

27. Rollo May, *The Springs of Creative Living* (New York: Abingdon-Cokesbury Press, 1940), pp. 223-225, 229.

28. Horton Davies, *Varieties of English Preaching, 1900-1960* (Englewood Cliffs: Prentice-Hall, 1963), p. 62.

29. George M. Gibson, *The Story of the Christian Year* (New York: Abingdon-Cokesbury Press, 1945), pp. 180-181.

30. Justin Martyr, *The First Apology*, trans. Thomas B. Falls (New York: Christian Heritage, 1948), p. 107.

31. Rollo May, *Creative Living*, p. 231.
32. Joseph Sittler, *The Ecology of Faith* (Philadelphia: Muhlenberg Press, 1961), pp. 12-14.
33. Eduard Schweizer, *Divine Service in the New Testament and Today* (Montreal: Presbyterian College, 1970), p. 15.
34. Richard Baxter, *The Reformed Pastor* (Richmond, Va.: John Knox Press, 1956), p. 34.
35. Charles Haddon Spurgeon, *Lectures to My Students*, First Series (London: Passmore and Alabaster, 1875), p. 55.

Chapter 9:   The Preparation of Sermons

1. Robert J. McCracken, *The Making of the Sermon* (New York: Harper & Brothers, 1956), p. 90. Cf. Charles L. Rice, *Interpretation and Imagination* (Philadelphia: Fortress Press, 1970), p. 103.
2. St. Augustine, *On Christian Doctrine* (New York: Liberal Arts Press, 1958), pp. 166-168.
3. Willard A. Pleuthner, *Building Up Your Congregation* (Chicago: Wilcox & Follett, 1951), pp. 117-118.
4. David Poling, *The Last Years of the Church* (Old Tappan, N.J.: Fleming H. Revell, 1970), p. 65.
5. Cf. Raymond W. Albright, *Focus on Infinity* (New York: Macmillan, 1961), pp. 172-173.
6. Charles A. McGlon, ed., "How I Prepare My Sermons," *The Quarterly Journal of Speech*, 40, no. 1 (February 1954).
7. George W. Webber, *The Congregation in Mission* (New York: Abingdon Press, 1964), pp. 77-84.
8. Dietrich Ritschl, *A Theology of Proclamation* (Richmond, Va.: John Knox Press, 1960), pp. 149-156, 165.
9. Yngve Brilioth, *A Brief History of Preaching*, trans. Karl E. Mattson (Philadelphia: Fortress Press, 1965), p. 153.
10. Fulton J. Sheen, *Treasure in Clay* (Garden City, N.Y.: Doubleday & Company, 1980), pp. 75-76.
11. Cf. Clyde E. Fant, *Preaching for Today* (New York: Harper & Row, 1975), pp. 118-126.

Chapter 10:   The Structure of Sermons

1. Marcus Fabius Quintilian, *Institutes of Oratory*, trans. John Selby Watson, (London: George Bell and Sons, 1892), II, p. 14.
2. Dietrich Ritschl, *A Theology of Proclamation* (Richmond, Va.: John Knox Press, 1960), pp. 135, 177, 135.
3. Phillips Brooks, *Lectures on Preaching* (London: Richard D. Dickinson, 1881), p. 115.

4. Fenelon, *Dialogues on Eloquence*, trans. Wilbur Samuel Howell (Princeton University Press, 1951), p. 111.
5. Aristotle, *De Poetica*, trans. Ingram Bywater, in Richard McKeon (ed.), *Introduction to Aristotle* (New York: Random House, 1947), p. 634.
6. Raymond W. Albright, *Focus on Infinity: A Life of Phillips Brooks* (New York: Macmillan Company, 1961), p. 173.
7. Gilbert Stillman MacVaugh, "A Structural Analysis of the Sermons of Dr. Harry Emerson Fosdick," *Quarterly Journal of Speech*, 18 November 1932: 531ff.
8. Marcus T. Cicero, *De Oratore*, trans. E. W. Sutton (Cambridge: Harvard University Press, 1948) II, 313-315.
9. Athanase Coquerel, *Observations Pratiques sur La Predication* (Paris: J. Cherbuliez, 1860), p. 166.
10. Edgar Allen Poe, *The Philosophy of Composition* (New York: Pageant Press, 1959), pp. 68, 69.
11. Harry Emerson Fosdick, "Animated Conversation," *If I Had Only One Sermon to Prepare*, ed. Joseph Fort Newton (New York: Harper & Brothers Publishers, 1932), pp. 112-113.
12. *The Guardian*, 18 September 1936, in Charles Smyth, *The Art of Preaching* (London: Society for Promoting Christian Knowledge, 1940), pp. 47-49.
13. A. Vinet, *Homiletics*, trans. and ed. Thomas H. Skinner (New York: Ivison & Philley, 1854), p. 285.
14. John Watson (Ian Maclaren), *The Cure of Souls* (Cincinnati, Ohio: Jennings and Graham, 1896), pp. 26-32.
15. Walter Russell Bowie, *Preaching* (New York: Abingdon Press, 1954), p. 168.
16. James S. Stewart, *The Gates of New Life* (New York: Charles Scribner's Sons, 1940), pp. 220-231.
17. Arthur E. Dalton, *Brief and to the Point* (London: James Clarke, 1961).
18. Clyde E. Fant, *Preaching for Today* (New York: Harper & Row, 1975), pp. 122-124.
19. Kenneth G. Hance, David C. Ralph, and Milton J. Wiskell, *Principles of Speaking* (Belmont, Calif.: Wadsworth Publishing Company, 1962), pp. 176-179.
20. Henri D'Espine, "Comment proclamer le message?" *Sinn und Wesen der Verkündigung* (Zürich: Evangelischer Verlag A. G. Zollikon, 1941), p. 71.

Chapter 11: Structural Options

1. James W. Cox, ed., *The Twentieth Century Pulpit*, vol. 1, (Nashville, Tenn.: Abingdon Press, 1978); James W. Cox and Patricia Parrent Cox, eds., *The Twentieth Century Pulpit*, vol. 2, (Nashville, Tenn.: Abingdon Press, 1981).
2. Cox, *Pulpit*, pp. 197-201.
3. Ibid., pp. 15-19.
4. Karl Barth, *Dogmatics in Outline* (New York: Philosophical Library, n.d.), p. 9.

5. Emil Brunner, *The Christian Doctrine of God: Dogmatics*, vol. 1, (Philadelphia: Westminster Press, 1950), pp. 9-11.
6. Cox, *Pulpit*, pp. 9-14.
7. Cox and Cox, *Pulpit*, pp. 194-203.
8. Cox, *Pulpit*, pp. 226-236.
9. Cox, *Pulpit*, pp. 75-81.
10. Cox and Cox, *Pulpit*, pp. 59-65.
11. St. Augustine, *On Christian Doctrine* (New York: Liberal Arts Press, 1958), pp. 118-119.
12. R. C. H. Lenski, *The Sermon: Its Homiletical Construction* (Columbus, Ohio: Lutheran Book Concern, n.d.), pp. 178-179.
13. Cox, *Pulpit*, pp. 115-123.
14. Ibid., pp. 197-201.
15. Ibid., pp. 188-196.
16. Harry Emerson Fosdick, *What Is Vital in Religion* (New York: Harper & Brothers, 1955), pp. 89-99.
17. See Joseph Fort Newton, *The New Preaching* (Nashville, Tenn.: Cokesbury Press, 1930); Fred B. Craddock, *As One Without Authority* (Nashville, Tenn.: Abingdon Press, 1979); Ralph L. Lewis and Gregg Lewis, *Inductive Preaching* (Westchester, Ill.: Crossway Books, 1983).
18. Harry A. Overstreet, *Influencing Human Behavior* (New York: The People's Institute Publishing Company, 1925), pp. 13-15.
19. Cox, *Pulpit*, pp. 30-35.
20. Cf. Walter Russell Bowie, *Preaching* (New York: Abingdon Press, 1954), pp. 173-174; Henry Grady Davis, *Design for Preaching* (Philadelphia: Muhlenberg Press, 1958), pp. 182-184; Milton Crum Jr., *Manual on Preaching* (Valley Forge: Judson Press, 1977), pp. 15-45.
21. Cox and Cox, *Pulpit*, pp. 53-58.
22. Cox and Cox, *Pulpit*, pp. 214-219.
23. Ibid., pp. 50-56.
24. Alan H. Monroe and Douglas Ehninger, *Principles and Types of Speech*, 6th ed., (Glenview, Ill.: Scott, Foresman and Company, 1967), pp. 264-289.
25. James T. Cleland, *Eight More Sermons* (Durham, N.C.: Divinity School of Duke University, 1959), pp. 2-5.

Chapter 12:   The Primacy of Story

1. Henry Ward Beecher, *Lectures on Preaching* (New York: J. B. Ford and Company, 1872), pp. 155-169.

Chapter 13:   Introduction, Conclusion, and Title

1. James S. Stewart, *The Gates of New Life* (New York: Charles Scribner's Sons, 1940), p. 132.

2. Harry Emerson Fosdick, *Riverside Sermons* (New York: Harper & Brothers, 1958), pp. 195-196.
3. Henry Grady Davis, *Design for Preaching* (Philadelphia: Muhlenberg Press, 1958), p. 191.
4. Charles R. Brown, *The Art of Preaching* (New York: Macmillan, 1922), p. 113.
5. D. W. Cleverley Ford, *A Theological Preacher's Notebook* (London: Hodder & Stoughton, 1962), pp. 49, 53, 60.
6. James W. Cox, ed., *The Twentieth Century Pulpit*, vol. 1 (Nashville, Tenn.: Abingdon Press, 1978), pp. 9-278.
7. Ibid., p. 57.
8. Thomas R. Lewis and Ralph G. Nichols, *Speaking and Listening* (Dubuque, Iowa: Wm. C. Brown Co., 1965), pp. 69-73.
9. Andrew W. Blackwood, *The Preparation of Sermons* (New York: Abingdon-Cokesbury Press, 1948), p. 162.
10. William James, *Talks to Teachers* (New York: Dover Publications, 1962), p. 36.
11. James S. Stewart, *Gates*, p. 41.
12. Dietrich Ritschl, *A Theology of Proclamation* (Richmond, Va.: John Knox Press, 1960), p. 138.
13. Harry Emerson Fosdick, *Riverside Sermons* (New York: Harper & Brothers, 1958), pp. 28, 46, 54, 63, 203.
14. G. Paul Butler, ed., *Best Sermons*, vol. 8 (Princeton, N.J.: D. Van Nostrand, 1962), p. 123.
15. Don M. Aycock, ed., *Preaching with Purpose and Power* (Macon, Ga.: Mercer University Press, 1982), p. 160.
16. George A. Buttrick, *Sermons Preached in a University Church* (New York: Abingdon Press, 1959), pp. 65, 89.
17. Halford E. Luccock, *Marching Off the Map* (New York: Harper & Brothers, 1952), pp. 25, 96.
18. Andrew Watterson Blackwood, ed., *The Protestant Pulpit* (New York: Abingdon Press, 1947), p. 198.
19. Fosdick, *Riverside Sermons*, p. 247.
20. Blackwood, *Protestant Pulpit*, pp. 86, 50.
21. Butler, *Best Sermons*, p. 157.
22. Fosdick, *Riverside Sermons*, pp. 195, 353.
23. Buttrick, *Sermons*, pp. 30, 72, 117, 195.
24. Butler, *Best Sermons*, pp. 279, 47.
25. Blackwood, *Protestant Pulpit*, pp. 63, 144, 173.

Chapter 14: The Factors of Attention and Interest

1. For the following discussion, compare Alan H. Monroe and Douglas-Ehninger, *Principles and Types of Speech* 6th ed. (Glenview, Ill.: Scott, Foresman and Company, 1969), pp. 209-223 and pp. 350-357; Arthur Edward Phillips, *Effective Speaking* (Chicago: Newton Company, 1914), pp. 63-78;

Percy H. Whiting, *How to Speak and Write with Humor*, (New York: McGraw-Hill Books Co., 1959), p. 28.

2. Cf. Clement F. Rogers, *The Parson Preaching* (New York: Macmillan Company, n.d.), p. 31.

3. D. W. Cleverley Ford, *An Expository Preacher's Notebook* (New York: Harper & Brothers, 1960), pp. 26, 47, 57, 67-68.

4. *King John*, act. 4, sc. 2, lines 11-16.

5. James W. Cox, ed., *The Twentieth Century Pulpit*, vol. 1 (Nashville, Tenn.: Abingdon Press, 1978), p. 71.

6. Frederick Buechner, *Peculiar Treasures* (San Francisco: Harper & Row, 1979).

7. Phillips, *Effective Speaking*, p. 64.

8. Halford Luccock, *In the Minister's Workshop* (New York: Abingdon-Cokesbury Press, 1944), pp. 142-143.

9. Harry Emerson Fosdick, *Riverside Sermons* (New York: Harper & Brothers, 1958), pp. 247-248.

10. Cox, *Pulpit*, pp. 214-219.

11. William D. Thompson and Gordon C. Bennett, eds., *Dialogue Preaching* (Valley Forge, Pa.: Judson Press, 1969), pp. 75-86.

12. James W. Cox and Patricia Parrent Cox, eds., *The Twentieth Century Pulpit*, vol. 2, (Nashville, Tenn.: Abingdon Press, 1981), pp. 20-25.

13. See also Chapter Eleven, "Structural Options." H. A. Overstreet, *Influencing Human Behavior* (New York: People's Institute Publishing Company, 1925), pp. 13-15.

14. Frank H. Caldwell, *Preaching Angles* (New York: Abingdon Press, 1954), pp. 113-116.

15. Merrill Abbey, *Preaching to the Contemporary Mind* (Nashville, Tenn.: Abingdon Press, 1963), pp. 66-81.

16. Harry Emerson Fosdick, *Living Under Tension* (New York: Harper & Brothers, 1941), pp. 102-112.

17. William Zinsser, *On Writing Well* (New York: Harper & Row, 1976), p. 134.

18. Larry Wilde, *How the Great Comedy Writers Create Laughter* (Chicago: Nelson-Hall, 1976), pp. 91-92.

19. Frederick Buechner, *Telling the Truth: The Gospel as Tragedy, Comedy, and Fairy Tale* (San Francisco: Harper & Row, 1977), p. 63.

20. Ambrose Bierce, *Devil's Dictionary* (1911; reprint ed., New York: Dover Publications, 1958), p. 22.

21. *The Reader's Digest Dictionary of Quotations* (New York: Funk & Wagnalls, 1968), p. 151.

22. *Fun Fare: A Treasury of Reader's Digest Wit and Humor* (New York: Simon and Schuster, 1949), p. 279.

23. Bob Bassindale, *How Speakers Make People Laugh* (West Nyack, N.Y.: Parker Publishing Company, 1976), p. 176.

24. Alexander Pope, *An Essay on Man*, Ep. ii, 1. 217.

25. H. W. Fowler, *A Dictionary of Modern English Usage*, 2nd ed., (New York: Oxford University Press, 1965), p. 492.

26. Dale Carnegie, *Effective Speaking*, ed. Dorothy Carnegie (New York: Association Press, 1962), p. 83.

27. Cf. V. A. Ketcham, "Seven Doors to the Mind," in William Phillips Sandford and Willard Hayes Yeager, *Business Speeches by Business Men* (McGraw-Hill Book Company, 1930), pp. 405-417.
28. James W. Cox, *Surprised by God* (Nashville, Tenn.: Broadman Press, 1979), pp. 17-23.

Chapter 15:   The Ethics of Motivation

1. William Sargant, *Battle for the Mind* (Garden City, N.Y.: Doubleday & Company, 1957), pp. 237-239.
2. Fritz Kunkel, *In Search of Maturity* (New York: Charles Scribner's Sons, 1946), p. 287.
3. Peter Brunner, *Worship in the Name of Jesus* (St. Louis, Mo.: Concordia Publishing House, 1968), pp. 132-133.
4. St. Augustine, *On Christian Doctrine*, (New York: Liberal Arts Press, 1958), Book 4.

Chapter 16:   The Forms of Development and Support

1. Henry Ward Beecher, *Lectures on Preaching* (New York: J. B. Ford and Company, 1872), p. 175.
2. Cf. Arthur Edward Phillips, *Effective Speaking* (Chicago: Newton Company, 1914), p. 92.
3. Ibid., pp. 95-96, quoting Alexander Maclaren.
4. George A. Buttrick, *Sermons Preached in a University Church* (New York: Abingdon Press, 1959), pp. 39, 41.
5. Quoted by Clement Rogers, *The Parson Preaching* (New York: Macmillan Company, n.d.), p. 30.
6. Gilbert Highet, *The Art of Teaching* (New York: Vintage Books, 1950), p. 239.
7. Harry Emerson Fosdick, "What Is the Matter with Preaching," *Harper's Magazine*, July 1928.
8. Paul Tillich, *The Eternal Now* (New York: Charles Scribner's Sons, 1963), p. 43.
9. Phillips, *Effective Speaking*, p. 104.
10. James W. Cox, ed., *The Twentieth Century Pulpit*, vol. 1 (Nashville, Tenn.: Abingdon Press, 1978), p. 198.
11. Ibid., p. 229.
12. Theodore Parker Ferris, *Selected Sermons* (Boston: Trinity Church, 1976), p. 72.
13. Phillips, *Effective Speaking*, p. 121.
14. Carlyle Marney, *These Things Remain* (New York: Abingdon-Cokesbury Press, 1953), p. 122.
15. Andrew W. Blackwood, *The Preparation of Sermons* (London: Church Book Room Press, 1951), pp. 160-161.

16. Phillips Brooks, *The Candle of the Lord* (New York: E. P. Dutton and Company, 1881), pp. 9, 274, 275.
17. Fred F. Brown, *The Church* (Atlanta: The Baptist Hour, 1942), p. 8. (A pamphlet.)
18. Cox, *Pulpit*, pp. 111, 143, 21.
19. Ibid., p. 264.
20. Ibid., pp. 239-240.
21. Ibid., pp. 21, 23.
22. Ibid., pp. 141-144.
23. Enid Saunders Candlin, *Christian-Science Monitor*, March 20, 1970, p. 12.
24. H. W. Fowler, *Modern English Usage*, 2nd ed. rev. (New York: Oxford University Press, 1965), pp. 361-362.
25. Porter G. Perrin, *An Index to English* (Chicago: Scott, Foresman, and Co., 1939), p. 390.
26. Charles W. Ferguson, *Say It with Words* (New York: Alfred A. Knopf, 1939), pp. 58-59.
27. Quoted by Edmund Fuller, ed., *Thesaurus of Anecdotes* (Garden City, N.Y.: Garden City Publishing Co., 1948), p. v.
28. Frederick Buechner, *Telling the Truth: The Gospel as Tragedy, Comedy, and Fairy Tale* (San Francisco: Harper & Row, 1977), p. 63.
29. H. Grady Davis, *Design for Preaching* (Philadelphia: Muhlenberg Press, 1958), p. 157.
30. Quoted by James W. Cox, *A Guide to Biblical Preaching* (Nashville, Tenn.: Abingdon Press, 1976), p. 53.

Chapter 17:   Style

1. H. W. Fowler, *A Dictionary of Modern English Usage*, 2nd ed. rev. (New York: Oxford University Press, 1965), p. 537.
2. Cited in Sir Ernest Gowers, *The Complete Plain Words* (Baltimore: Penguin Books, 1954), p. 80.
3. Rudolf Flesch, *How to Write, Speak, and Think More Effectively* (New York: Harper & Brothers, 1960), p. 30.
4. Henry Grady Davis, *Design for Preaching* (Philadelphia: Muhlenberg Press, 1958), pp. 282-293.
5. Paul B. Bull, *Preaching and Sermon Construction* (New York: Macmillan Company, 1922), p. 131.
6. James W. Cox, *Surprised by God* (Nashville, Tenn.: Broadman Press, 1979), pp. 39-42.
7. William Strunk, Jr., and E. B. White, *The Elements of Style*, 3rd ed. (New York: Macmillan Publishing Co., 1979), p. 31.
8. After John C. Hodges with Mary E. Whitten, *Harbrace College Handbook*, (New York: Harcourt, Brace & World, 1962), p. 318.
9. Ralph Waldo Emerson, "Eloquence," *Society and Solitude* (Boston: Houghton, Mifflin and Company, 1904), p. 90.
10. Paul Scherer, *For We Have This Treasure* (New York: Harper & Brothers, 1944), p. 196.

11. Cf. V. A. Ketcham, "Seven Doors to the Mind," in William Phillips Sandford and Willard Hayes Yeager, *Business Speeches by Business Men* (McGraw-Hill Book Co., 1930), pp. 407-417.
12. Paul Scherer, *The Place Where Thou Standest* (New York: Harper & Brothers, 1942), p. 97.
13. Flesch, *How to Write*, pp. 145-146.
14. John Albert Broadus, *Sermons and Addresses* (Baltimore, Md.: H. L. Wharton and Co., 1886), p. 39.
15. Saint Augustine, *On Christian Doctrine* (New York: Liberal Arts Press, 1958), pp. 145-146.
16. Gorham Munson, *The Written Word* (New York: Collier Books, 1962), pp. 83-85.
17. Theodore Parker Ferris, *Go Tell the People* (New York: Charles Scribner's Sons, 1951), pp. 56-57.
18. Paul Scherer, *The Word God Sent* (New York: Harper & Row, 1965), p. 52.
19. See Walt Whitman, *Leaves of Grass* (New York: New American Library, 1964), pp. 227-228.
20. Albert Edward Phillips. *Effective Speaking* (Chicago: Newton Company, 1914), pp. 81-82.
21. Jacques Barzun, *Simple & Direct: A Rhetoric for Writers* (New York: Harper & Row, 1975), p. 12.
22. Adela Rogers St. Johns, *How to Write and Story and Sell It* (Garden City, N.Y.: Doubleday & Co., 1956), pp. 147, 148.
23. Harry Emerson Fosdick, *The Living of These Days* (New York: Harper & Brothers, 1956), p. 100.
24. Scherer, *This Treasure*, p. 179.
25. Peter Elbow, *Writing with Power* (New York: Oxford University Press, 1981), p. 13, 14-15.

Chapter 18:   The Mastery of the Message

1. Charles A. McGlon, ed., "How I Prepare My Sermons: A Symposium," *Quarterly Journal of Speech* 40, no. 1 (February 1954): 51-52.
2. Edmund Holt Linn, *Preaching as Counseling* (Valley Forge, Pa.: Judson Press, 1966), pp. 148-149.
3. Cicero, *De Oratore*, III, 59, quoted by John A. Broadus, *On the Preparation and Delivery of Sermons*, ed. Jesse Burton Weatherspoon (New York: Harper & Brothers, 1944), pp. 350-351.
4. M. Bautain, *The Art of Extempore Speaking* (New York: Blue Ribbon Books, 1940), p. 141.
5. John Albert Broadus, "Essay on the Best Mode of Preparing and Delivering Sermons," *Religious Herald*, 14 December 1854.
6. R. S. Storrs, *Preaching Without Notes* (New York: Dodd and Mean, 1875), pp. 116-117.
7. Harry Emerson Fosdick, *The Living of These Days* (New York: Harper & Brothers, 1956), p. 84.
8. McGlon, "How I Prepare," p. 55.

9. See Chelsey V. Young, *The Magic of a Mighty Memory* (West Nyack: Parker Publishing Co., 1971), pp. 71-73.
10. Cf. Jack Valenti, *Speak Up with Confidence* (New York: William Morrow and Co., 1982), pp. 61-62.
11. An example of this format may be found in Marshall's sermon in James W. Cox, ed. *The Twentieth Century Pulpit*, vol. 1 (Nashville, Tenn.: Abingdon Press, 1978).
12. William Osler, *A Way of Life* (New York: Dover Publications, 1951), pp. 237-249.

Chapter 19: The Use of Voice and Body

1. Virgil A. Anderson, *Training the Speaking Voice*, 3rd ed. (New York: Oxford University Press, 1977), p. 3.
2. Dwight E. Stevenson and Charles F. Diehl, *Reaching People from the Pulpit* (New York: Harper & Brothers, 1958), p. 29.
3. Henry Ward Beecher, *Lectures on Preaching* (New York: J. B. Ford and Co., 1872), pp. 131-132.
4. Raymond W. Albright, *Focus on Infinity*, (New York: Macmillan Company, 1961), p. 169.
5. Beecher, *Lectures*, pp. 134, 133-134.
6. Charles Reynolds Brown, *The Art of Preaching* (New York: Macmillan Company, 1922), pp. 156-157.
7. Helmut Thielicke, ed., *Encounter with Spurgeon* (Philadelphia: Fortress Press, 1963), pp. 160-161.

Chapter 20: The Preacher's Personality

1. Markus Barth, *Conversation with the Bible* (New York: Holt, Rinehart and Winston, 1964), pp. 9-10.
2. Hans Lietzmann, quoted by Jerome Hamer, *Karl Barth* (Westminster, Md.: Newman Press, 1962), p. 115.
3. Henri J. M. Nouwen, *The Wounded Healer* (Garden City, N.Y.: Doubleday & Co., 1972), p. 95.
4. Theodor Bovet, *That They May Have Life*, trans. John A. Baker (London: Darton, Longman & Todd, 1964), p. 216.
5. Adapted by permission from an article by James W. Cox in *Proclaim*, July 1980, p. 43. © Copyright 1980 The Sunday School Board of the Southern Baptist Convention. All rights reserved.
6. William Osler, *A Way of Life* (New York: Dover Publications, 1951), pp. 240-242, 247.
7. Frederick W. Robertson, *Sermons* (New York: Harper & Brothers, Publishers, n.d.), p. 177.
8. Stopford A. Brooke, ed., *Life and Letters of Frederick W. Robertson, M.A.* (New York: Harper & Brothers, Publishers, n.d.), p. 86.

9. R. E. C. Browne, *The Ministry of the Word* (London: SCM Press, 1958), pp. 69-71.
10. George Arthur Buttrick, *The Christian Fact and Modern Doubt* (New York: Charles Scribner's Sons, 1935), p. 16.
11. Alexander Pope, *An Essay on Man*, 1. 217.
12. Paul Tournier, *The Person Reborn*, trans. Edwin Hudson (New York: Harper & Row, Publishers, 1966), p. 217.
13. Cf. article by James W. Cox, *The Upper Room*, May-June 1977, p. 44.
14. See Tournier, *Person Reborn*, p. 221.
15. John Bunyan, *Grace Abounding to the Chief of Sinners* (London: SCM Press, 1955), p. 83.

For Further Reading and Reference

Introduction:

RHETORIC

Burke, Kenneth. *A Rhetoric of Motives*. New York: Prentice-Hall, 1950.

Campbell, George. *The Philosophy of Rhetoric*. Rev. ed. Boston: Charles Ewer, 1823.

Cicero, Marcus Tullius. *De Oratore*. 2 Vols. Cambridge, Mass: Harvard University Press, 1942.

*Cooper, Lane. *The Rhetoric of Aristotle*. New York: D. Appleton and Co., 1932.

Corbett, Edward P. J. *Classical Rhetoric for the Modern Student*. 2d ed. New York: Oxford University Press, 1971.

Quintilian. *Institutes of Oratory*. Translated by John Selby Watson. London: George Bell and Sons, 1892.

Richards, Ivor Armstrong. *The Philosophy of Rhetoric*. New York: Oxford University Press, 1964.

Whately, Richard. *Elements of Rhetoric*. Carbondale, Illinois: Southern Illinois University Press, 1963.

HOMILETICS

*Augustine, Saint. *On Christian Doctrine*. Trans. with introduction by D. W. Robertson, Jr. New York: Liberal Arts Press, 1958.

Barth, Karl. *The Preaching of the Gospel*. Translated by B. E. Hooke. Philadelphia: The Westminster Press, 1963.

Baxter, Batsell Barrett. *The Heart of the Yale Lectures*. New York: The Macmillan Co., 1947.

Black, James M. *The Mystery of Preaching*. New York: Fleming H. Revell, 1924.

Blackwood, Andrew W. *The Preparation of Sermons*. New York: Abingdon-Cokesbury Press, 1948.

———. *The Protestant Pulpit*. Nashville: Abingdon-Cokesbury Press, 1947.

Bohren, Rudolf. *Predigtlehre*. 3 Auflage. München: Chr. Kaiser Verlag, 1974.

Bowie, Walter Russell. *Preaching*. Nashville: Abingdon Press, 1954.

*Especially recommended

Brilioth, Yngve T. *A Brief History of Preaching.* Translated by Karl E. Mattson. Philadelphia: Fortress Press, 1965.

*Broadus, John A. *On the Preparation and Delivery of Sermons.* 4th ed., rev. by Vernon L. Stanfield. San Francisco: Harper & Row, 1979.

Brooks, Phillips. *Lectures on Preaching.* New York: E. P. Dutton, 1877.

Brown, H. C., Jr., H. Gordon Clinard, and Jesse J. Northcutt. *Steps to the Sermon.* Nashville: Broadman Press, 1963.

Browne, Robert E. C. *The Ministery of the Word.* Philadelphia: Fortress Press, 1976.

Buttrick, George A. *Jesus Came Preaching.* New York: Charles Scribner's Sons, 1931.

Caemmerer, Richard R. *Preaching for the Church.* St. Louis: Concordia Publishing House, 1959.

Coquerel, Athanase Josué. *Observations Pratiques sur la Prédication.* Paris: J. Cherbuliez, 1860.

Cox, James W. *A Guide to Biblical Preaching.* Nashville: Abingdon Press, 1976.

*Cox, James W., ed. *The Twentieth Century Pulpit.* 2 vols. Nashville: Abingdon Press, 1978–81.

Crum, Milton, Jr. *Manual on Preaching.* Valley Forge, Pa.: Judson Press, 1977.

Dargan, Edwin Charles. *A History of Preaching.* Vols. I and II. New York: A. C. Armstrong & Son, 1905–12.

*Davis, H. Grady. *Design for Preaching.* Philadelphia: Fortress Press, 1958.

Fant, Clyde E. *Bonhoeffer: Worldly Preaching.* Nashville: T. Nelson, 1975.

———. *Preaching for Today.* New York: Harper & Row, 1975.

*Fant, Clyde E., and William M. Pinson, Jr., eds. *Twenty Centuries of Great Preaching.* 12 vols. plus index vol. Waco, Texas: Word Books, 1971.

*Farmer, H. H. *The Servant of the Word.* London: Nisbet & Co., 1941.

Fénelon, Francois de Salignac de la Mothe. *Dialogues Concerning Eloquence.* Trans. by William Stevenson. Glasgow: R. and A. Foulis, 1760.

Ford, D. W. Cleverley. *The Ministry of the Word.* London: Hodder and Stoughton, 1979.

*Forsyth, P. T. *Positive Preaching and the Modern Mind.* London: Hodder and Stoughton, 1907.

Holland, DeWitte. *Preaching in American History.* Nashville: Abingdon Press, 1969.

Holland, DeWitte, ed. *Sermons In American History.* Nashville: Abingdon Press, 1971.

Hyperius, Andreas Gerhard. *Die Homiletik und Die Katechetik.* Verdeutscht und mit Einleitungen versehen von E. Chr. Achelis und Eugen Sachsse. Berlin: Reuther & Reichard, 1901.

*Killinger, John. *Fundamentals of Preaching.* Philadelphia: Fortress Press, 1985.

Linn, Edmund Holt. *Preaching as Counseling.* Valley Forge, Pennsylvania: Judson Press, 1966.

Miller, Donald G. *The Way to Biblical Preaching.* New York: Abingdon Press, 1957.

Mitchell, Henry H. *Black Preaching.* Philadelphia: Lippincott, 1970.

Phelps, Austin. *Theory of Preaching.* New York: Charles Scribner's Sons, 1881.

Robinson, Haddon W. *Biblical Preaching.* Grand Rapids, Michigan: Baker Book House, 1980.

Rogers, Clement Francis. *The Parson Preaching*. New York: Macmillan, 1947.

Scherer, Paul. *For We Have This Treasure*. New York: Harper & Bros. 1944.

Skinner, Craig. *The Teaching Ministry of the Pulpit*. Grand Rapids, Michigan: Baker Book House, 1973.

Spurgeon, Charles H. *Lectures to my Students*. London: Passmore and Alabaster, 1875. (first series)

Stewart, James S. *Heralds of God*. New York: Charles Scribner's Sons, 1946.

Sweazey, George E. *Preaching the Good News*. Englewood Cliffs, N.J.: Prentice-Hall, Inc., 1976.

Tizard, Leslie James. *Preaching: the Art of Communication*. Foreword by Leslie E. Cook. New York: Oxford University Press, 1958.

Trillhaas, Wolfgang. *Evangelische Predigtlehre*. Fünfte, Neubearbeitete Auflage. München: Chr. Kaiser Verlag, 1964.

Turnbull, Ralph G. *A History of Preaching*. Vol III. Grand Rapids, Michigan: Baker Book House, 1974.

Vinet, Alexander R. *Homiletics*. Trans. and ed. by Thomas H. Skinner. Chicago: Ivison, Blakeman, Taylor & Co., 1854.

Wiersbe, Warren W. *Treasury of the World's Great Sermons*. Grand Rapids, Michigan: Kregel Publications, 1977.

Part I: The Importance of Preaching

*Barth, Karl. *Church Dogmatics*. Vol I, *The Doctrine of the Word of God*. Trans. by G. T. Thomson. Edinburgh: T. & T. Clark, 1936.

*Dodd, C. H. *The Apostolic Preaching*. London: Hodder & Stoughton, 1936.

Ebeling, Gerhard. *Theology and Proclamation: Dialogue with Bultmann*. Trans. by John Riches. Philadelphia: Fortress Press, 1966.

Kraus, Hans-Joachim. *Predigt aus Vollmacht*. Neukirchen-Vluyn: Neukirchener Verlag des Erziehungsvereins, 1966.

Rust, Eric C. *The Word and Words*. Macon: Mercer University Press, 1982.

Scherer, Paul. *The Word God Sent*. New York: Harper & Row, 1965.

Sittler, Joseph. *The Ecology of Faith*. Philadelphia: Muhlenberg Press, 1961.

Smith, Charles W. F. *Biblical Authority for Modern Preaching*. Philadelphia: The Westminster Press, 1960.

Stewart, James S. *A Faith to Proclaim*. New York: Charles Scribner's Sons, 1953.

Wingren, Gustaf. *The Living Word*. Translated by Victor C. Pogue. Philadelphia: Muhlenberg Press, 1960.

Part II: The Context of Preaching

*Berlo, David K. *The Process of Communication*. New York: Holt, Rinehart and Winston, 1960.

Book of Common Prayer. New York: The Church Hymnal Corporation and the Seabury Press, 1977.

Buber, Martin. *I and Thou*. Translated by Ronald Gregor Smith. Edinburgh: T. & T. Clark, 1937.

Burke, Kenneth. *A Rhetoric of Motives*. New York: Prentice-Hall, 1950.

Cairns, David S. *The Faith That Rebels*. 2nd ed. New York: Doubleday, Doran, & Co., 1928.

Craig, Archibald C. *Preaching in a Scientific Age*. London: SCM Press, 1954.

*Gibson, George M. *The Story of the Christian Year*. New York: Abingdon-Cokesbury Press, 1945.

Hoon, Paul W. *The Integrity of Worship*. Nashville: Abingdon Press, 1971.

Howe, Reuel. *The Miracle of Dialogue*. Greenwich, Conn.: Seabury Press, 1963.

MacGregor, Geddes. *The Sense of Absence*. Philadelphia: J. B. Lippincott Co., 1968.

*Oates, Wayne E. *The Psychology of Religion*. Waco, Texas: Word Books, 1973.

Paquier, Richard. *Dynamics of Worship*. Philadelphia: Fortress Press, 1967.

Rust, Eric C. *Religion, Revelation and Reason*. Macon, Georgia: Mercer University Press, 1981.

*_____. *Science and Faith*. New York: Oxford University Press, 1967.

Segler, Franklin M. *Christian Worship*. Nashville: Broadman Press, 1967.

Underhill, Evelyn. *Worship*. New York: Harper & Brothers, 1957.

*Wainwright, Geoffrey. *Doxology: The Praise of God in Worship, Doctrine and Life: A Systematic Theology*. London: Epworth Press, 1980.

Part III: The Content of Sermons

Common Lectionary. New York: The Church Hymnal Corporation, 1983.

*Cox, James W., ed. *Biblical Preaching: An Expositor's Treasury*. Philadelphia: The Westminster Press, 1983.

Frör, Kurt. *Biblische Hermeneutik*. München: Chr. Kaiser Verlag, 1961.

Fuller, Reginald H. *The Use of the Bible in Preaching*. Philadelphia: Fortress Press, 1981.

Hayes, John H., and Carl R. Holladay. *Biblical Exegesis*. Atlanta: John Knox Press, 1982.

*Mounce, Robert H. *The Essential Nature of New Testament Preaching*. Grand Rapids, Michigan: Wm. B. Eerdmans, 1960.

Ritschl, Dietrich. *A Theology of Proclamation*. Richmond: John Knox Press, 1960.

Smart, James D. *The Interpretation of Scripture*. Philadelphia: Westminster Press, 1961.

*Stewart, James S. *A Faith to Proclaim*. London: Hodder and Stoughton, 1953.

Westermann, Claus, ed. *Essays on Old Testament Hermeneutics*. Translated by James Luther Mays. Richmond: John Knox Press, 1963.

Wink, Walter. *The Bible in Human Transformation*. Philadelphia: Fortress Press, 1973.

_____. *Transforming Bible Study*. Nashville: Abingdon Press, 1980.

Part IV: The Making of the Sermon

Aho, Gerhard. *The Lively Skeleton: Thematic Approaches and Outlines*. St. Louis: Concordia Publishing House, 1977.

Cleland, James T. *Preaching To Be Understood*. New York: Abingdon Press, 1965.

*Flesch, Rudolf F. *How to Write, Speak and Think More Effectively*. New York: Harper & Row, 1960.

*Lenski, R. C. H. *The Sermon: Its Homiletical Construction*. Columbus, Ohio: Lutheran Book Concern, n.d.

Linn, Edmund Holt. *Preaching As Counseling*. Valley Forge, Pennsylvania: Judson Press, 1966.

Lowry, Eugene L. *The Homiletical Plot*. Atlanta: John Knox Press, 1980.

Luccock, Halford E. *In the Minister's Workship*. New York: Abingdon-Cokesbury Press, 1944.

Mitchell, Henry H. *The Recovery of Preaching*. San Francisco: Harper & Row, 1977.

*Monroe, Alan H. *Principles and Types of Speech*. Rev. ed. New York: Scott, Foresman and Co., 1939.

Pearce, J. Winston. *Planning Your Preaching*. Nashville: Broadman Press, 1967.

*Phillips, A. E. *Effective Speaking*. Chicago: The Newton Co., 1908.

Robertson, Haddon W. *Biblical Preaching*. Grand Rapids, Michigan: Zondervan Press, 1980.

Sangster, William Edwin. *The Craft of the Sermon*. London: The Epworth Press, 1954.

*Schweizer, Eduard. *God's Inescapable Nearness*. Translated and edited by James W. Cox. Waco, Texas: Word Books, 1971.

Strunk, William, Jr., and E. B. White. *The Elements of Style*. New York: The Macmillan Co., 1959.

Part V: The Delivery of Sermons

*Anderson, Virgil A. *Training the Speaking Voice*. New York: Oxford University Press, 1942.

*Baillie, John. *A Diary of Private Prayer*. London: Oxford University Press, 1936.

Baumann, J. Daniel. *An Introduction to Contemporary Preaching*. Grand Rapids, Michigan: Baker Book House, 1972.

Baxter, Richard. *The Reformed Pastor*. Ed. by William Brown. 5th ed. London: Religious Tract Society, 1862.

Doberstein, John W., ed. *Minister's Prayer Book*. Philadelphia: Muhlenberg Press, n.d.

Fant, Clyde E. *Preaching for Today*. New York: Harper & Row, 1975.

Lessac, Arthur. *The Use and Training of the Human Voice*. New York: DBS Publications, Inc., 1967.

*Niles, Daniel T. *The Preacher's Calling to Be Servant*. London: Lutterworth Press, 1959.

Nouwen, Henri J. M. *Creative Ministry*. Garden City, New York: Doubleday, 1971.

Spurgeon, Charles H. *Lectures to My Students*. London: Passmore and Alabaster, 1875.

*Stevenson, Dwight E., and Charles F. Diehl. *Reaching People from the Pulpit*. New York: Harper & Row, 1958.

Index